CASES AND MATERIALS ON A

D0505135

AUSTRALIA
Law Book Co.
Sydney

CANADA and USA
Carswell
Toronto

HONG KONG
Sweet & Maxwell Asia

NEW ZEALAND
Brookers
Wellington

SINGAPORE and MALAYSIA
Sweet & Maxwell Asia
Singapore and Kuala Lumpur

CASES AND MATERIALS ON AS LEVEL LAW

First edition

by

Martin Hunt

LONDON
SWEET & MAXWELL
2004

Published in 2004 by
Sweet & Maxwell Limited of
100 Avenue Road
London NW3 3PF
http://www.sweetandmaxwell.co.uk

Typeset by LBJ Typesetting Ltd, Kingsclere
Printed in Great Britain by
Ashford Colour Print, Hants

No natural forests were destroyed
to make this product; only farmed
timber was used and replanted

ISBN 0 421 876 808

A CIP catalogue record for this book
is available from the British Library

For Ariane,
in love and friendship

Acknowledgements

Grateful acknowledgement is made to the following authors, publishers and organisations for their permission to quote from their works:

The Incorporated Council of Law Reporting for England and Wales.

The Bar Council.

MIDDLETON, Christopher: "Bench test". October 3, 2001. © Christopher Middleton.

VERKAIK, Robert: "Pay survey for solicitors shows women get 15% less". November 5, 2003. © The Independent.

The article is to be credited to the author and carry a clear copyright by-line to The Independent, with the date the article first appeared.

Extracts from the All England Law Reports were reproduced by permission of Reed ELsevier (UK) Limited trading as LexisNexis UK.

Extracts from the New Law Journal were reproduced courtesy of LexisNexis UK. © LexisNexis UK.

Parliamentary copyright material is reproduced with the permission of the Controller of Her Majesty's Stationery Office on behalf of Parliament.

Extracts from *http://www.cabinet-office.gov.uk/parliamentary-counsel* reproduced courtesy of The Parliamentary Council.

Extract from *http://www.conveyancer.org.uk* reproduced courtesy of the Council for Licensed Conveyancers.

Extract from *http://www.ccrc.gov.uk* reproduced courtesy of the Criminal Cases Review Commission.

Extract from *http://www.magistrates-association.org.uk* reproduced courtesy of the Magistrates Association.

Extract from *http://www.barprobono.org.uk* reproduced courtesy of the Bar Pro Bono unit.

Preface

This new book provides students with a range of source materials and cases, together with related exercises and activities, complementing the material available in *A Level and AS Level Law: A Study Guide* by the same author (2nd edition, Sweet & Maxwell, 2003). It has been written specifically to cover the specifications for AS Law from both the AQA and OCR examination boards. Each chapter begins with a list of issues to explore, setting out clear learning objectives for the student. The **How to use this book** section details the contents of both the AQA and OCR specifications and matches this to the chapters in the book.

The book has been designed to enhance students' understanding and develop their legal skills in a number of ways:

- By introducing students to primary legal resources, such as cases and legislation, along with reports and articles. This will be especially beneficial for the OCR Sources of Law examination.

- By providing activities in each chapter that will enable students to develop their portfolio evidence for Key Skills Communication at Level 3.

- By incorporating the materials and exercises into classroom activities, students will be able to demonstrate clear evidence of learning and achievement.

I would like to thank my 2003–4 AS Law students at Yeovil College for their help and feedback in "classroom testing" this new material. I would also like to take this opportunity to thank all my colleagues, past and present, and friends (especially Rob Whiteman and Ariane Sherine), whose encouragement and support made this book possible. I would also like to thank my editors at Sweet & Maxwell for their unfailing support and efficiency in its preparation and publication.

Martin Hunt, Lecturer in Law, Yeovil College
Yeovil, December 11, 2003

Contents

Table of Cases

Table of Statutes

Table of Statutory Instruments

Table of European materials

How to use this book

To help you find the information you need for your AS Level studies, below are tables listing the contents of both the AQA and OCR specifications (current as at date of publication) and identifying in which chapter you will find the relevant information:

AQA AS Modules:

Module 1: Law Making	Chapter
European Legislative Process and Institutions: Treaties, regulations, directives and decisions. The way in which European Law takes effect. The functions of the Council, Commission, Parliament and the European Court of Justice. Art.234 references.	3
Domestic Legislative Process and Institutions: Formal processes of statute creation; roles of House of Commons in formulating and introducing Bills, the House of Lords in acting as a check on the Government's power, the constitutional position of the Crown acting as "The Queen in Parliament". The doctrine of parliamentary supremacy, having the power to make or unmake any law, and limitations on it, such as the European Treaties, European Convention on Human Rights and Human Rights Act 1998.	1
Delegated legislation: Statutory Instruments (Orders in Council and Ministerial Regulations), bye-laws (Local Authority, professional and public bodies/services/utilities). Control of delegated legislation: judicial, such as *ultra vires* and reasonableness, and parliamentary, such as the role of the Scrutiny Committee, positive and negative processes, Ministerial approval. Advantages and disadvantages of delegated legislation.	2
Influences upon Parliament: The role of the Law Commission in initiating research and proposing reform. The work of Royal Commissions investigating and proposing changes in specific areas. Political considerations and power through the manifesto and electoral mandate. The media and the pressure of events. Pressure groups, including, for example, lobbying by Trade Unions and agricultural, scientific, industrial, and commercial concerns.	1
Statutory Interpretation: Approaches to interpretation: literal, golden and mischief "rules", purposive approach, integrated approach. Intrinsic and extrinsic aids.	4

The Doctrine of Judicial Precedent: The hierarchy of the courts, *ratio decidendi* and *obiter dicta*, law reporting. The obligations and powers of the courts in following, overruling, distinguishing and disapproving precedents, supported by examples drawn from any area of law and illustrating the differing approaches adopted by judges.	5
Module 2: Dispute Solving	
The court structure: Original and appellate jurisdiction of civil and criminal courts: outline knowledge of civil process: promotion of pre-trial settlement, allocation of claims to tracks/courts, relative informality of small claims track and routes and grounds of appeal. Outline knowledge of criminal process: distinction between bail and remand, classification of offences (summary, indictable and "either way"), mode of trial, committal, administrative hearing, routes and grounds of appeal.	7 9
Alternatives to courts: Tribunals, arbitration, mediation, conciliation, negotiation. Comparison of these alternatives with each other and with civil courts: issues of cost, time, privacy, appeals, formality, representation, accessibility and appropriateness for particular issues.	10
The legal profession: The work of barristers, solicitors and legal executives. Training and regulation.	11
Finance of advice and representation: Private finance, insurance, conditional fees, *pro bono* work. Statutory provision of Legal Help and Legal Representation in civil and criminal matters. Alternative sources of advice, *e.g.* CAB, media.	14
The judges: Selection and appointment, training, role, independence and immunity, dismissal.	12
Lay people: Magistrates: selection and appointment, training, role, powers. Jurors: qualification and selection, role.	13

OCR AS Modules:

Module 2568: Machinery of Justice	Chapter
Civil courts: County Court and High Court; jurisdiction at first instance: small claims; fast track; multi-track. Appeals and appellate courts. Problems of using the courts.	9
Alternatives to the courts: Arbitration; conciliation; mediation. Role and composition of administrative tribunals in outline.	10

European Court of Justice: Article 234 (formerly A.177) referrals; relationship to English courts.	3
Police powers: Powers to stop and search; powers of arrest; powers of detention and the treatment of suspects at the police station. Balance of individual rights and the need for investigative powers.	6
Criminal courts: Pre-trial matters: bail, mode of trial, committal proceedings. Jurisdiction of Magistrates' Courts, Youth Courts and Crown Courts at first instance. Appeals. Role of the Criminal Cases Review Commission.	7
Principles of sentencing: Aims of sentencing; purpose and effect of sentences; reoffending rates.	8
Powers of the courts: An understanding of different types of sentences, *e.g.* custodial, community, fines and discharges; compensation and other powers.	8
Module 2569: Legal Personnel	
Judiciary: Appointment; tenure; independence; role, including role in judicial review and enforcement of human rights in outline; role of the Lord Chancellor. The theory of the separation of powers.	12
Barristers and solicitors: Training; work; supervisory role of Bar Council and Law Society. Role of paralegals in outline. Legal Services Ombudsman.	11
Crown Prosecution Service: Role; personnel; Director of Public Prosecutions.	11
Lay magistrates: Appointment; social background; training; role; evaluation and criticism. Role of the magistrates' clerk in outline.	13
Juries: Qualifications of jurors; selection of jury panels; role in criminal and civil cases; evaluation and criticism. Alternatives to jury.	13
Government funding: Legal Aid Board/Legal Services Commission; Community Legal Service; Criminal Defence Service; funding of civil and criminal cases; advice schemes in civil and criminal cases. Access to justice.	14
Advice agencies: Purpose and role of Citizens' Advice Bureaux; law centres; other advice agencies in outline only.	14
Role of legal profession: Private funding of cases; conditional fees.	14
Module 2570: Sources of Law:	
Mechanics of precedent: Precedent as operated in the English Legal System; *stare decisis; obiter dicta; ratio decidendi;* hierarchy of the courts; binding and persuasive precedent; overruling; reversing; and distinguishing.	5
Law-making potential: Original precedent; the Practice Statement 1966; distinguishing; the role of the judges.	5
Acts of Parliament: Green papers, White Papers, legislative stages in Parliament.	2

Delegated legislation: Orders in Council; Statutory Instruments; byelaws; control of delegated legislation including Parliamentary Scrutiny Committees and Judicial Review; reasons for delegating legislative powers.	2
Statutory interpretation: Literal rule, Golden rule, Mischief rule, purposive approach; rules of language; presumptions; intrinsic and extrinsic aids; effects of membership of the European Union on interpretation.	4
European Institutions: The law-making functions of the Council, Commission, Parliament; the role and composition of the European Court of Justice.	3
Primary and secondary sources of EU Law: Treaties, regulations, directives and decisions; their implementation by the courts; the impact of European Union law on domestic legal institutions and law.	3
Impetus for law reform: The role of Parliament; the role of the judges; effect of public opinion and pressure groups.	1
Law reform agencies: The role of the Law Commission; Royal Commissions and other agencies in outline.	1

SECTION ONE: LAW MAKING

1 | Primary Legislation

? Issues to Explore

? How are Acts of Parliament made?

? How effective are the law reform agencies such as the Law Commission?

? What are the advantages and disadvantages of pressure groups?

? How effective is the consultation process?

? How effective is the drafting process?

? What is the relationship between the House of Commons and the House of Lords?

Definition:

PRIMARY LEGISLATION:	Primary legislation refers to Acts of Parliament. As Parliament is the sovereign institution in Britain, Acts of Parliament are the highest form of law.

- The process of making an Act of Parliament involves the pre-parliamentary stages of the enactment process—**proposal**, **consultation**, and **drafting**—and the parliamentary stages of **enactment** in the House of Commons, House of Lords and Royal Assent.

- Most proposals for new legislation come from the **Government** (in the form of **Public Bills**), **law reform agencies** (such as the **Law Commission** and **Royal Commisions**), pressure or **interest groups**, and **individual MPs** (in the form of **Private Members Bills**).

What is a Bill?

Types of Bill

A Bill is a proposal for a new piece of legislation that, if approved by a majority in both the House of Commons and House of Lords, will become an Act of Parliament and law of the land.

Most important bills are introduced by a government minister and relate to public policy. Such bills are known as Public Bills.

Private Members' Bills are introduced by backbench MPs, normally to raise awareness of a particular issue—they often stand little chance of becoming law. However, some do make it through parliament and onto the statute book, such as the 1967 Abortion Act sponsored by David Steel.

Private Members' Bills are a type of Public Bill and should not be confused with Private Bills. Rarely introduced, Private Bills normally affect specific private interests and are often introduced by MPs on behalf of companies. They are used, for example, to facilitate plans to build a railway line, rather than for matters of public policy.

(Adapted from BBC News: A–Z of Parliament.)

Private Members' Bills

Individual Members of Parliament, sometimes referred to as Private Members, have the power to introduce their own legislation under the Private Members' Bill procedure.

There are three types of Private Members' Bill:

- The most important is the balloted bill. Each year a ballot is held at the start of the session and the 20 MPs whose names come out top are allowed to introduce legislation on a subject of their choice. The six or seven MPs at the top of this list are given time by the Government to have their proposals discussed in detail in the House. Measures which gain strong cross party support can stand a good chance of becoming law.

- Members may also introduce Private Members' Bills in the form of Ten Minute Rule Bills on Tuesday and Wednesday afternoons. The sponsoring MP may make a speech lasting 10 minutes in support of his or her bill. These bills are not allocated time for further discussion and stand little chance of becoming law.

- The third type of Private Members' Bill is the Presentation Bill. A Member introducing this type of bill is not able to speak in support of it and the bill stands almost no chance of becoming law.

These bills are used by MPs largely as a method of publicising a particular issue.

(Adapted from BBC News: A—Z of Parliament.)

Complete this table, giving a brief explanation of each type of Bill, with examples

Type of Bill	Explanation	Examples
Public		

Private Members		
Private		

The Law Commission

What is the Law Commission?

The Law Commission is the independent body set up by Parliament in 1965 to keep the law of England and Wales under review and to recommend reform when it is needed. Our law is a combination of the common law—decisions of the higher courts—and of statute law enacted or authorised by Parliament; sometimes those decisions and statutes may go back many centuries.

Substantial reform of the law is a task for Parliament. Although proposals for reform may well not be satisfactory unless they are preceded by research and by wide consultation with experts and with those who may be affected by the reforms. Our job is to carry out this research and consultation, and to modernise, improve and simplify the law by formulating proposals on a systematic basis for consideration by Parliament.

What does the Law Commission do?

Our main work is the reform of the law, but we also work on consolidation of statutes and statute law revision. The Commission does not give legal advice to individuals or investigate complaints about the law or about lawyers.

Who are the members of the Commission?

There are five Commissioners, all of whom work full-time at the Commission. The Chairman is a High Court judge. The other four Commissioners are experienced judges, barristers, solicitors or teachers of law. They are appointed by the Secretary of State for Constitutional Affairs (formerly the Lord Chancellor) for up to five years, and their appointments can be extended. They are supported by the Chief Executive of the Commission and about 20 other members of the Government Legal Service, four or five Parliamentary Counsel (who draft the Bills to reform and consolidate the law), and around 15 research assistants (usually recently qualified law graduates), as well as a librarian and administrative staff.

Reform of what?

The Law Commissions Act requires the Commission to keep "all the law" under review. In choosing the projects on which to work, we and the Government are guided by the views of judges, lawyers, government departments and the general public, who tell us of the difficulties they have experienced in applying the law or in seeking legal remedies. We take account of the importance of the issues involved and their suitability for consideration by the Commission, as well as the availability of resources.

The main areas of law on which we work include: trust and property law; criminal law; contract; tort; commercial law; the law of landlord and tenant; and damages.

A full list of all the Commission's consultation papers and reports, together with the legislation resulting from them, is available on the Internet. Some examples of such legislation are: the Land Registration Act 2002, providing for electronic conveyancing and revolutionising the land registration system; the Trustee Act 2000, modernising aspects of the law of trusts; the Family Law Act 1996, changing the law of domestic violence; the Computer Misuse Act 1990, introducing new criminal offences about the misuse of computers; the Children Act 1989, rewriting the whole of the law on children; the Consumer Protection Act 1987, covering liability for defective products; and the Family Law Reform Act 1987, removing the legal disadvantages attached to illegitimacy.

Codification

In most countries whole areas of law are contained in a single code rather than, as in England, being divided between the common law, which is derived from decisions of judges over the centuries, and statute law enacted by Parliament. It has always been the Commission's objective that parts of English law should similarly be governed by a series of statutory codes, to make the law more accessible to the citizen and easier for the courts and litigants to understand and handle. For instance, in family law much of the Commission's work has resulted in the production of what is in effect a code, though contained in a series of separate Acts of Parliament.

More particularly, for some years the Commission has had in hand a project to produce a criminal code, such as exists in almost every other country in the world. In 1989 we published a Draft Code in rational and modern form and language, and since then we have produced a series of draft Bills which, if enacted, could form the nucleus of such a Code as well as improving the substance of the law. The Government has said that it sees the enactment of a Code as an important part of its plans to modernise the criminal justice system.

Consolidation of statutes

Another of the Commission's important activities is the consolidation of statute law. This involves putting together in one Act of Parliament, or in a group of Acts, all the existing statutory provisions previously located in several different Acts. The existing provisions are repealed by the new Act or Acts. For example, the Powers of Criminal Courts (Sentencing) Act 2000 brought together in a single piece of legislation sentencing powers which were previously to be found in more than a dozen Acts. The law itself remains unchanged, but those who use it—lawyers and the courts, and the general public—can now find it all in one place.

Is it all worth it?

The Commission's recommendations for law reform have a profound practical effect on the legal rights, duties and liabilities of a large number of people—but only if they are implemented by Parliament. We can make recommendations, but only Parliament can change the law. So far, over 100 (more than two-thirds of the Commission's law reform reports) have been implemented, and a number await the Government's reactions, or Parliamentary time. As a result of the Commission's ongoing work, large areas of the law have been the subject of systematic investigation and improvement. Antiquated laws have been abolished, and new remedies devised appropriate for the times in which we live. Much has already been done, but there is still much more to do.

(Adapted from The Law Commission's website.)

Quinquennial Review of the Law Commission

by John Halliday CB (March 2003)

Overview: The Law Commission's contribution to improvements in the law is held in high esteem by the wide variety of its stakeholders who were consulted during this review. The review has found no grounds for disturbing the present functions of the Commission, or for proposing fundamental changes in its methods of working. The thrust of this report is that the recent developments made by both the Commission and Government to strengthen working processes should be taken further over the coming years. The aim of such developments should be to maximise the public benefits to be derived from law reform: the delivery of public benefit should become a "golden thread" running through all processes, from project selection, through project management, recommendations, implementation, and final evaluation of outcomes. . .

The Law Commission has many strengths, especially the high quality of its output. These need to be sustained during any future improvement programme. Scope for improvement lies predominantly in the timeliness and impact of the Commission's work, rather than its quality. . .

Implementation of reports: Once a Law Commission report is published, it is the responsibility of the lead Government Department to accept or reject its recommendations and to implement them, where appropriate. Of the 91 law reform reports produced between 1985 and 2001, 82 called for legislation: 39 of those 82 reports (48 per cent) have been enacted. . . In addition to the 48 per cent of reports that have been implemented through primary legislation, one rejected report and part of a second report under consideration have been implemented through Court of Appeal judgments. This gives a total of 50 per cent of reports that have been implemented. . . If 50 per cent of reports have been implemented then it stands that 50 per cent have not. Out of the 82 reports calling for legislation 15 per cent have been rejected, 13 per cent have been accepted and 17 per cent remain under consideration. The status of the remaining 5 per cent of reports is unknown. As this review has indicated, the Law Commission is concerned about the number of outstanding reports. . .

Time taken to implement reports: As well as the level of implementation, it is important to consider the speed of implementation. The average time taken from the publication to the implementation of a report (between 1985 and 2001) was three years and one month. . . an assessment of *all* of the reports currently under consideration paints a bleaker picture. On average the reports were published four years and seven ago. This raises the question of whether those reports, which have been under consideration for some time, are ever likely to be accepted and implemented. . .

The search for new procedural devices to facilitate Parliamentary scrutiny of Law Commission Bills needs to be invigorated. Without new procedures there will be continuing risks of worthwhile law reforms, including codified criminal law, not being implemented, or being implemented only after long delays. . .

Recommendation 30: The Lord Chancellor's Department—in consultation with the Law Commission, other Government Departments (including the Government's business managers) and the relevant Parliamentary authorities—should initiate a project aimed at identifying special Parliamentary procedures to facilitate scrutiny of Law Commission Bills. . .

(Adapted from The Department for Constitutional Affairs website.)

The Law Commission	
What is the Law Commission?	
Who works for the Commission?	
What does the Commsission do?	
Examples of the Commission's work?	

What are the strengths and weaknesses of the Law Commission?	
Strengths	Weaknesses

Royal commissions

Royal commissions are *ad hoc* advisory committees established by the government—though formally appointed by the Crown (hence the "royal" monikor) to investigate any subject that the administration of the day sees fit to refer one to. They are often used for non-party political issues, or for issues that a government wishes to be seen as addressing in a non-party political way. A government is not bound to accept the advice of any royal commission.

In practice, royal commissions have sometimes been established to deal with issues that a government feels may be too controversial to be seen tackling itself. For example, in recent years various politicians have campaigned for a royal commission to examine the issue of the decriminalisation of cannabis. But some royal commissions have also been seen as ways of side-lining issues.

The size of a royal commission, (its chairperson, membership and remit) is set by the government. Most commissions take evidence, deliberate and then produce a final report. The government usually outlines at the time of its establishment when it expects a royal commission to produce its final conclusions. The average duration from establishment to report is between two and four years.

(Adapted from BBC News: A—Z of Parliament.)

Royal commissions	
Explanation	
Advantages	

Disadvantages	

Pressure groups

Pressure groups are organisations which aim to influence Parliament and government in the way that decisions are made and carried out. They have become much more important in politics in recent years, with many people no longer choosing to involve themselves in the traditional political parties and instead to work through single-issue groups.

There are a huge range of pressure groups, campaigning on issues including animal welfare, education, the environment, equality for ethnic minorities, health, housing, rural affairs and welfare rights.

Some pressure groups work through radical protest; others seek influence in more traditional ways such as encouraging people to write to their MPs or petition the government.

(Adapted from An Introduction to Parliament: Making New Law—UK Parliament website.)

New law to trap parents who murder

By Jo Dillon, Deputy Political Editor

A new charge of joint homicide is to be introduced to close a loophole that allows parents to escape justice by covering up for each other when children are killed or seriously injured at home.

Latest figures show that three children under 10 are killed or seriously injured each week. But while 90 per cent of adult murders are solved and result in convictions, almost two-thirds of cases of child murder or serious assault never get to court, and of those that do, just 27 per cent result in a conviction. Only a tiny number are found guilty of murder or manslaughter. It is a record that even the police admit is "appalling". Now the Government has signalled it is ready to change the law. Home Office minister Hilary Benn, in a Commons written answer last week, said it accepted the "need for the law to be strengthened so that people jointly accused cannot evade justice by protecting each other". He said a number of possibilities were being considered, including changes to procedures in the wake of a child death. A Home Office spokeswoman said the Government would "legislate at the earliest possible opportunity".

Ministerial action will be assisted by two reports—one from the Law Commission, the other from the National Society for the Prevention of Cruelty to Children. The NSPCC report, entitled Which of You Did It?, records the findings of a working party led by Judge Isobel Plumstead, to look into the problems of bringing child killers to justice. English case law determines that if it cannot be proved which parent was responsible for the death or serious injury of a child then there is no case to answer.

(Adapted from The Independent, February 23, 2003.)

Activity ❶

Working in **pairs** or **small groups**, and using the information in the articles above, together with any other information you may find (*e.g.* in books, journals, newspapers or on the internet), prepare the case for or against the involvement of pressure groups in making new law. In preparing this activity, you should also read **Chapter 1** of *A Level and AS Level Law: a Study Guide*. You might also find it helpful to complete the **table**, below. You should then **debate** this issue as a whole class.

(Evidence: Communications: C3.1a, C3.2)

Pressure groups	
Explanation	
"Cause" groups— examples	
"Interest" groups— examples	
Advantages	
Disadvantages	

Activity ❷

Using the information you have gathered for Activity 1 and any further information you have gained as a result of the debate, prepare an **appropriate document** (*e.g.* an article of approximately 1000 words for a broadsheet newspaper) that outlines the main arguments for and against the involvement of pressure groups in making new law. This document must include at least one **image**.

(Evidence: Communications: C3.2, C3.3)

Consultation

Who is consulted about changes to the law?

Before Bills are introduced into Parliament, there has often been consultation or discussion with interested parties such as professional bodies, voluntary organisations and pressure groups. Proposals for legislative changes may be contained in government **White Papers**. These may be preceded by consultation papers, sometimes called **Green Papers**, which set out government proposals that are still taking shape and seek comments from the public. There is no requirement for there to be a White or Green Paper before a Bill is introduced into Parliament.

(Adapted from An introduction to Parliament: making new law—UK Parliament website.)

Green Papers

A Green Paper is a consultation document issued by the government which contains policy proposals for debate and discussion before a final decision is taken on the best policy option. A Green Paper will often contain several alternative policy options. Following this consultation the government will normally publish firmer recommendations in a White Paper.

White Papers

A White Paper is a document issued by a government department which contains detailed proposals for legislation. It is the final stage before the government introduces its proposals to Parliament in the form of a Bill. When a White Paper is issued, it is often accompanied by a statement in the House from the secretary of state of the department sponsoring the proposals.

(Adapted from BBC News: A–Z of Parliament.)

Consultation	
Who is consulted?	
What are Green Papers?	
What are White Papers?	

Why is consultation important?

Drafting

The Parliamentary Counsel Office

The Parliamentary Counsel are a specialised team of around 50 lawyers with their own Office in Whitehall. Their main work is drafting government Bills for introduction into Parliament and related Parliamentary business. The PCO handle all government Bills apart from one or two specialised types, and those relating only to Scotland. Members of the PCO are also loaned (usually for two years at a time) to the Law Commission where they are mainly engaged on the preparation of law reform Bills and consolidation Bills. The PCO also lends members (again for about two years at a time) to the Inland Revenue, where they help on a project designed to simplify tax legislation.

A Bill is drafted on instructions from the legal branch of the government department concerned. The functions of Parliamentary Counsel are not confined to the choice of language, but include (to a greater or lesser extent) the clarification and detailed working out, in consultation with lawyers and administrators in the department, of the policy to be given effect to by the Bill and of the conceptual and legislative structure appropriate for this purpose. The work on a Bill includes: drafting amendments to be moved by the government in the course of the Bill's passage through Parliament; drafting any necessary financial and other resolutions; advising the department concerned with the Bill on opposition and back-bench amendments and on questions of Parliamentary procedure; attending, as required, sittings of both Houses (and Committees of those Houses) when a Bill is under discussion; and co-operation with officers of both Houses.

Parliamentary Counsel operate for the most part in teams of two or three. The instructions for a Bill are allocated to one of the senior Counsel, who then takes full responsibility for it and handles it together with one or two of the junior Counsel. The Counsel correspond and confer as necessary with the department or departments involved, and with the Law Officers on matters of concern to them. With the exception of the annual Finance Bills, specialisation is not encouraged; any one of the Counsel is expected to be able to deal with a Bill on any subject.

(Adapted from The Parliamentary Counsel Office website.)

How are proposals for new legislation translated into Bills to be presented to Parliament?

The enactment process

Public Bills can be introduced into either the House of Commons or the House of Lords. As a rule, government bills likely to raise political controversy start in the Commons, while those of a technical but less party-political nature often go to the Lords first. Bills with a mainly financial purpose are always introduced in the Commons. If the main object of a Public Bill is to create a public charge—involving new taxation or public spending—it must be introduced by a government minister in the Commons.

First reading

The **first reading** of a Public Bill is a formality. Once formally presented, a Bill is printed and proceeds to a second reading. Amendments can be made at the committee and subsequent stages.

Second reading

Following its first reading, a government Bill will usually have its second reading within the next fortnight if time permits. This provides the first main occasion for **debate on the general principles of a Bill**—detailed discussion being reserved for the committee stage.

On second reading the Bill is normally proposed by a government minister (often the senior minister) in the department responsible for the measure. He or she outlines the main principles of the Bill and summarises the most important clauses. The official Opposition spokesman then responds and during the debate the views of other opposition parties and backbenchers are heard. The debate normally concludes with a response from another government minister and he or she deals with some of the major points raised in the debate.

Unless the Bill is non-controversial the Opposition in the Commons will usually decide to vote against a government bill on its second reading, or to move an amendment to the motion "that the Bill be read a second time".

If the House votes against the Bill at second reading, it can progress no further, but this virtually never happens.

Committee stage

When a Bill has passed its second reading in the House of Commons, it is usually referred to a **standing committee** for detailed, **clause-by-clause examination**. In some cases a bill may be referred to a **Committee of the Whole House** instead. Bills which have their committee stage on the floor of the House generally fall into one of the following categories:

- Bills of major constitutional importance (*e.g.* those concerned with the ratification of the treaties constituting the European Union, or with the government of parts of the UK).

- Bills which the government needs to pass with unusual speed (*e.g.* when the courts have found a previous Act defective, and this has major financial or political consequences, or there is a state of emergency).

- Bills which are of a very uncontroversial nature (*e.g.* those consolidating existing law) of which the committee stage is expected to be very short and where it would not be worthwhile to establish a standing committee.

- Private Members' Bills which are not opposed and of which all the stages are taken without debate.

Report stage

A fortnight after a standing committee has examined a Bill it then **reports its decisions for consideration by the House** as a whole. The report stage is an opportunity for members not serving on the standing committee to propose further amendments or new clauses to a Bill. All members may speak and vote and for lengthy or complex Bills the debate may be spread over several days. Bills which have had their committee stage entirely on the floor of the House do not normally receive a full report stage debate.

In the House of Commons the report stage is usually followed immediately (*i.e.* as the next item of business) by the Bill's third reading debate.

Third reading

At the third reading a Bill is **reviewed in its final form** including amendments made at earlier stages. **In the Commons** substantive amendments cannot be made to a Bill at this stage and the third reading debate is generally short.

After passing its third reading in one House a Bill is sent to the other House.

Agreement of both Houses

Having received its third reading in one House, a Bill is sent to the other House where it passes through all the stages once more. Financial legislation is not scrutinised in detail by the Lords.

The passage through the second House is not a formality, and Bills can be further amended. Amendments made by the second House must be agreed by the first, or a compromise agreement reached, such that both Houses have agreed the same text, before a Bill can receive Royal Assent.

Bills with contentious amendments pass back and forth between the Houses before agreement is reached. If each House insists on its amendments, then a Bill may be lost.

Limitations on the power of the Lords

Most government Bills introduced and passed in the Lords pass through the Commons without difficulty, but a Bill from the Lords which proved unacceptable to the Commons would not become law. The Lords do not generally prevent bills from the Commons becoming law, although they will often amend them and return them for further consideration by the Commons.

The assent of the Lords is not essential, subject to certain conditions, in the case of "money Bills". Bills dealing solely with taxation or expenditure must become law within one month of being sent to the Lords.

If, after the process of considering amendments, it proves impossible to reach agreement on a non-financial Bill, then the Bill may be lost. Alternatively, the Commons can use its powers to present a Bill originating in the House of Commons for Royal Assent after one year and in a new session, even if the Lords' objections are maintained.

These limitations to the powers of the Lords are contained in the Parliament Acts of 1911 and 1949. They are based on the belief that the main legislative function of the non-elected House is to act as a chamber of revision, complementing but not rivalling the elected House.

Royal Assent

When a Bill has completed all its parliamentary stages, it receives Royal Assent from the Queen. Royal Assent nowadays is generally declared to both Houses by their Speakers and is listed in *Hansard*, the official record of proceedings in Parliament.

After this the Bill becomes part of the law of the land and is known as an **Act of Parliament**. Royal Assent was last given in person by the Sovereign in 1854. The Royal Assent has not been refused since 1707, when Queen Anne refused a Bill for settling the militia in Scotland.

(Adapted from An introduction to Parliament: making new law—UK Parliament website.)

The Parliament Acts

The Parliament Acts of 1911 and 1949 restrict the power of the House of Lords to block legislation introduced by the government. Under the Acts, those Bills which have been approved by the House of Commons can be given Royal Assent without passing through the House of Lords. If the Lords refuse to agree to a Bill which has already been approved by the Commons then the government can pass the Bill into law, after a delay of one year, without seeking the Lords' agreement. The powers granted in the Parliament Acts were used to force through the War Crimes Act in 1991 and the Sexual Offences (Amendment) Act in 2000. The Parliament Acts also provide that Money Bills, such as the Finance Bill, do not require the Lords' consent before gaining Royal Assent. The Parliament Acts do not apply to Bills introduced by Lords, or Bills to extend the life of Parliament beyond five years.

(Adapted from BBC News: A–Z of Parliament.)

 ## Activity ❸

You have been asked to give a short **presentation** to a group of politics students about how Parliament passes laws. Using the material in the extracts above, and any other relevant information you can find, prepare and deliver this presentation. In preparing this activity, you should also read **Chapter 1** of **A Level and AS Level Law: a Study Guide**. You might also find it helpful to complete the table, below. Make sure that your presentation covers:

- The production of Bills.

- The passage of Bills through Parliament.

- The need for Royal Assent.

- What happens if the House of Commons and House of Lords disagree.

You must also produce a **one-page handout** for the audience, giving the main points of your presentation and where they can find further information. Your handout, in addition to the text, must include at least **one image**.

(Evidence: Communications: 3.1b, C3.2, C3.3)

The enactment process	
First reading	
Second reading	
Committee stage	
Report stage	
Third reading	
Other House	
What if the Commons and Lords cannot agree?	
Royal Assent	

2 | Delegated Legislation

? Issues to Explore

? What is delegated legislation?

? What are the different types of delegated legislation?

? What are the advantages and disadvantages of delegated legislation?

? How effective are the controls over the use of delegated powers?

Definition:

DELEGATED LEGISLATION:	Delegated legislation is law made by individuals or institutions acting under a grant of legislative power from Parliament.

- Powers to make delegated legislation are generally granted in an **enabling Act**.

- The enabling Act will establish a framework of general principles and grant delegated legislative powers to others to fill in the details.

- The three main types of delegated legislation are **Statutory Instruments**, **Byelaws**, and **Orders in Council**.

Below is an example of a **Statutory Instrument**.

STATUTORY INSTRUMENTS

2000 No. 1502

SEA FISHERIES, ENGLAND

CONSERVATION OF SEA FISH

The Undersized Spider Crabs Order 2000

Made	*7th June 2000*
Laid before Parliament	*8th June 2000*
Coming into force	*30th June 2000*

The Minister of Agriculture, Fisheries and Food and the Secretaries of State respectively concerned with the sea fishing industry in Scotland and Wales, acting jointly, in exercise of the powers conferred on them by sections 1(1), (4) and (6) of the Sea Fish (Conservation) Act 1967 and of all other powers enabling them in that behalf, and the said Minister, the said Secretaries of State and the Secretary of State concerned with the sea fishing industry in Northern Ireland, acting jointly, in exercise of the powers conferred upon them by section 15(3) of the said Act, and of all other powers enabling them in that behalf, hereby make the following Order. . .

Prescribed minimum size for landing spider crabs in England

3.—(1) For the purposes of section 1(1) of the Act (which prohibits the landing in England and Wales of any sea fish of any description, being a fish of a smaller size than such size as may be prescribed in relation to sea fish of that description), there is hereby prescribed as the minimum size for male spider crabs a size of 130 millimetres.

Complete this table by answering the questions using the information in the above extract.	
What does the Order prohibit?	
What do you think this is intended to achieve?	
What is the enabling Act under which this Order is made?	
What is the general purpose of that Act?	
How do the detailed rules in the Order relate to that general purpose?	
Why do we use delegated legislation for this? Why not include the detailed rules in the Act itself?	

Delegated or secondary legislation

In order to reduce pressure on parliamentary time, Acts of Parliament often give government ministers or other authorities the power to regulate administrative details by means of "delegated" or secondary legislation. This mostly takes the form of Orders in Council, Regulations and Rules known as **Statutory Instruments (SIs)**. These are as much the law of the land as are Acts of Parliament. SIs are normally drafted by the legal department of the ministry concerned and may be subject, when in draft, to consultations with interested parties. About 3,000 SIs are issued each year.

To minimise any risk that delegating powers to the executive might undermine the authority of Parliament, such powers are normally only delegated to authorities directly accountable to Parliament. The relevant Acts sometimes provide for some measure of direct parliamentary control over proposed delegated legislation, by giving Parliament the opportunity to affirm or annul it. Parliament always has the right to consider whether the SI is made in accordance with the powers that it delegated.

(Adapted from An introduction to Parliament: making new law—UK Parliament website.)

Nature of subordinate legislation

Subordinate legislation is made under powers conferred by or under statute on Her Majesty in Council or on a Minister, Department, the National Assembly for Wales or other body or person. It is also called delegated or secondary legislation, and the statute conferring the power is referred to as the enabling or empowering or "parent" Act.

Limits of delegated powers

Provisions in subordinate legislation must be *intra vires*, that is they must be within the scope of the enabling power. If they are *ultra vires* they are invalid. The draftsman may, for example, have to consider whether there is power to impose or increase taxation, or to sub-delegate, or to give the instrument retrospective effect, or to repeal or amend provisions in statutes, or to bind the Crown.

(Adapted from Statutory Instrument Practice, Cabinet Office/HMSO, 3rd Ed., 2003.)

Statutory Instruments

Statutory Instruments (SIs) are rules and regulations made by ministers under powers given to them by Acts of Parliament. They are sometimes known as secondary legislation. The legal changes contained in SIs are generally matters of detail and do not require lengthy debate in either House. Around 3,000 Statutory Instruments are brought before Parliament every year. Only a small number of these are debated in Parliament. They may be debated on the floor of the House or in a Statutory Instrument Committee for up to one and a half hours. MPs can vote to reject SIs but they cannot be amended.

(Adapted from BBC News: A–Z of Parliament.)

Orders in Council

Orders in Council are classified as secondary legislation. They are issued by the Privy Council and often relate to the regulation of professional bodies, or the transfer of responsibilities between government departments. Usually, alterations to legislation are made by using Statutory Instruments, which are made under the authority of a parent Act of Parliament, but in cases where this is inappropriate Orders in Council are used.

(Adapted from BBC News: A–Z of Parliament.)

Byelaws

Domestic Records Information 84

1. Introduction

Byelaws are rules made by a local authority, corporation or association for the regulation, administration or management of a certain district, property or undertaking. They usually deal with matters of internal regulation, and are binding on all persons within the area or organisation to which they relate. Local authorities may make byelaws for the good rule and government of the whole or any part of the district for which they are responsible. Corporations may make byelaws for the better government of their own body or for the regulation of their dealings with the public: in modern times, such byelaws have commonly been made by railway companies and other commercial undertakings in the exercise of powers expressly conferred by statute . . . Byelaws require confirmation by a Secretary of State.

(Adapted from The Public Record Office website.)

Byelaws

Local authorities have power under certain Acts of Parliament to make byelaws, which are local laws that create criminal offences. Before they can come into effect, byelaws must be confirmed by a Secretary of State. This branch deals with applications from local authorities and parish and town councils for confirmation of byelaws for which the Deputy Prime Minister as First Secretary of State is the confirming authority. The byelaws and their enabling powers are listed below.

Byelaw	*Enabling Power*
Good rule and government and the prevention and suppression of nuisances	Local Government Act 1972 (s.235)
Public walks and pleasure grounds	Public Health Act 1875 (s.164)
Open spaces and disused burial grounds	Open Spaces Act 1906 (ss.12/15)

Pleasure fairs, amusement premises, etc.	Public Health Act 1961 (s.75) as amended by s.22, Local Government (Miscellaneous Provisions) Act 1976
Seashore and promenades	Public Health Acts Amendment Act 1907 (ss.82 and 83)
Public bathing	Public Health Act 1936 (s.231)
Markets	Food Act 1984 (s.60)
Hairdressers and barbers	Public Health Act 1961 (s.77)

Procedure for making byelaws

1. These notes explain the procedure for making byelaws as laid down in s.236 of the Local Government Act 1972.

2. Following the general election on June 7, responsibility for the confirmation of certain byelaws was transferred from the Home Secretary to the Secretary of State for Transport, Local Government and the Regions. These responsibilities were transferred to the Office of the Deputy Prime Minister on May 29, 2002. Home Office Circular 25/1996 (which remains in use until further notice) sets out the procedures for drafting byelaws either by a standard or a fast-track process, using model byelaws.

Making the byelaws

3. When the council has formally resolved to adopt any byelaws, they should be made under the common seal of the authority. The seal should be placed after any schedule or plan which is to be included in the byelaws. The document should also be signed and dated.

4. Where the byelaws are made by a parish or community council not having a seal, they should be made under the hands and seals of two members of the council1. In this case, a suitable subscription to the byelaws would be:

Given under our hands and seals this ... ... day of ... ...

(Signed) ... ... (Seal)

(Signed) ... ... (Seal)

Members of the ... ... Parish/Town Council.

5. If members of the parish or town council who sign the byelaws do not possess personal seals, the imprint of a signet ring, coin or thumb will suffice. Sealing wax and parchment seals may be obtained from legal stationers.

6. In order to provide sufficient room for the official stamp and the seal of the Secretary of State, at least 15 centimetres (six inches) of space should be left after the council's seal.

Advertising the byelaws and holding them on deposit

7. After the byelaws have been sealed, a notice of the council's intention to apply for their confirmation must be given in one or more newspapers circulating in the area to which the byelaws are to apply.

8. The usual wording for the newspaper notice is shown below.

9. For at least one month after the date of the publication of the newspaper(s), a copy of the byelaws must be held on deposit at the offices of the council for inspection by the public at all reasonable hours.

10. It is sometimes overlooked that it is a "copy of the byelaws" which has to be held on deposit. The period of deposit, therefore, cannot begin until the byelaws have been brought into existence by being sealed. To avoid confusion, councils are advised to ensure that the byelaws are advertised **after** they have been sealed.

11. The council must provide any person who applies with a copy of the byelaws or with a copy of any part of the byelaws. A fee of not more than 10 pence should be charged for every 100 words contained in any copy supplied.

COUNTY/DISTRICT/PARISH/TOWN OF ... ...
CONFIRMATION OF BYELAWS

Notice is hereby given that the County/District/Parish/Town Council of ... ... intends after the expiry of the period mentioned below to apply to the Secretary of State for confirmation of byelaws made by the Council [insert here a brief description of the byelaws].

Copies of the byelaws will be kept at the offices of the Council at ... ... and will be open to inspection without payment on any weekday during the usual office hours for one calendar month from and after the date of the [first] publication of this notice. Copies of the byelaws will also be supplied on receipt of an application accompanied by a fee of ... ... for each copy.

Any objection to the confirmation of the byelaws may be made by letter addressed to the Office of the Deputy Prime Minister (DLL), Eland House (5/B1), Bressenden Place, London SW1E 5DU before the byelaws are confirmed.

(Signed) ... ... Proper Officer of the Council
(Dated) ... ...

Applying for confirmation of the byelaws

12. Application to the ODPM for confirmation should not be made until the month of deposit has expired. Two sealed documents are required by the Department.

13. The application should state that a copy of the sealed byelaws as forwarded has been deposited for inspection for a full calendar month since publication of the newspaper(s). A photocopy or clipping of the newspaper(s) should also be enclosed.

14. On receipt of the sealed byelaws, provided that no objections have been received, they will normally be confirmed and returned to you within two weeks. Where objections have been received, copies may be forwarded to you for the council's comments before a decision is taken.

15. In contentious cases, particularly those where the arguments are finely balanced, it is open to the Secretary of State to order a public inquiry to be held. Such inquiries are rare and, in the normal course, the Secretary of State would hope that the issues—and any scope for compromise—might be determined locally between the council and objectors.

Date of operation of the byelaws

16. When he confirms byelaws, the Secretary of State may fix the date upon which they are to come into force. The date will normally be one month from the point of confirmation, unless there are special circumstances which make an earlier date desirable. If this is the case, a request and reasons should accompany your application.

(Adapted from The Office of the Deputy Prime Minister website.)

Delegated Legislation—Explanation			
Type	Explanation?	Made by?	National or Local Effect?
Statutory Instruments			
Orders in Council			
Byelaws			

Activity ❶

You have been asked to give a short **presentation** to a group of new local councillors about delegated legislation. Using the material in the extracts above, and any other relevant information you can find (e.g. from the UK Parliament website), prepare and deliver this presentation. In preparing this activity, you should also read **Chapter 2** of **A Level and AS Level Law: a Study Guide**. Make sure that your presentation covers:

● What is delegated legislation?

● How are law-making powers delegated to bodies like local councils?

● What are the different types of delegated legislation?

● What type of delegated legislation are the councilors likely to be involved in making?

The presentation must include at least **one image**.

You must also produce a **one-page handout** for the audience, giving the main points of your presentation and where they can find further information. Your handout, in addition to the text, must include at least **one image**.

(Evidence: Communications: 3.1b, C3.2, C3.3)

Varieties of parliamentary control

Class	Procedure
(i) (ii) (iii)	**Affirmative procedures** The instrument is laid in draft, and cannot be made unless the draft is approved by Parliament (or the House of Commons). The instrument is laid after making, but cannot come into force unless and until so approved. The instrument is laid after making, but cannot remain in force after a specified period (usually 28 days, sometimes a month or 40 days, from the date on which it was made) unless approved within that period.
(iv) (v)	**Negative procedures** The instrument is laid in draft, and cannot be made if the draft is disapproved within 40 days. The instrument is laid after making, subject to revocation if a resolution for annulment is passed within 40 days.
(vi) (vii)	**Other procedures** The instrument is required to be laid before Parliament after being made, but there is no provision for further parliamentary proceedings. The instrument is not required to be laid.

Use of affirmative procedure

Affirmative procedure is less common than the negative procedure . . . but provides the more stringent form of parliamentary control, since the Statutory Instrument or draft must receive positive approval.

Use of negative procedure

Negative procedure provides a less stringent form of parliamentary control than affirmative: the instrument will remain in force, or may be made in the form of the draft, unless a Member introduces a negative resolution . . . and the resolution is agreed to. The procedure applicable to negative instruments (class (iv)) is relatively uncommon, but that applicable to negative instruments (class (v)) is much the most common form of parliamentary control.

(Adapted from Statutory Instrument Practice, Cabinet Office/HMSO, 3rd Ed. 2003.)

Joint Committee on Statutory Instruments

Remit:

The Joint Committee on Statutory Instruments is responsible for scrutinising all statutory instruments made in exercise of powers granted by Act of Parliament.

The Joint Committee is empowered to draw the special attention of both Houses to an instrument on any one of a number of grounds specified in the Standing Order under which it operates; or on any other ground which does not impinge upon the merits of the instrument or the policy behind it.

(Adapted from The UK Parliament website.)

Activity ❷

Working in **pairs** or **small groups**, and using the information in the articles above, together with any other information you may find (e.g. in books, journals, newspapers or on the internet), prepare the case for or against the growth in the amount of delegated legislation. In preparing this activity, you should also read **Chapter 2** of *A Level and AS Level Law: a Study Guide*. You might also find it helpful to complete the **table** below. You should then **debate** this issue as a whole class.

(Evidence: Communications: C3.1a, C3.2)

Delegated legislation—evaluation	
Advantages	
Disadvantages	
Parliamentary controls	
Judicial controls	

Activity ❸

Using the information you have gathered for Activity 2 and any further information you have gained as a result of the debate, prepare an **extended document** (e.g. an article of approximately 1000 words for a broadsheet newspaper) that outlines the main arguments for and against the growth in the amount of delegated legislation. This document must include at least one **image**.

(Evidence: Communications: C3.2, C3.3)

3 | European Legislation

? Issues to Explore

? What are the main institutions of the European Union?

? What are the main types of European legislation?

? What is the effect of EU membership on the sovereignty of Parliament?

? What is the relationship between the English courts and the European Court of Justice?

Definition:

EUROPEAN LEGISLATION:	European legislation is law made by the European Union and applies either directly or indirectly, to all the Member States.

- The **European Union** (as it is now known) was formed in the 1950s to encourage European co-operation, mainly in the economic sphere.

- Britain joined the Union in 1973.

- In order to achieve its objectives, the Union has had to establish its own legal institutions and law—a **European Legal Order**.

- The main governing and law-making institutions of the Union are the **Council of Ministers**, the **Commission**, the **Parliament**, and the **Court of Justice**.

The Council of the European Union

The Council is the EU's main decision-making body. Like the European Parliament, the Council was set up by the founding treaties in the 1950s. It represents the Member States, and its meetings are attended by one minister from each of the EU's national governments.

Which ministers attend which meeting depends on what subjects are on the agenda. If, for example, the Council is to discuss environmental issues, the meeting will be attended by the Environment Minister from each EU country and it will be known as the "Environment Council".

Each minister in the Council is empowered to commit his or her government. In other words, the minister's signature is the signature of the whole government. Moreover, each minister in the Council is answerable to his or her national parliament and to the citizens that parliament represents. This ensures the democratic legitimacy of the Council's decisions.

The Council has six key responsibilities:

1. To pass European laws. In many fields it legislates jointly with the European Parliament.

2. To co-ordinate the broad economic policies of the Member States.

3. To conclude international agreements between the EU and one or more States or international organisations.

4. To approve the EU's budget, jointly with the European Parliament.

5. To develop the EU's Common Foreign and Security Policy based on guidelines set by the European Council.

6. To co-ordinate co-operation between the national courts and police forces in criminal matters.

Most of these responsibilities relate to the "Community" domain, *i.e.* areas of action where the member states have decided to pool their sovereignty and delegate decision-making powers to the EU institutions. This domain is the "first pillar" of the European Union.

However, the last two responsibilities relate largely to areas in which the Member States have not delegated their powers but are simply working together. This is called "intergovernmental co-operation" and it covers the second and third "pillars" of the European Union (CFSP and police and judicial co-operation in criminal matters).

(Adapted from Europa: The European Union On-Line.)

Council of Ministers

Officially called the Council of the European Union, the Council of Ministers is the only EU institution which represents the Member States' national governments. It is made up of government ministers from the [Member] States, creating a kind of cabinet of cabinets. Which ministers attend the Council depends on the subject under discussion, *e.g.* the agriculture ministers will make up the council for discussions on farming.

The presidency of the Council rotates between each Member State every six months. . . Together with the European Parliament, the Council has the power to make EU laws and decide the budget. The Council is responsible for the common foreign and security policy headed by its Secretary-General and High Representative. . . It also co-ordinates co-operation on police and judicial questions.

The way the council votes depends on the matter under discussion. For some sensitive issues, for example taxation, the council must vote unanimously but other decisions require a simple majority or a qualified majority.

(Adapted from BBC News: A–Z of Europe.)

The European Commission

The Commission is the politically independent institution that represents and upholds the interests of the EU as a whole. It is the driving force within the EU's institutional system: it proposes legislation, policies and programmes of action and it is responsible for implementing the decisions of Parliament and the Council. Like the Parliament and Council, the European Commission was set up in the 1950s under the EU's founding treaties.

The term "Commission" is used in two senses. First, it refers to the "Members of the Commission", *i.e.* the team of 20 men and women appointed by the Member States and Parliament to run the institution and take its decisions. Secondly, the term "Commission" refers to the institution itself and to its staff. Informally, the Members of the Commission are known as "commissioners". They have all held political positions in their countries of origin, and many have been government ministers, but as Members of the Commission they are committed to acting in the interests of the Union as a whole and not taking instructions from national governments. A new Commission is appointed every five years, within six months of the elections to the European Parliament.

The Commission remains politically answerable to Parliament, which has the power to dismiss it by adopting a motion of censure. The Commission attends all the sessions of Parliament, where it must clarify and justify its policies. It also replies regularly to written and oral questions posed by MEPs. The day-to-day work of the Commission is done by its administrative officials, experts, translators, interpreters and secretarial staff. There are approximately 24,000 of these European civil servants. That may sound a lot, but in fact it is fewer than the number of staff employed by most medium-sized city councils in Europe. Far from being faceless bureaucrats, these people are ordinary citizens from every EU country, selected through competitive examinations and working together to build a strong and successful European Union.

The European Commission has four main roles:

1. to propose legislation to Parliament and the Council;

2. to manage and implement EU policies and the budget;

3. to enforce European law (jointly with the Court of Justice); and

4. to represent the European Union on the international stage, for example by negotiating agreements between the EU and other countries.

(Adapted from Europa: The European Union On-Line.)

European Commission

The Commission is the EU's civil service, made up of 20 commissioners and a subsidiary staff of about 27,000, making it the biggest of the European institutions. The commission's main job is to initiate new policy measures.

After consultation with interest groups and experts, it proposes legislation to the Council of Ministers and the European Parliament who then decide on it. Once legislation is passed, the Commission is then responsible for implementing it.

It also acts as the guardian of the EU treaties to ensure that EU legislation is applied correctly by the Member States. If necessary, it can institute legal proceedings against member states or businesses that fail to comply with European law and, as a last resort, bring them before the European Court of Justice.

Commissioners are accountable to the European Parliament, which is the only body with the power to sack them. The commissioners come from all 15 Member States, but have to promise to follow the interests of the EU, not their own country. Each has responsibility for a policy area, *e.g.* enlargement, agriculture, etc. At present the big countries have two commissioners and the smaller countries only one. This will change with enlargement. At the 2000 Nice Summit, the big countries agreed to give up their second commissioner. Once the union has 27 Member States, countries will take turns to appoint commissioners.

(Adapted from BBC News: A–Z of Europe.)

The European Parliament

The members of the European Parliament (MEPs) sit in Europe-wide political groups that bring together all the main political parties operating in the EU member states rather than national blocks.

The origins of the Parliament go back to the 1950s and the founding treaties. Since 1979, MEPs have been directly elected by the citizens they represent. Parliamentary elections are held every five years, and every EU citizen who is registered as a voter is entitled to vote. So Parliament expresses the democratic will of the Union's 374 million citizens, and it represents their interests in discussions with the other EU institutions.

The Parliament has three main roles:

1. It shares with the Council the power to legislate. The fact that is a directly-elected body helps guarantee the democratic legitimacy of European law.

2. It exercises democratic supervision over all EU institutions, and in particular the Commission. It has the power to approve or reject the nomination of commissioners, and it has the right to censure the Commission as a whole.

3. It shares with the Council authority over the EU budget and can therefore influence EU spending. At the end of the procedure, it adopts or rejects the budget in its entirety.

(Adapted from Europa: The European Union On-Line.)

European Parliament

The Parliament is the only directly elected body in the European Union and the only elected international assembly in the world. Every five years, Europe's 375 million citizens have the chance to vote for 626 representatives.

The Parliament is split between Brussels, Luxembourg and Strasbourg. For one week every month it holds a session with all its deputies in Strasbourg. It has a secretariat in Luxembourg and its committees spend two weeks a month meeting in Brussels.

Although it began as a discussion forum, Parliament now has significant powers, deciding together with the Council of Ministers on legislation and the EU's budget. But on some sensitive matters, such as taxation, it can still only give its opinion.

Parliament is also the democratic watchdog over the European Commission. Commissioners must be approved by Parliament before they can be appointed and Parliament has the power to sack the Commission—a fate the Commission only escaped in 1999 by its mass resignation.

(Adapted from BBC News: A–Z of Europe.)

The Court of Justice

The Court of Justice of the European Communities (often referred to simply as "the Court") was set up in 1952 under the Treaty of Paris (establishing the European Coal and Steel Community). Its job is to ensure that EU legislation (technically known as "Community law") is interpreted and applied in the same way by each Member State. In other words, that it is always identical for all parties and in all circumstances. The Court has the power to settle legal disputes between Member States, EU institutions, businesses and individuals.

The Court is composed of one judge *per* Member State, so that all the EU's national legal systems are represented. Even after enlargement there will still be one judge *per* Member State, but for the sake of efficiency the Court will be able to sit as a "Grand Chamber" of just 13 judges instead of always having to meet in a plenary session attended by all the judges. The Court is assisted by eight "advocates-general". Their role is to present reasoned opinions on the cases brought before the Court. They must do so publicly and impartially.

To help the Court of Justice cope with the thousands of cases brought before it, and to offer citizens better legal protection, a "Court of First Instance" was created in 1989. This Court (which is attached to the Court of Justice) is responsible for giving rulings on certain kinds of case, particularly actions brought by private individuals and cases relating to unfair competition between businesses. The Court of Justice and the Court of First Instance each have a President, chosen by their fellow-judges to serve for a term of three years.

The Court gives rulings on cases brought before it. The four most common types of case are:

1. requests for a preliminary ruling;

2. proceedings for failure to fulfil an obligation;

3. proceedings for annulment; and

4. proceedings for failure to act.

(Adapted from Europa: The European Union On-Line.)

European Court of Justice

Together with the national courts, the Court of Justice is the judicial power of the European Union. Its job is to make sure that European law is understood in the same way across the European Union. It can also settle disputes between the union's different institutions and Member States. The Court has [had an important influence on] laws in such fields as employment, the environment, consumer protection and the free movement of goods and services. It was set up at the very beginning of European integration when the European Coal and Steel Community was established in 1951. An individual European citizen can bring a case before the ECJ if the case concerns a decision taken by a European institution. In 1989, a Court of First Instance was established to take on some of the Court of Justice's workload but cases are still subject to lengthy delays.

(Adapted from BBC News: A-Z of Europe.)

Summarise the nature and roles of the main European Institutions:	
Council of Ministers	
Commission	
Parliament	
Court of Justice	

Direct applicability and direct effect

Before considering the different forms of **Union law**, we must understand two central concepts of the European legal order:

- **Direct applicability**—a provision of Union law is directly applicable where it **automatically** forms part of the national law of each Member State. There is no need for the Member States to enact national legislation to incorporate it.

- **Direct effect**—a provision of Union law is directly effective where it creates individual rights enforceable in national courts. There are two forms of direct effect:

  (a) **vertical direct effect**—this creates individual rights against the State; and
  (b) **horizontal direct effect**—this creates individual rights against other individuals.

- In examining each of the different types of Union law, it is important to identify whether it is directly applicable and whether it is capable of direct effect.

Sources of Union Law

Treaty of Rome—Art. 249 (Formerly Art. 189)

In order to carry out their task and in accordance with the provisions of this Treaty, the European Parliament acting jointly with the Council, the Council and the Commission shall make regulations and issue directives, take decisions, make recommendations or deliver opinions.

A regulation shall have general application. It shall be binding in its entirety and directly applicable in all Member States.

A directive shall be binding, as to the result to be achieved, upon each Member State to which it is addressed, but shall leave to the national authorities the choice of form and methods.

A decision shall be binding in its entirety upon those to whom it is addressed.

Recommendations and opinions shall have no binding force.

(Adapted from Europa: The European Union On-Line.)

Van Duyn v Home Office (No.2) [1975] 3 All E.R. 190

COURT OF JUSTICE OF THE EUROPEAN COMMUNITIES
JUDGES LECOURT (PRESIDENT), O DALAIGH, MACKENZIE STUART, DONNER, MON-
ACO, MERTENS DE WILMARS, PESCATORE, KUTSCHER AND SØRENSEN
OCTOBER 23, NOVEMBER 13, DECEMBER 4, 1974

European Economic Community—treaty provisions—direct application in Member States—circumstances in which rights conferred by treaty provisions directly enforceable by individuals in courts of member states—provisions imposing precise obligations—provisions not requiring the adoption of further measures for implementation.

European Economic Community—directives—direct application in Member States—circumstances in which rights conferred by directives enforceable by individuals in courts of Member States—directive imposing unconditional obligation on Member States—directive not requiring further measure for its implementation.

In 1968 the Minister of Health stated in the House of Commons that the Government considered that the practice of Scientology was socially harmful, and that work permits and employment vouchers would not be issued to foreign nationals for work at Scientology establishments. No legal restrictions were, however, placed on the practice of Scientology in the UK nor on British nationals who wished to become members of the Church of Scientology or to take employment with it. In 1973 the plaintiff, who was a Dutch national and a practising Scientologist, was offered employment as a secretary with the Church of Scientology at its college at East Grinstead. The plaintiff decided to take up the post but on arrival at Gatwick airport she was refused leave to enter the UK on the ground that the Home Office "considered it undesirable to give anyone leave to enter the UK on the business of or in the employment of the Church of Scientology."

The Advocate General (M Henri Mayras) delivered the following opinion:

My Lords, the first question need not long detain us. The criteria which the court has evolved over the past years for the purpose of determining whether a provision of Community law and, in particular, a rule set out in the EEC Treaty, is directly applicable so as to confer on individuals rights enforceable by them in the national courts, are clearly laid down: the provision must impose a clear and precise obligation on member states; it must be unconditional, in other words subject to no limitation; if, however, a provision is subject to certain limitations, their nature and extent must be exactly defined; finally, the implementation of a Community rule must not be subject to the adoption of any subsequent rules or regulations on the part either of the Community institutions or of the member states, so that, in particular, member states must not be left any real discretion with regard to the application of the rule in question.

There is less certainty regarding the solution of the second question which, as has been seen, is concerned with the direct applicability of . . . directive[s]. Article 189 of the EEC Treaty distinguishes in fact between regulations, which are not only binding but also directly applicable in the member states, and directives, which are also binding on the states but which have, in principle, no direct effect inasmuch as they leave to the states the choice of methods for their implementation. Nevertheless, looking beyond formal legal categories, the court [has] declared that, apart from regulations, other Community acts mentioned in Art. 189 may have direct effect, particularly in cases where the Community authorities have imposed on member states the obligation to adopt a particular course of conduct. The court stated that the positive effect of these acts would be lessened if individuals were unable, in such a case, to enforce through the courts rights conferred on them by decisions of this nature, even though such decisions were not taken in the form of regulations.

The Council has . . . imposed on member states a clear and precise obligation. The first condition for direct effect is satisfied. The second is also. The rule is sufficient in itself. It is not subject either to the adoption of subsequent acts on the part either of the Community authority or of member states. The fact that the latter have, in accordance with the principle relating to directives, the choice of form and methods which accord with their national law does not imply that the Community rule is not directly applicable. On the contrary, it is so closely linked to the implementation of Art. 48, as regards employed persons, that it seems to me to be inseparable from and of the same nature as the provision of the EEC Treaty . . . These considerations lead me to conclude that the provision in question confers on Community nationals rights which are enforceable by them in the national courts and which the latter must protect."

THE COURT:

First question

4. By the first question, the court is asked to say whether Art. 48 of the EEC Treaty is directly applicable so as to confer on individuals rights enforceable by them in the courts of a member state.

5. It is provided, in Art. 48(1) and (2), that freedom of movement for workers shall be secured by the end of the transitional period and that such freedom "shall entail the abolition of any discrimination based on nationality between workers of the Member States as regards employment, remuneration and other conditions of work and employment".

6. These provisions impose on Member States a precise obligation which does not require the adoption of any further measure on the part either of the Community institutions or of the member states and which leaves them, in relation to its implementation, no discretionary power.

7. Paragraph 3, which defines the rights implied by the principle of freedom of movement for workers, subjects them to limitations justified on grounds of public policy, public security or public health. The application of these limitations is, however, subject to judicial controls, so that a Member State's right to invoke the limitations does not prevent the provisions of Art. 48, which enshrine the principle of freedom of movement for workers, from conferring on individuals rights which are enforceable by them and which the national courts must protect.

8. The reply to the first question must therefore be in the affirmative.

Second question

9. The second question asks the court to say whether EEC Directive 64/221 of February 25, 1964 on the co-ordination of special measures concerning the movement and residence of foreign nationals which are justified on grounds of public policy, public security or public health is directly applicable so as to confer on individuals rights enforceable by them in the courts of a Member State.

11. The UK observes that, since Art. 189 of the EEC Treaty distinguishes between the effects ascribed to regulations, directives and decisions, it must therefore be presumed that the Council, in issuing a directive rather than making a regulation, must have intended that the directive should have an effect other than that of a regulation and accordingly that the former should not be directly applicable.

12. If, however, by virtue of the provisions of Art. 189 regulations are directly applicable and, consequently, may by their very nature have direct effects, it does not follow from this that other categories of acts mentioned in that Article can never have similar effects. In would be incompatible with the binding effect attributed to a directive by Art. 189 to exclude, in principle, the possibility that the obligation which it imposes may be invoked by those concerned. In particular, where the Community authorities have, by directive, imposed on Member States the obligation to pursue a particular course of conduct, the useful effect of such an act would be weakened if individuals were prevented from relying on it before their national courts and if the latter were prevented from taking it into consideration as an element of Community law.

15. Accordingly, in reply to the second question, Art. 3(1) of EEC Directive 64/221 of February 25, 1964 confers on individuals rights which are enforceable by them in the courts of a member state and which the national courts must protect.

(Adapted from The All England Law Reports.)

Marshall v Southampton and South West Hampshire Area Health Authority (Teaching) [1986] 2 All E.R. 584

COURT OF JUSTICE OF THE EUROPEAN COMMUNITIES JUDGES Lord MACKENZIE STUART (PRESIDENT), EVERLING, BAHLMANN (PRESIDENTS OF CHAMBERS), BOSCO, KOOPMANS, DUE AND O'HIGGINS, ADVOCATE GENERAL SIR GORDON SLYNN JUNE 5, SEPTEMBER 18, 1985, FEBRUARY 26, 1986

European Economic Community—directives—circumstances in which rights conferred by directives enforceable by individuals in courts of Member States.

THE COURT OF JUSTICE:

. . . It is necessary to recall that, according to a long line of decisions of the court . . . wherever the provisions of a directive appear, as far as their subject matter is concerned, to be unconditional and sufficiently precise, those provisions may be relied on by an individual against the State where that State fails to implement the directive in national law by the end of the period prescribed or where it fails to implement the directive correctly.

(Adapted from The All England Law Reports.)

Faccini Dori v Recreb Srl [1995] All E.R. (EC) 1

COURT OF JUSTICE OF THE EUROPEAN COMMUNITIES JUDGES DUE (PRESIDENT), MANCINI, MOITINHO DE ALMEIDA, DÍEZ DE VELASCO, EDWARD (PRESIDENTS OF CHAMBERS), KAKOURIS, JOLIET (RAPPORTEUR), SCHOCKWEILER, RODRÌGUEZ IGLESIAS, GRÉVISSE, ZULEEG, KAPTEYN AND MURRAY ADVOCATE GENERAL LENZ MARCH 16, 1993, FEBRUARY 9, JULY 14, 1994

European Community—directives—direct application in Member States—consumer protection—directive concerning protection of consumer in respect of contracts negotiated away from business premises—Member State failing to transpose directive into national law within prescribed time limit—whether consumer entitled to rely on right of cancellation provided for by directive—whether provisions of directive concerning right of cancellation unconditional and sufficiently precise—if so, whether directive capable of being invoked in proceedings between consumer and trader.

On January 19, 1989 D entered into an agreement with a company marketing English language correspondence courses. The contract was concluded at a railway station, away from the company's business premises. Some days later, by registered letter dated January 23, D informed the company that she was cancelling her order. The company replied on June 3, that it had assigned its claim to a second company, R. D accordingly wrote to R on June 24, confirming that she had cancelled her subscription to the course in reliance on Art. 5 of Council Directive (EEC) 85/577, which, in the case of contracts negotiated away from the trader's business premises, granted consumers a right of cancellation for a period of up to seven days to enable them to assess the obligations arising under the contract.

The COURT OF JUSTICE:

1. The directive requires the Member States to adopt certain rules intended to govern legal relations between traders and consumers. In view of the nature of the dispute, which is

between a consumer and a trader, the question submitted by the national court raises two issues, which should be considered separately. The first is whether the provisions of the directive concerning the right of cancellation are unconditional and sufficiently precise. The second is whether a directive which requires the Member States to adopt certain rules specifically intended to govern relations between private individuals may be relied on in proceedings between such persons in the absence of measures to transpose the directive into national law.

2. The second issue raised by the national court relates more particularly to the question whether, in the absence of measures transposing the directive within the prescribed time limit, consumers may derive from the directive itself a right of cancellation against traders with whom they have concluded contracts and enforce that right before a national court. As the court has consistently held . . . a directive cannot of itself impose obligations on an individual and cannot therefore be relied upon as such against an individual.

3. It would be unacceptable if a state, when required by the Community legislature to adopt certain rules intended to govern the State's relations—or those of State entities—with individuals and to confer certain rights on individuals, were able to rely on its own failure to discharge its obligations so as to deprive individuals of the benefits of those rights.

4. The effect of extending that case law to the sphere of relations between individuals would be to recognise a power in the Community to enact obligations for individuals with immediate effect, whereas it has competence to do so only where it is empowered to adopt regulations.

5. It follows that, in the absence of measures transposing the directive within the prescribed time limit, consumers cannot derive from the directive itself a right of cancellation as against traders with whom they have concluded a contract or enforce such a right in a national court.

6. It must also be borne in mind that, as the court has consistently held since its judgment in *Von Colson v Land Nordrhein-Westfalen*, the Member States' obligation arising from a directive to achieve the result envisaged by the directive and their duty under Art. 5 of the Treaty to take all appropriate measures, whether general or particular, is binding on all the authorities of member states, including, for matters within their jurisdiction, the courts. The judgments of the court in *Marleasing SA v La Comercial Internacional de Alimentación* and *Wagner Miret v Fondo de Garantia Salarial* make it clear that, when applying national law, whether adopted before or after the directive, the national court that has to interpret that law must do so, as far as possible, in the light of the wording and the purpose of the directive so as to achieve the result it has in view and thereby comply with the third para. of Art. 189 of the Treaty.

7. If the result prescribed by the directive cannot be achieved by way of interpretation, it should also be borne in mind that, in terms of the judgment in *Francovich v Italy*, Community law requires the Member States to make good damage caused to individuals through failure to transpose a directive, provided that three conditions are fulfilled. First, the purpose of the directive must be to grant rights to individuals. Secondly, it must be possible to identify the content of those rights on the basis of the provisions of the directive. Finally, there must be a causal link between the breach of the State's obligation and the damage suffered.

8. So, as regards the second issue raised by the national court, the answer must be that in the absence of measures transposing the directive within the prescribed time limit consumers cannot derive from the directive itself a right of cancellation as against traders with whom they have concluded a contract or enforce such a right in a national court.

However, when applying provisions of national law, whether adopted before or after the directive, the national court must interpret them as far as possible in the light of the wording and purpose of the directive.

(Adapted from BBC News: A-Z of Parliament.)

Source of law	Directly applicable?	Vertical and/or horizontal direct effect?
Treaty provisions		
Regulations		
Directives		
Decisions		
What is meant by indirect effect (see "*Faccini Dori*", para.6)?		
What is meant by State liability in damages (see "*Faccini Dori*", para.7)?		

Union membership and the sovereignty of Parliament

The Community view

Costa v ENEL [1964] CMLR 425

. . . By contrast with ordinary international treaties, the EEC Treaty has created its own legal system which, on the entry into force of the Treaty, became an integral part of the legal systems of the Member States and which their courts are bound to apply. By creating a Community of unlimited duration, having its own institutions, its own personality, its own legal capacity and capacity of representation on the international plane and, more particularly, real powers stemming from a limitation of sovereignty or a transfer of powers from the States to the Community, the Member States have limited their sovereign rights, albeit within limited fields, and have thus created a body of law which binds both their nationals and themselves. The integration into the laws of each Member State of provisions which derive from the Community, and more generally the terms and the spirit of the Treaty, make it impossible for the States, as a corollary, to accord precedence to a unilateral and subsequent measure over a legal system accepted by them on a basis of reciprocity. Such a measure cannot therefore be inconsistent with that legal system. The executive force of Community law cannot vary from one State to another in deference to subsequent domestic laws, without jeopardizing the attainment of objectives of the Treaty . . . The obligations undertaken under the Treaty establishing the Community would not be unconditional, but merely contingent, if they could be called in question by subsequent legislative acts of the signatories. Wherever the Treaty grants the States the right to act unilaterally, it does this by clear and precise provisions . . . It follows from all these observations that the law stemming from the Treaty, an independent source of law, could not, because of its special and original nature, be overridden by domestic legal provisions, however framed, without being deprived of its character as Community law and without the legal basis of the Community itself being called into question. The transfer by the States from their domestic legal system to the Community legal system of the rights and obligations arising under the Treaty carries with it a permanent limitation of their sovereign rights, against which a subsequent unilateral act incompatible with the concept of the Community cannot prevail . . .

(Adapted from The Common Market Law Reports.)

Amministrazione delle Finanze dello Stato v Simmenthal SpA [1978] 3 CMLR 263

. . . any national court must, in a case within its jurisdiction, apply Community law in its entirety and protect rights which the latter confers on individuals and must accordingly set aside any provision of national law which may conflict with it, whether prior or subsequent to the Community rule.

(Adapted from The Common Market Law Reports.)

What is the Community view on national sovereignty?

What should national courts do where there is a conflict between Community and national laws?

The UK View

European Communities Act 1972

Section 2 General Implementation of Treaties

(1) All such rights, powers, liabilities, obligations and restrictions from time to time created or arising by or under the Treaties, and all such remedies and procedures from time to time provided for by or under the Treaties, as in accordance with the Treaties are without further enactment to be given legal effect or used in the United Kingdom shall be recognised and available in law, and be enforced, allowed and followed accordingly; and the expression "enforceable Community right" and similar expressions shall be read as referring to one to which this subsection applies.

(4) . . . any enactment passed or to be passed, other than one contained in this Part of this Act, shall be construed and have effect subject to the foregoing provisions of this section; . . .

Garland v British Rail Engineering Ltd [1982] 2 All E.R. 402

HOUSE OF LORDS
LORD DIPLOCK, LORD EDMUND-DAVIES, LORD FRASER OF TULLYBELTON, LORD RUSSELL OF KILLOWEN AND LORD SCARMAN
NOVEMBER 26, 1980, APRIL 22, 1982

LORD DIPLOCK:
. . . My Lords, even if the obligation to observe the provisions of Art. 119 were an obligation assumed by the United Kingdom under an ordinary international treaty or convention and there were no question of the treaty obligation being directly applicable as part of the law to be applied by the courts in this country without need for any further enactment, it is a principle of construction of United Kingdom statutes, now too well established to call for citation of authority, that the words of a statute passed after the Treaty has been signed and

dealing with the subject matter of the international obligation of the United Kingdom, are to be construed, if they are reasonably capable of bearing such a meaning, as intended to carry out the obligation and not to be inconsistent with it . . . The instant appeal does not present an appropriate occasion to consider whether, having regard to the express direction as to the construction of enactments "to be passed" which is contained in s.2(4), anything short of an express positive statement in an Act of Parliament passed after January 1, 1973 that a particular provision is intended to be made in breach of an obligation assumed by the United Kingdom under a Community treaty would justify an English court in construing that provision in a manner inconsistent with a Community treaty obligation of the United Kingdom however wide a departure from the *prima facie* meaning of the language of the provision might be needed in order to achieve consistency.

(Adapted from The All England Law Reports.)

Litster v Forth Dry Dock and Engineering Co. Ltd [1989] 1 All E.R. 1134

HOUSE OF LORDS
LORD KEITH OF KINKEL, LORD BRANDON OF OAKBROOK, LORD TEMPLEMAN, LORD OLIVER OF AYLMERTON AND LORD JAUNCEY OF TULLICHETTLE
FEBRUARY 1, 2, MARCH 16, 1989

LORD OLIVER OF AYLMERTON:
My Lords, this appeal raises, not for the first time, the broad question of the approach to be adopted by courts in the United Kingdom to domestic legislation enacted in order to give effect to this country's obligations under the EEC Treaty . . . If the legislation can reasonably be construed so as to conform with those obligations, obligations which are to be ascertained not only from the wording of the relevant directive but from the interpretation placed on it by the Court of Justice of the European Communities, such a purposive construction will be applied even though, perhaps, it may involve some departure from the strict and literal application of the words which the legislature has elected to use.

(Adapted from The All England Law Reports.)

Macarthys Ltd v Smith [1979] 3 All E.R. 325

COURT OF APPEAL, CIVIL DIVISION
LORD DENNING M.R., LAWTON AND CUMMING-BRUCE L.JJ.
MAY 23, 24, 25, JULY 19, 25, 1979

LORD DENNING M.R.:
I pause here, however, to make one observation on a constitutional point. Thus far I have assumed that our Parliament, whenever it passes legislation, intends to fulfil its obligations under the Treaty. If the time should come when our Parliament deliberately passes an Act with the intention of repudiating the Treaty or any provision in it or intentionally of acting inconsistently with it and says so in express terms then I should have thought that it would be the duty of our courts to follow the statute of our Parliament. I do not however envisage any

such situation . . . Unless there is such an intentional and express repudiation of the Treaty, it is our duty to give priority to the Treaty.

(Adapted from The All England Law Reports.)

Factortame Ltd v Secretary of State for Transport (No.2) [1991] 1 All E.R. 70

HOUSE OF LORDS
LORD BRIDGE OF HARWICH, LORD BRANDON OF OAKBROOK, LORD OLIVER OF AYLMERTON. LORD GOFF OF CHIEVELEY AND LORD JAUNCEY OF TULLICHETTLE
APRIL 17, 18, 19, 20, 24, 25, 26, 27, 1989, JULY 2, 3, 4, 5, 9, 25, 26, OCTOBER 11, 1990

Some public comments on the decision of the Court of Justice, affirming the jurisdiction of the courts of Member States to override national legislation if necessary to enable interim relief to be granted in protection of rights under Community law, have suggested that this was a novel and dangerous invasion by a Community institution of the sovereignty of the United Kingdom Parliament. But such comments are based on a misconception. If the supremacy within the European Community of Community law over the national law of Member States was not always inherent in the EEC Treaty it was certainly well established in the jurisprudence of the Court of Justice long before the United Kingdom joined the Community. Thus, whatever limitation of its sovereignty Parliament accepted when it enacted the European Communities Act 1972 was entirely voluntary. Under the terms of the 1972 Act it has always been clear that it was the duty of a United Kingdom court, when delivering final judgment, to override any rule of national law found to be in conflict with any directly enforceable rule of Community law. Similarly, when decisions of the Court of Justice have exposed areas of United Kingdom statute law which failed to implement Council directives, Parliament has always loyally accepted the obligation to make appropriate and prompt amendments. Thus there is nothing in any way novel in according supremacy to rules of Community law in those areas to which they apply and to insist that, in the protection of rights under Community law, national courts must not be inhibited by rules of national law from granting interim relief in appropriate cases is no more than a logical recognition of that supremacy.

(Adapted from The All England Law Reports.)

Thoburn v Sunderland City Council and other appeals [2002] 4 All E.R. 156

QUEEN'S BENCH DIVISION (DIVISIONAL COURT)
LAWS L.J. AND CRANE J.
NOVEMBER 20–22, 2001, FEBRUARY 18, 2002

LAWS L.J.:
. . . The present state of our domestic law is such that substantive Community rights prevail over the express terms of any domestic law, including primary legislation, made or passed

after the coming into force of the 1972 Act, even in the face of plain inconsistency between the two . . . Where does this leave the constitutional position? . . . We should recognise a hierarchy of Acts of Parliament: as it were "ordinary" statutes and "constitutional" statutes. The two categories must be distinguished on a principled basis. In my opinion a constitutional statute is one which: (a) conditions the legal relationship between citizen and State in some general, overarching manner; or (b) enlarges or diminishes the scope of what we would now regard as fundamental constitutional rights; (a) and (b) are of necessity closely related: it is difficult to think of an instance of (a) that is not also an instance of (b). The special status of constitutional statutes follows the special status of constitutional rights. Examples are the Magna Carta, the Bill of Rights 1689, the Act of Union, the Reform Acts which distributed and enlarged the franchise, the Human Rights Act 1998, the Scotland Act 1998 and the Government of Wales Act 1998. The 1972 Act clearly belongs in this family. It incorporated the whole corpus of substantive Community rights and obligations, and gave overriding domestic effect to the judicial and administrative machinery of Community law. It may be there has never been a statute having such profound effects on so many dimensions of our daily lives. The 1972 Act is, by force of the common law, a constitutional statute.

Ordinary statutes may be impliedly repealed. Constitutional statutes may not. For the repeal of a constitutional Act or the abrogation of a fundamental right to be effected by statute, the court would apply this test: is it shown that the legislature's *actual*—not imputed, constructive or presumed—intention was to effect the repeal or abrogation? I think the test could only be met by express words in the later statute, or by words so specific that the inference of an actual determination to effect the result contended for was irresistible. The ordinary rule of implied repeal does not satisfy this test. Accordingly, it has no application to constitutional statutes . . . A constitutional statute can only be repealed, or amended in a way which significantly affects its provisions touching fundamental rights or otherwise the relation between citizen and State, by unambiguous words on the face of the later statute.

In my judgment (as will by now be clear) the correct analysis . . . involves and requires these following four propositions. (1) All the specific rights and obligations which EU law creates are by the 1972 Act incorporated into our domestic law and rank supreme: that is, anything in our substantive law inconsistent with any of these rights and obligations is abrogated or must be modified to avoid the inconsistency. This is true even where the inconsistent municipal provision is contained in primary legislation. (2) The 1972 Act is a constitutional statute: that is, it cannot be impliedly repealed. (3) The truth of (2) is derived, not from EU law, but purely from the law of England: the common law recognises a category of constitutional statutes. (4) The fundamental legal basis of the United Kingdom's relationship with the EU rests with the domestic, not the European, legal powers. In the event, which no doubt would never happen in the real world, that a European measure was seen to be repugnant to a fundamental or constitutional right guaranteed by the law of England, a question would arise whether the general words of the 1972 Act were sufficient to incorporate the measure and give it overriding effect in domestic law. But that is very far from this case.

(Adapted from The All England Law Reports.)

What is the effect of ss.2(1) and 2(4) of the European Communities Act 1972?	
How has this affected the approach of the courts to the interpretation of UK legislation?	
What is the status of the 1972 Act (see "*Thorburn*")?	
What are the consequences of this (see "*Macarthys*", "*Factortame*", and "*Thorburn*")?	

The UK Courts and the European Court of Justice

Treaty of Rome—Art. 234 (formerly Art. 177)

(1) The Court of Justice shall have jurisdiction to give preliminary rulings concerning:

(a) the interpretation of this Treaty;

(b) the validity and interpretation of acts of the institutions of the Community and of the ECB;

(c) the interpretation of the statutes of bodies established by an act of the Council, where those statutes so provide.

(2) Where such a question is raised before any court or tribunal of a Member State, that court or tribunal may, if it considers that a decision on the question is necessary to enable it to give judgment, request the Court of Justice to give a ruling thereon.

(3) Where any such question is raised in a case pending before a court or tribunal of a Member State against whose decisions there is no judicial remedy under national law, that court or tribunal shall bring the matter before the Court of Justice.

(Adapted from Europa: The European Union On-Line.)

H P Bulmer Ltd v J Bollinger SA [1974] 2 All E.R. 1226

COURT OF APPEAL, CIVIL DIVISION
LORD DENNING M.R., STAMP AND STEPHENSON L.JJ.
APRIL 4, 5, 8, 9, MAY 22, 1974

LORD DENNING M.R.:
Article 177 shows that, if a question of interpretation or validity is raised, the European Court is supreme. It is the ultimate authority. Even the House of Lords has to bow down to it. If a question is raised before the House of Lords on the interpretation of the treaty—on which it is necessary to give a ruling—the House of Lords is bound to refer it to the European Court. Article 177(3) of the treaty uses that emphatic word "shall". The House has no option. It must refer the matter to the European Court . . . But short of the House of Lords, no other English court is bound to refer a question to the European Court at Luxembourg. Not even a question on the *interpretation* of the treaty. Article 177(2) uses the permissive word "may" in contrast to "shall" in Art. 177(3). In England the trial judge has complete *discretion*. If a question arises on the interpretation of the treaty, an English judge can decide it for himself. He need not refer it to the court at Luxembourg unless he wishes. He can say: "It will be too costly", or "It will take too long to get an answer" or "I am well able to decide it myself". If he does decide it himself, the European Court cannot interfere. None of the parties can go off to the European Court and complain. The European Court would not listen to any party who went moaning to them. The European Court take the view that the trial judge has a complete discretion to refer or not to refer. If a party wishes to challenge the decision of the trial judge in England—to refer or not to refer—he must appeal to the Court of Appeal in England. The judges of the

Court of Appeal, in their turn, have complete discretion. They can interpret the treaty themselves if they think fit. If the Court of Appeal do interpret it themselves, the European Court will not rebuke them for doing so. If a party wishes to challenge the decision of the Court of Appeal—to refer or not to refer—he must get leave to go to the House of Lords and go there. It is only in that august place that there is no discretion. If the point of interpretation is one which is "necessary" to give a ruling, the House *must* refer it to the European Court at Luxembourg. The reason behind this imperative is this. The cases which get to the House of Lords are substantial cases of the first importance. If a point of interpretation arises there, it is assumed to be worthy of reference to the European Court at Luxembourg. Whereas the points in the lower courts may not be worth troubling the European Court about.

Whenever any English court thinks it would be helpful to get the view of the European Court—on the interpretation of the treaty—there is a *condition precedent* to be fulfilled. It is a condition which applies to the House of Lords as well as to the lower courts. It is contained in the same paragraph of Art. 177(2) of the treaty and applies in Art. 177(3) as well. It is this. An English court can only refer the matter to the European Court "*if it considers* that a decision on the question is necessary to enable it to give judgment". Note the words "if *it* considers". That is, "if the *English court* considers'. On this point again the opinion of the English courts is final, just as it is on the matter of discretion. An English judge can say either: "I consider it necessary", or 'I do not consider it necessary'. His discretion in that respect is final. Let me take the two in order.

(i) If the English judge considers it *necessary* to refer the matter, no one can gainsay it save the Court of Appeal. The European Court will accept his opinion. It will not go into the grounds on which he based it.

(ii) If the English judge considers it *not necessary* to refer a question of interpretation to the European Court—but instead decides it itself—that is the end of the matter. It is no good a party going off to the European Court. They would not listen to him. They are conscious that the treaty gives the final word in this respect to the English courts. From all I have read of their cases, they are very careful not to exceed their jurisdiction. They never do anything to trespass on any ground which is properly the province of the national courts.

Guidelines as to whether a decision is necessary:

The point must be conclusive. The English court has to consider whether "a decision of the question is *necessary* to enable it to give *judgment*". That means judgment in the very case which is before the court. The judge must have got to the stage when he says to himself: "This clause of the treaty is capable of two or more meanings. If it means *this*, I give judgment for the plaintiff. If it means *that*, I give judgment for the defendant." In short, the point must be such that, whichever way the point is decided, it is conclusive of the case.

Previous ruling. In some cases, however, it may be found that the same point—or substantially the same point—has already been decided by the European Court in a previous case. In that event it is not necessary for the English court to decide it. It can follow the previous decision without troubling the European Court.

Acte claire. In other cases the English court may consider the point is reasonably clear and free from doubt. In that event there is no need to interpret the treaty but only to apply it, and that is the task of the English court.

(Adapted from *The All England Law Reports.*)

Under Art. 234, when *may* a national court refer a question to the European Court for a "preliminary ruling"?

Under Art. 234, when *must* a national court refer a question to the European Court for a "preliminary ruling"?

What guidance does Lord Denning offer on these questions?

Activity ❶

You have been asked to give a short **presentation** to a group of politics students about European Union legislation. Using relevant information (e.g. from the Europa website) prepare and deliver this presentation. In preparing this activity, you should also read **Chapter 3** of *A Level and AS Level Law: a Study Guide*. Make sure that your presentation covers:

- The main institutions of the European Union.

- The role of these institutions in making European Union legislation.

- The different types of European Union legislation.

- How this legislation becomes part of English law and that it includes at least **one image**.

You must also produce a **one-page handout** for the audience, giving the main points of your presentation and where they can find further information. Your handout, in addition to the text, must include at least **one image**.

(Evidence: Communications: 3.1b, C3.2, C3.3)

Activity ❷

As a group, and using any relevant information you may find (e.g. in books, journals, newspapers or on the internet), prepare the case for or against the view that European Union membership has weakened British sovereignty. You should then contribute these ideas in a class **debate** on this issue.

(Evidence: Communications: C3.1a, C3.2)

Activity ❸

Using the information you have gathered for Activity 2 and any further information you have gained as a result of the debate, prepare an **extended document** (e.g. an article of approximately 1000 words for a broadsheet newspaper) that outlines the main arguments for and against the view that European Union membership has weakened British sovereignty. This document must include at least one **image**.

(Evidence: Communications: C3.2, C3.3)

4 | Statutory Interpretation

? Issues to Explore

? Why is interpretation necessary?

? What are the main approaches to interpretation used by judges?

? What aids are available to the judges to help them interpret legislation?

? What are the advantages and disadvantages of the different approaches?

? How effective are the judges in interpreting legislation?

Definition:

STATUTORY INTERPRETATION:	Statutory interpretation is the process by which judges understand and apply legislation to individual cases.

- While Parliament (or those delegated by Parliament) makes legislation, it is the judges who have the task of interpreting and applying that legislation.
- Due to issues such as technicality, complexity and ambiguity, this can be a difficult task, as judges must try not to cross the line between interpretation and law-making.
- The main approaches developed by the judges have been the **literal** approach, the **golden** approach, the **mischief or purposive** approach, and **modern unitary** approach.
- A number of **internal (intrinsic)** and **external (extrinsic)** aids are available to the judges to help them interpret legislation.

Why is interpretation necessary?

Helping the reader of Bills and Acts

Christopher Jenkins summarises the background to explanatory notes, designed to improve the accessibility of statutes

. . . Clarity must always be the aim of anyone who drafts legislation. If the meaning of a provision is not clear, people cannot be sure of complying with it until the courts have interpreted it following litigation. So in drafting Acts of Parliament "it is not enough to attain to a degree of precision which a person reading in good faith can understand; but it is necessary to attain, if possible, to a degree of precision which a person reading in bad faith cannot misunderstand. It is all the better if he cannot pretend to misunderstand it."

Clarity will, of course, be enhanced if legislation is kept simple. But legislation about a complex topic is bound to be complex. And even in simple areas the law sometimes has to be set out in considerable detail. . .

There are reasons other than complexity why Acts of Parliament can be difficult to understand. One set of reasons relates to the conditions under which Acts are prepared. The time available for drafting is rarely enough to permit the constant examination and re-ordering of ideas and words which is necessary for maximum clarity. Many Acts are amended, either during their passage as Bills through Parliament or by later Acts, in a way which subverts their original structure. . .

There are other constraints which are not the result of political or Parliamentary pressures but which are inherent in the nature of legislation. The only task of legislation is to change the law, to be the law. Explanatory material, highly desirable though it may be, is not intended to have legal effect. It has no place in the legislation itself, and including it introduces a risk of changing the meaning.

This factor means that the drafter of legislation cannot generally make use of a number of techniques which are used in other forms of communication to make the message easier to grasp. For example . . . to give worked examples . . . or setting out some of the background . . . [or] simply saying it more than once in different ways . . .

None of these techniques can ordinarily be attempted in legislation. They introduce into the text words which are not strictly required for changing the law, and are therefore unsafe.

(Adapted from The New Law Journal, May 28, 1999, p.798.)

End of the road for Go-Peds

High court ruling forces scooters off highway

By Keith Perry

Go-Peds, the trendy motorised scooters that have achieved cult status were effectively driven off the roads yesterday after the high court ruled they had the same legal status as motor vehicles. The decision means scooter aficionados will need a driving licence and third party insurance to use them on public highways. But as no insurance company is prepared to cover them for road use because of their inadequate braking system and lack of lights or proper steering, driving them on the public highway is liable to prosecution.

Lord Justice Pill and Mr Justice Bell ruled that a Middlesbrough restaurateur, Michael Saddington, who was arrested in a "Keystone Cops" chase through Harrogate should have been convicted of driving while disqualified. The judges overruled magistrates who dismissed the charges against Mr Saddington, 38. They allowed an appeal by the chief constable of North Yorkshire against the magistrates' decision.

Lord Justice Pill said he was satisfied that a Go-Ped was a mechanically propelled vehicle and in the eyes of the law was intended for road use. Therefore a driving licence and third party insurance would be needed. At an earlier hearing he said the public may need protection from the Go-Ped craze because of a loophole in the law which allowed their uncontrolled use. . . Lord Justice Pill added: "The test is not whether a reasonable person would use a Go-Ped on a road which in ordinary circumstances he probably would not because of the dangers involved. The test is whether a reasonable person would say that one of its uses would be on the roads. That person must consider whether some general use on the roads must be contemplated and not merely isolated use or use by a man losing his senses." The judge added that, in his opinion, people would be tempted to use Go-Peds on the road. They would ignore manufacturer's warnings not to do so, and the court's opinion that they are not roadworthy.

(Adapted from The Guardian, October 27, 2000.)

Chief Constable of the North Yorkshire Police v Saddington

Civil Procedure—Appeal by way of case stated against justices decision—Whether an unregistered motor scooter is a motor vehicle—Road Traffic Act 1988, s.185(1).

QUEEN'S BENCH DIVISION (ADMINISTRATIVE COURT)
PILL L.J., BELL J.
OCTOBER 26, 2000

PILL L.J.:

In the afternoon of March 23, 1999 a police officer was on mobile patrol duty in Harrogate Town Centre. He observed the respondent ride past him in the left hand inside lane on a motorised scooter, pass through traffic lights which were showing red and turn left. The police officer followed him activating his vehicles blue flashing lights and two-tone horn. The respondent failed to stop and, so the Justices found, attempted to avoid apprehension by riding through a narrow gap between parked cars before picking up his machine and running with it into a nearby public house. He was found to be disqualified from holding or obtaining a driving licence and was arrested. The respondent was not the owner of the scooter, known as a Go-Ped, which had not been altered in any way from its original manufactured state. The Go-Ped had been propelled under its own engine power and was equipped with an independent braking system . . .

The issue in the appeal is whether what is described in the informations as an unregistered motor scooter is a motor vehicle within the meaning of that term in s.185(1) of the Road Traffic Act 1988 ("the 1988 Act"). Motor vehicle is defined in s.185 of the 1988 Act as "a mechanically propelled vehicle intended or adapted for use on roads".

We are told . . . that considerable numbers of scooters of this and similar design are in circulation. I would take judicial notice of that and would expect justices to do the same. The temptation to use Go-Peds on the roads is considerable, notwithstanding their limitations. They provide a ready means of getting through traffic on short journeys on busy urban roads and, for that matter, on less busy suburban roads.

The test is not whether a reasonable person would use a Go-Ped on a road, which in ordinary circumstances he probably would not because of the dangers involved. The test is whether a reasonable person would say that one of its uses would be use on the roads. That person must consider whether some general use on the roads must be contemplated and not merely isolated use or use by a man losing his senses. The design and capabilities of the Go-Ped and the possibilities it offers will be considered and considered in the context of an assessment of peoples' wish to get quickly through traffic and the pressure of time upon many people.

In my judgment the conclusion must be that general use on the roads is to be contemplated. The distributors' advice not to use the Go-Ped on the roads will in practice be ignored to a considerable extent. Surrender to the temptation to use it on the roads will not be an isolated occurrence even though the vehicle may not be roadworthy in the sense used by the Justices.

(Adapted from The All England Official Transcripts.)

Briefly describe the reasons why it necessary for judges to interpret legislation

The literal approach

Fisher v Bell [1960] 3 All E.R. 731

QUEEN'S BENCH DIVISION
LORD PARKER C.J., ASHWORTH AND ELWES JJ.
NOVEMBER 10, 1960

Criminal law—dangerous weapons—flick knife—knife displayed in shop window with price attached—whether "offer for sale"—s.1(1) of the Restriction of Offensive Weapons Act 1959.

A shopkeeper displayed in his shop window a knife with a price ticket behind it. He was charged with offering for sale a flick knife, contrary to s.1(1) of the Restriction of Offensive Weapons Act, 1959.

Held—The shopkeeper was not guilty of the offence with which he was charged because the displaying of the knife in the shop window was merely an invitation to treat and the shopkeeper had not thereby offered the knife for sale, within the meaning of s.1(1) of the Act of 1959.

LORD PARKER C.J.:

. . . Section 1(1) of the Act provides: "Any person who manufactures, sells of hires or offers for sale or hire, or lends or gives to any other person—(a) any knife which has a blade which opens automatically by hand pressure applied to a button, spring or other device in or attached to the handle of the knife, sometimes known as a "flick knife". . . shall be guilty of an offence . . ."

The sole question is whether the exhibition of that knife in the window with the ticket constituted an offer for sale within the statute. I think that most lay people would be inclined to the view (as, indeed, I was myself when I first read these papers), that if a knife were displayed in a window like that with a price attached to it, it was nonsense to say that that was not offering it for sale. The knife is there inviting people to buy it, and in ordinary language it is for sale; but any statute must be looked at in the light of the general law of the country, for Parliament must be taken to know the general law. It is clear that, according to the ordinary law of contract, the display of an article with a price on it in a shop window is merely an invitation to treat. It is in no sense an offer for sale the acceptance of which constitutes a contract. That is clearly the general law of the country. Not only is that so, but it is to be observed that, in many statutes and orders which prohibit selling and offering for sale of goods, it is very common, when it is so desired, to insert the words "offering or exposing for sale", "exposing for sale" being clearly words which would cover the display of goods in a shop window. Not only that, but it appears that under several statutes—we have been referred in particular to the Prices of Goods Act, 1939, and the Goods and Services (Price Control) Act 1941—Parliament, when it desires to enlarge the ordinary meaning of those words, has a definition section enlarging the ordinary meaning of "offer for sale" to cover other matters including, be it observed exposure of goods for sale with the price attached.

In those circumstances I, for my part, though I confess reluctantly, am driven to the conclusion that no offence was here committed. At first sight it appears absurd that knives of this sort may not be manufactured, they may not be sold, they may not be hired, they may not be lent, they may not be given, but apparently they may be displayed in shop windows; but even if this is a *casus omissus*—and I am by no means saying that it is—it is not for this court to supply the omission.

(Adapted from The All England Law Reports.)

What is the literal approach?	
How was it applied in this case?	

The golden approach

Adler v George [1964] 1 All ER 628

QUEEN'S BENCH DIVISION
LORD PARKER C.J., PAULL AND WIDGERY JJ.
JANUARY 30, 1964

Criminal law—official secrets—interference with officer of police or member of HM forces "in the vicinity of" a prohibited place—vicinity—whether offence could be committed by person in prohibited place—s.3 of the Official Secrets Act 1920.

LORD PARKER C.J.:

Section 3 of the Official Secrets Act 1920, provides that: "No person in the vicinity of any prohibited place shall obstruct, knowingly mislead or otherwise interfere with or impede, the chief officer or a superintendent or other officer of police, or any member of His Majesty's forces engaged on guard, sentry, patrol, or other similar duty in relation to the prohibited place, and, if any person acts in contravention of, or fails to comply with, this provision, he shall be guilty of a misdemeanour."

In the present case the appellant had obtained access—it matters not how—to, and was on, Marham Royal Air Force station on May 11, 1963, and it was found that he there and then obstructed a member of Her Majesty's Royal Air Force.

The sole point here, and a point ably argued by the appellant, is that if he was on the station he could not be in the vicinity of the station, and that it is an offence under this section to obstruct a member of Her Majesty's forces only while the accused is in the vicinity of the station. The appellant has referred to the natural meaning of "vicinity", which I take to be quite generally the state of being near in space, and he says that it is inapt and does not cover being in fact on the station in the present case. For my part I am quite satisfied that this is a case where no violence is done to the language by reading the words "in the vicinity of "as meaning "in or in the vicinity of". Here is a section in an Act of Parliament designed to prevent interference with, amongst others, members of Her Majesty's forces who are engaged on guard, sentry, patrol or other similar duty in relation to a prohibited place such as this station. It would be extraordinary, and I venture to think that it would be absurd, if an indictable offence was thereby created when the obstruction took place outside the precincts of the station, albeit in the vicinity, and no offence at all was created if the obstruction occurred on the station itself . . . There may be of course many contexts in which "vicinity" must be confined to its literal meaning of "being near in space", but, under this section, I am quite clear that the context demands that the words should be construed in the way which I have stated. I would dismiss this appeal.

What is the golden approach?	
How was it applied in this case?	

The purposive approach

Smith v Hughes [1960] 2 All E.R. 859

QUEEN'S BENCH DIVISION
LORD PARKER C.J., HILBERY AND DONOVAN JJ.
JUNE 16, 1960

Criminal law—soliciting for the purposes of prostitution—whether soliciting from window or balcony is soliciting ''in a street''—s.1(1) of the Street Offences Act, 1959.

LORD PARKER C.J.:

. . . The facts, to all intents and purposes, raise the same point in each case; there are minute differences. The appellants in each case were not themselves physically in the street but were in a house adjoining the street. In one case the appellant was on a balcony and she attracted the attention of men in the street by tapping and calling down to them. In other cases the appellants were in ground-floor windows, either closed or half open, and in another case in a first-floor window.

The sole question here is whether in those circumstances each appellant was soliciting in a street or public place. The words of s.1(1) of the Act are in this form: "It shall be an offence for a common prostitute to loiter or solicit in a street or public place for the purpose of prostitution." Observe that it does not say there specifically that the person who is doing the soliciting must be in the street. Equally it does not say that it is enough if the person who receives the solicitation or to whom it is addressed is in the street. For my part, I approach the matter by considering what is the mischief aimed at by this Act. Everybody knows that this was an Act intended to clean up the streets, to enable people to walk along the streets without being molested or solicited by common prostitutes. Viewed in that way, it can matter little whether the prostitute is soliciting while in the street or is standing in a doorway or on a balcony, or at a window, or whether the window is shut or open or half open; in each case her solicitation is projected to and addressed to somebody walking in the street. For my part, I am content to base my decision on that ground and that ground alone. I think that the magistrate came to a correct conclusion in each case, and that these appeals should be dismissed.

(Adapted from The All England Law Reports.)

What is the purposive approach?	
How was it applied in this case?	
All three judgements were given by Lord Parker in the 1960s— what does this tell us about the approach of the judges?	

Jones v Wrotham Park Settled Estates [1979] 1 All E.R. 286

HOUSE OF LORDS
LORD DIPLOCK, LORD SALMON, LORD EDMUND-DAVIES, LORD FRASER OF TULLYBELTON AND LORD RUSSELL OF KILLOWEN
OCTOBER 30, 31, NOVEMBER 2, 6, DECEMBER 13, 1978

LORD DIPLOCK:

. . . My Lords, I am not reluctant to adopt a purposive construction where to apply the literal meaning of the legislative language used would lead to results which would clearly defeat the purposes of the Act. But in doing so the task on which a court of justice is engaged remains one of construction, even where this involves reading into the Act words which are not expressly included in it . . . three conditions . . . must be fulfilled in order to justify this course. . . First, it [must be] possible to determine from a consideration of the provisions of the Act read as a whole precisely what the mischief was that it was the purpose of the Act to remedy; secondly, it [must be] apparent that the draftsman and

Parliament had by inadvertence overlooked, and so omitted to deal with, an eventuality that required to be dealt with if the purpose of the Act was to be achieved; and thirdly, it [must be] possible to state with certainty what were the additional words that would have been inserted by the draftsman and approved by Parliament had their attention been drawn to the omission before the Bill passed into law. Unless this third condition is fulfilled any attempt by a court of justice to repair the omission in the Act cannot be justified as an exercise of its jurisdiction to determine what is the meaning of a written law which Parliament has passed. Such an attempt crosses the boundary between construction and legislation. It becomes a usurpation of a function which under the constitution of this country is vested in the legislature to the exclusion of the courts. . .

(Adapted from The All England Law Reports.)

Inco Europe Ltd v First Choice Distribution (a firm) [2000] 2 All E.R. 109

HOUSE OF LORDS
LORD NICHOLLS OF BIRKENHEAD, LORD JAUNCEY OF TULLICHETTLE, LORD STEYN, LORD CLYDE AND LORD MILLETT
FEBRUARY 11, MARCH 9, 2000

LORD NICHOLLS OF BIRKENHEAD:

. . . Unfortunately, the new para.(g), read literally, also made a major legislative change which was not consequential on any provision of the 1996 Act. . . I am left in no doubt that, for once, the draftsman slipped up. . . It has long been established that the role of the courts in construing legislation is not confined to resolving ambiguities in statutory language. The court must be able to correct obvious drafting errors. In suitable cases, in discharging its interpretative function the court will add words, or omit words or substitute words.

This power is confined to plain cases of drafting mistakes. The courts are ever mindful that their constitutional role in this field is interpretative. They must abstain from any course which might have the appearance of judicial legislation. A statute is expressed in language approved and enacted by the legislature. So the courts exercise considerable caution before adding or omitting or substituting words. Before interpreting a statute in this way the court must be abundantly sure of three matters: (1) the intended purpose of the statute or provision in question; (2) that by inadvertence the draftsman and Parliament failed to give effect to that purpose in the provision in question; and (3) the substance of the provision Parliament would have made, although not necessarily the precise words Parliament would have used, had the error in the Bill been noticed. The third of these conditions is of crucial importance. Otherwise any attempt to determine the meaning of the enactment would cross the boundary between construction and legislation. . .

(Adapted from The All England Law Reports.)

What do these two cases tell us about the limits of a purposive approach?

The unitary approach

Attorney General's Reference (No.1 of 1988) [1989] 1 All E.R. 321

COURT OF APPEAL, CRIMINAL DIVISION
LORD LANE C.J., HUTCHISON AND TUCKER JJ.
SEPTEMBER 26, OCTOBER 18, 1988

Company—insider dealing—prohibition on stock exchange deals by insiders, etc.—person who obtains insider information—obtain—whether "obtains" restricted to acquiring by purpose and effort—whether person who receives unsolicited inside information prohibited from dealing in company's securities—s.1(3)(4)(a) of the Company Securities (Insider Dealing) Act 1985.

LORD LANE C.J.:

On April 11, 1988 the respondent appeared in the Crown Court at Southwark and pleaded not guilty to two offences of dealing in the securities of a company as a prohibited person, contrary to s.1(3) and (4)(a) of the Company Securities (Insider Dealing) Act 1985.

The material facts were as follows. In the autumn of 1985 the respondent held himself out as a possible purchaser of company A. He was put in touch with Miss M, an employee of the company's merchant bankers. He asked her to provide him with financial information about the company. In the event the type of information envisaged did not reach the respondent until after the date of the offences alleged.

On the morning of December 5, 1985 the chairman of the company agreed with representatives of company B for their take-over of company A. The merchant bank took no part in the negotiation of this agreement.

Miss M, on hearing of the agreed take-over and with the chairman's blessing, informed the respondent of the agreement and that an announcement would be made shortly. She told the respondent that the information she was imparting to him was sensitive and highly confidential and that as a result of what she was saying to him he would be an 'insider'. Ten minutes later the respondent telephoned to his stockbroker and placed an order for 10,000 shares in company A. In the event he actually purchased two blocks of shares, 5,000 shares at one price and 1,000 shares at another price.

The next day a public announcement of the take-over was made. The share price rose quickly and five weeks later he sold his two blocks of shares at a handsome profit.

The prosecution conceded that the respondent had taken no step directly or indirectly to secure, procure or acquire the information given to him by Miss M. . .

. . . The first task in these circumstances is to discover the ordinary meaning of the word "obtained". . . There are, it is clear from the lexicographers and one's own experience, two such meanings. The definition in the *Shorter Oxford English Dictionary* is: "To procure or gain, as the result of purpose and effort; hence, generally, to acquire, get." *Black's Law Dictionary* (5th ed., 1979) is not dissimilar: "to get hold of by effort; to get possession of; to procure; to acquire, in any way." Thus the word is capable of supporting the contention of either party: that of the Attorney General, who argues that it means to "acquire in any way", and that of the respondent that it means to "procure as the result of purpose or effort".

The Attorney General, to support his submission that it is the latter, broader, meaning which the draftsman was intending to adopt, draws our attention to the scheme of the 1985 Act. This shows that potential offenders are divided into classes. The first target of s.1 is the primary insider. Broadly speaking, subject to the defences in s.3, any individual who is or at any time in the preceding six months has been knowingly connected with a company may not deal on a recognised stock exchange in securities of that company if he is in possession of inside information as defined in the section. It is not necessary for the prosecution to establish that the inside information was actually used by the person in reaching his decision to deal.

The other class is the secondary insider. It was to this class that the respondent was alleged to have belonged. As already indicated, to succeed against such a defendant the prosecution must prove that he had information which he knowingly obtained directly or indirectly from another individual who was connected with a particular company, or who was so connected at any time during the preceding six months, who the defendant knew or had reasonable cause to believe, held the information by virtue of being so connected that the information was, in short, confidential and that it was price sensitive. As with the primary insider, the offence is committed when he deals in the securities of that company.

Thus, in the case of each type of insider, the offence is not one of using information but of dealing in the securities while being in possession of the relevant information.

The Attorney General submits that, looking at the Act as a whole, as one is entitled to do in construing the relevant word, one should conclude that the vice aimed at is the exploitation of an unfairly privileged advantage gained from a particular source. If so, why, he asked rhetorically, should the unsoliciting "tippee" (to adopt the inelegant but convenient expression used by the editors of *Gore-Brown on Companies* (44th ed., 1986) be any less culpable than the person who has deliberately sought out the information? The vice lies in the way the information is used, not in the method of its receipt. . .

. . . We had our attention drawn to the history of the 1985 Act. Its effect was to consolidate earlier enactments, including the provisions of the Companies Act 1980. . . Preceding the 1980 Act was a White Paper on *The Conduct of Company Directors* (Cmnd 7037), which dealt, *inter alia*, with the subject of insider dealing. That type of conduct was not then subject to any legal sanctions, although it was causing serious concern not only in business circles. . . We are invited to look at the contents of that paper in order to see the mischief which it was desired by Parliament to remedy. . . Our attention was drawn particularly to the expressions "the . . . information . . . will generally be in his possession" and "someone in such a position has provided him . . . with the information", as indicative of the broad rather than the narrow approach to the problem which we have to decide. What is in our view much more significant is the obvious and understandable concern which the paper shows about the damage to public confidence which insider dealing is likely to cause and the clear intention to prevent so far as possible what amounts to cheating when those with inside knowledge use that knowledge to make a profit in their dealing with others. . .

. . . Now, so far as gaining an unfair advantage of or, put bluntly, cheating the other party to a transaction is concerned, it makes no difference to the person cheated whether the information on which the "tippee" is basing the cheating was sought out by him or came his way by unsolicited gift. Against the background of public and government concern it would indeed have been surprising if Parliament had intended that persons such as, for example, the respondent in the instant case should be free to make a profit from their insider information simply because of the way in which they came by the information. It would do nothing to increase the confidence of the public in the probity of the business world if behaviour such as that of the respondent were to be free from sanction. . . In other words, if one construes the key word "obtained" in the light of the purpose behind the Act, the conclusion must, in our judgment, be that it means no more than "received".

Counsel for the respondent, however, submits that this broad construction of the word provides inadequate protection for the involuntary recipient of information. We disagree. The involuntary recipient does not, in our view, require protection. There is no crime in receiving information. He can protect himself from prosecution by the simple expedient of not dealing in the relevant securities. . .

. . . We have not found the decision easy, but taking all these matters into account, we have reached the conclusion that Parliament intended to penalise the recipient of inside information who deals in the relevant securities, whether he procures the information from the primary insider by purpose and effort or comes by it without any positive action on his part.

This conclusion will have the advantage of avoiding the fine distinctions which would otherwise have to be drawn between what is and what is not a sufficient purpose or effort to satisfy the narrow meaning of "obtain". These would have been distinctions so fine as to be almost imperceptible, and would have done nothing to enhance the reputation of the business world for honesty or of the criminal law for clarity.

(Adapted from The All England Law Reports.)

What approaches does Lord Lane use in this case?

What is the overriding factor in his final decision?	
What sources of information, other than the Act itself, does Lord Lane use?	

Which approach should the judges use?

Seaford Court Estates Ltd v Asher [1949] 2 All E.R. 155

COURT OF APPEAL
Lord GREENE M.R., ASQUITH and DENNING L.JJ.
MAY 2, 3, JUNE 1, 1949

DENNING L.J.:

. . . Whenever a statute comes up for consideration it must be remembered that it is not within human powers to foresee the manifold sets of facts which may arise, and, even if it were, it is not possible to provide for them in terms free from all ambiguity. The English language is not an instrument of mathematical precision. Our literature would be much the poorer if it were. This is where the draftsmen of Acts of Parliament have often been unfairly criticised. A judge, believing himself to be fettered by the supposed rule that he must look to the language and nothing else, laments that the draftsmen have not provided for this or that, or have been guilty of some or other ambiguity. It would certainly save the judges trouble if Acts of Parliament were drafted with divine prescience and perfect clarity. In the absence of it, when a defect appears a judge cannot simply fold his hands and blame the draftsman. He must set to work on the constructive task of finding the intention of Parliament, and he must do this not only from the language of the statute, but also from a consideration of the social conditions which gave rise to it and of the mischief which it was passed to remedy, and then he must supplement the written word so as to give "force and life" to the intention of the legislature. . . A judge should ask himself the question how, if the makers of the Act had themselves come across this ruck in the texture of it, they would have straightened it out? He must then do as they would have done. A judge must not alter the material of which the Act is woven, but he can and should iron out the creases. . .

(Adapted from The All England Law Reports.)

Magor and St Mellons Rural District Council v Newport Corporation [1950] 2 All E.R. 1226

COURT OF APPEAL
SOMERVELL, COHEN AND DENNING L.JJ.
NOVEMBER 3, 27, 1950

DENNING L.J.:

. . . This was so obviously the intention of the Minister's Order that I have no patience with an ultra-legalistic interpretation which would deprive them of their rights altogether. . . We do not sit here to pull the language of Parliament and of Ministers to pieces and make nonsense of it. That is an easy thing to do, and it is a thing to which lawyers are too often prone. We sit here to find out the intention of Parliament and of Ministers and carry it out, and we do this better by filling in the gaps and making sense of the enactment than by opening it up to destructive analysis. . .

(Adapted from The All England Law Reports.)

Magor and St Mellons Rural District Council v Newport Corporation [1951] 2 All E.R. 839

HOUSE OF LORDS
LORD SIMONDS, LORD GODDARD, LORD MORTON OF HENRYTON, LORD RADCLIFFE AND LORD TUCKER
JULY 4, 5, OCTOBER 25, 1951

LORD SIMONDS:

My Lords, I have had the advantage of reading the opinion which my noble and learned friend, Lord Morton of Henryton, is about to deliver, and I fully concur in his reasons and conclusion, as I do in those of Parker J. and the majority of the Court of Appeal. Nor should I have thought it necessary to add any observations of my own were it not that the dissenting opinion of Denning L.J. appears to invite some comment.

My Lords, the criticism which I venture to make of the judgment of the learned lord justice is not directed at the conclusion that he reached. It is after all a trite saying that on questions of construction different minds may come to different conclusions and I am content to say that I agree with my noble and learned friend. But it is on the approach of the lord justice to what is a question of construction and nothing else that I think it desirable to make some comment, for at a time when so large a proportion of the cases that are brought before the courts depend on the construction of modern statutes it would not be right for this House to pass unnoticed the propositions which the learned lord justice lays down for the guidance of himself and, presumably, of others. He said: "We sit here to find out the intention of Parliament and of Ministers and carry it out, and we do this better by filling in the gaps and making sense of the enactment than by opening it up to destructive analysis."

The first part of this passage appears to be an echo of what was said in *Heydon's* Case three hundred years ago and, so regarded, is not objectionable. But the way in which the learned lord justice summarises the broad rules laid down by Sir Edward Coke in that case may well induce grave misconception of the function of the court. The part which is played in the judicial interpretation of a statute by reference to the circumstances of its passing is too well known to need re-statement. It is sufficient to say that the general proposition that it is the duty of the court to find out the intention of Parliament—and not only of Parliament but of Ministers also—cannot by any means be supported. The duty of the court is to interpret the words that the legislature has used. Those words may be ambiguous, but, even if they are, the power and duty of the court to travel outside them on a voyage of discovery are strictly limited. . . . The second part of the passage that I have cited from the judgment of the learned lord justice is, no doubt, the logical sequel of the first. The court, having discovered the intention of Parliament and of Ministers too, must proceed to fill in the gaps. What the legislature has not written, the court must write. This proposition . . . cannot be supported. It appears to me to be a naked usurpation of the legislative function under the thin disguise of interpretation, and it is the less justifiable when it is guesswork with what material the legislature would, if it had discovered the gap, have filled it in. If a gap is disclosed, the remedy lies in an amending Act.

(Adapted from The All England Law Reports.)

Activity ❶

Working in **pairs** or **small groups**, and using the information in the articles above, together with any other information you may find (e.g. in books, journals, newspapers or on the internet), prepare the case for or against the purposive approach to statutory interpretation. In preparing this activity, you should also read **Chapter 4** of *A Level and AS Level Law: a Study Guide*. You might also find it helpful to complete the **table** below. You should then **debate** this issue as a whole class.

(Evidence: Communications: C3.1a, C3.2)

Approach?	Arguments for?	Arguments against?
Literal		

Golden		
Purposive		
Unitary		

Aids to interpretation

- When interpreting legislation, the courts may refer to certain **internal (intrinsic)** and **external (extrinsic)** aids to help in discovering the correct interpretation.

- It might seem obvious for the courts to refer to what was said in Parliament during the passing of the Act. These debates are reported in the official record known as **Hansard**. However, the judges have had difficulty over the years in deciding whether they should be allowed to refer to these debates.

Black-Clawson International Ltd v Papierwerke Waldhof-Aschaffenburg AG [1975] 1 All E.R. 810

HOUSE OF LORDS
LORD REID, VISCOUNT DILHORNE, LORD WILBERFORCE, LORD DIPLOCK AND LORD SIMON OF GLAISDALE
OCTOBER 14, 15, 16, 17, 18, 21, 22, 1974, MARCH 5, 1975

Statute—construction—aids to construction—report—report of committee presented to Parliament— committee recommending legislation—report giving statement of existing law—draft bill appended to report—report containing commentary an draft bill—commentary indicating that clause in draft bill intended to state but not alter common law—draft bill enacted without alteration—whether reference may be made to report to determine mischief which statute intended to cure—whether reference may be made to report for a direct statement as to meaning of statute.

LORD REID:

My Lords, the main question at issue in this case is the proper interpretation of s.8 of the Foreign Judgments (Reciprocal Enforcement) Act 1933. . . In this case it appears to me to be unusually important to consider as aids to construction all other material which the law allows us to look at, and I shall first state my view on that matter. We often say that we are looking for the intention of Parliament, but that is not quite accurate. We are seeking the meaning of the words which Parliament used. We are seeking not what Parliament meant but the true meaning of what they said. In the comparatively few cases where the words of a statutory provision are only capable of having one meaning, that is an end of the matter and no further enquiry is permissible. But that certainly does not apply to s.8.

One must first read the words in the context of the Act as a whole, but one is entitled to go beyond that. The general rule in construing any document is that one should put oneself "in the shoes" of the maker or makers and take into account relevant facts known to them when the document was made. The same must apply to Acts of Parliament subject to one qualification. An Act is addressed to all the lieges and it would seem wrong to take into account anything that was not public knowledge at the time. That may be common knowledge at the time or it may be some published information which Parliament can be presumed to have had in mind.

It has always been said to be important to consider the "mischief" which the Act was apparently intended to remedy. The word "mischief" is traditional. I would expand it in this way. In addition to reading the Act you look at the facts presumed to be known to Parliament when the Bill which became the Act in question was before it, and you consider whether there is disclosed some unsatisfactory state of affairs which Parliament can properly be supposed to have intended to remedy by the Act. There is a presumption which can be stated in various ways. One is that in the absence of any clear indication to the contrary Parliament can be presumed not to have altered the common law farther than was necessary to remedy the "mischief". Of course it may and quite often does go farther. But the principle is that if the enactment is ambiguous, that meaning which relates the scope of the Act to the mischief should be taken rather than a different or wider meaning which the contemporary situation did not call for. The mischief which this Act was intended to remedy may have been common knowledge 40 years ago. I do not think that it is today. But it so happens that a committee including many eminent and highly skilled members made a full investigation of the matter and reported some months before the Act was passed.

I think that we can take this report as accurately stating the "mischief" and the law as it was then understood to be, and therefore we are fully entitled to look at those parts of the report which deal with those matters.

But the report contains a great deal more than that. It contains recommendations, a draft Bill and other instruments intended to embody those recommendations, and comments on what the committee thought the Bill achieved. The draft Bill corresponds in all material respects with the Act so it is clear that Parliament adopted the recommendations of the committee. But nevertheless I do not think that we are entitled to take any of this into account in construing the Act.

Construction of the provisions of an Act is for the court and for no one else. This may seem technical but it is good sense. Occasionally we can find clear evidence of what was intended, more often any such evidence, if there is any, is vague and uncertain. If we are to take into account evidence of Parliaments' intention the first thing we must do is to reverse our present practice with regard to consulting *Hansard.* I have more than once drawn attention to the practical difficulties that would involve but the difficulty goes deeper. The questions which give rise to debate are rarely those which later have to be decided by the courts. One might take the views of the promoters of a Bill as an indication of the intention of Parliament but any view the promoters may have had about questions which later come before the court will not often appear in Hansard and often those questions have never occurred to the promoters. At best we might get material from which a more or less dubious inference might be drawn as to what the promoters intended or would have intended if they had thought about the matter, and it would I think generally be dangerous to attach weight to what some other members of either House may have said. The difficulties in assessing any references there might have been in Parliament to the question before the court are such that in my view our best course is to adhere to present practice.

If we are to refrain from considering expressions of intention in Parliament it appears to me that a *fortiori* we should disregard expressions of intention by committees or royal commissions which reported before the Bill was introduced. I may add that we did in fact examine the whole of this report—it would have been difficult to avoid that—but I am left in some doubt as to how the committee would have answered some of the questions which we have now to answer, because I do not think that they were ever considered by the committee. . .

(Adapted from The All England Law Reports.)

Apart from *Hansard*, what aids to interpretation can the courts refer to, and for what purpose?

Davis v Johnson [1978] 1 All E.R. 841

COURT OF APPEAL, CIVIL DIVISION
Lord DENNING M.R., SIR GEORGE BAKER P, GOFF, SHAW AND CUMMING-BRUCE L.JJ.
NOVEMBER 17, 18, 21, 22, 28, 1977

LORD DENNING M.R.:

. . . Some may say, and indeed have said, that judges should not pay any attention to what is said in Parliament. They should grope about in the dark for the meaning of an Act without switching on the light. I do not accede to this view. In some cases Parliament is assured in the most explicit terms what the effect of a statute will be. It is on that footing that members assent to the clause being agreed to. It is on that understanding that an amendment is not pressed. In such cases I think the court should be able to look at the proceedings. . . And it is obvious that there is nothing to prevent a judge looking at these debates himself privately and getting some guidance from them. Although it may shock the purists, I may as well confess that I have sometimes done it. I have done it in this very case. It has thrown a flood of light on the position . . .

(Adapted from The All England Law Reports.)

Davis v Johnson [1978] 1 All E.R. 1132

HOUSE OF LORDS
LORD DIPLOCK, VISCOUNT DILHORNE, LORD KILBRANDON, LORD SALMON AND LORD SCARMAN
JANUARY 16, 17, MARCH 9, 1978

VISCOUNT DILHORNE:

It is a well and long established rule that counsel cannot refer to Hansard as an aid to the construction of a statute. What is said by a Minister or by a member sponsoring a Bill is not a legitimate aid to the interpretation of an Act. . .

If it was permissible to refer to Hansard, in every case concerning the construction of a statute counsel might regard it as necessary to search through the Hansards of all the proceedings in each House to see if in the course of them anything relevant to the construction had been said. If it was thought that a particular Hansard had anything relevant in it and the attention of the court was drawn to it, the court might also think it desirable to look at the other Hansards. The result might be that attention was devoted to the interpretation of ministerial and other statements in Parliament at the expense of considera-tion of the language in which Parliament had thought to express its intention. While, of course, anyone can look at Hansard, I venture to think that it would be improper for a judge to do so before arriving at his decision and before this case I have never known that done. It cannot be right that a judicial decision should be affected by matter which a judge has seen but to which counsel could not refer and on which counsel had no opportunity to comment.

LORD SCARMAN:

There are two good reasons why the courts should refuse to have regard to what is said in Parliament or by Ministers as aids to the interpretation of a statute. First, such material is an unreliable guide to the meaning of what is enacted. It promotes confusion, not clarity. The cut and thrust of debate and the pressures of executive responsibility, essential features of open and responsible government, are not always conducive to a clear and unbiased explanation of the meaning of statutory language. And the volume of parliamentary and ministerial utterances can confuse by its very size. Secondly, counsel are not permitted to refer to Hansard in argument. So long as this rule is maintained by Parliament (it is not the creation of the judges), it must be wrong for the judge to make any judicial use of proceedings in Parliament for the purpose of interpreting statutes.

(Adapted from The All England Law Reports.)

Pepper (Inspector of Taxes) v Hart and related appeals [1993] 1 All E.R. 42

HOUSE OF LORDS
LORD BRIDGE OF HARWICH, LORD GRIFFITHS, LORD EMSLIE, LORD OLIVER OF AYLMER-TON AND LORD BROWNE-WILKINSON
NOVEMBER 4, 1991

LORD MACKAY OF CLASHFERN L.C., LORD KEITH OF KINKEL, LORD BRIDGE OF HARWICH, LORD GRIFFITHS, LORD ACKNER, LORD OLIVER OF AYLMERTON AND LORD BROWNE-WILKINSON
JUNE 8, 9, 10, 11, 17, 18, NOVEMBER 26, 1992

LORD GRIFFITHS:

My Lords, I have long thought that the time had come to change the self-imposed judicial rule that forbade any reference to the legislative history of an enactment as an aid to its interpretation. The ever-increasing volume legislation must inevitably result in ambiguities of statutory language which are not perceived at the time the legislation is enacted. The object of the court in interpreting legislation is to give effect so far as the language permits to the intention of the legislature. If the language proves to be ambiguous I can see no sound reason not to consult Hansard to see if there is a clear statement of the meaning that the words were intended to carry. The days have long passed when the courts adopted a strict constructionist view of interpretation which required them to adopt the literal meaning of the language. The courts now adopt a purposive approach which seeks to give effect to the true purpose of legislation and are prepared to look at much extraneous material that bears on the background against which the legislation was enacted. Why then cut ourselves off from the one source in which may be found an authoritative statement of the intention with which the legislation is placed before Parliament. . .

I cannot agree with the view that consulting Hansard will add so greatly to the cost of litigation that on this ground alone we should refuse to do so. Modern technology greatly facilitates the recall and display of material held centrally. I have to confess that on many occasions I have had recourse to Hansard, of course only to check if my interpretation had conflicted with an express parliamentary intention, but I can say that it does not take long to recall and assemble the relevant passages in which the particular section was dealt with in Parliament, nor does it take long to see if anything relevant was said. Furthermore if the search resolves the ambiguity it will in future save all the expense that would otherwise be incurred in fighting the rival interpretations through the courts. We have heard no suggestion that recourse to parliamentary history has significantly increased the cost of litigation in Australia or New Zealand and I do not believe that it will do so in this country. . .

LORD BROWNE-WILKINSON:
. . . the reasons put forward for the present rule are, first, that it preserves the constitutional proprieties, leaving Parliament to legislate in words and the courts (not parliamentary speakers) to construe the meaning of the words finally enacted, second, the practical difficulty of the expense of researching parliamentary material which would arise if the material could be looked at, third the need for the citizen to have access to a known defined text which regulates his legal rights and, fourth, the improbability of finding helpful guidance from Hansard. . .

My Lords, I have come to the conclusion that, as a matter of law, there are sound reasons for making a limited modification to the existing rule (subject to strict safeguards). . . In my judgment. . .reference to parliamentary material should be permitted as an aid to the construction of legislation which is ambiguous or obscure or the literal meaning of which leads to an absurdity. Even in such cases references in court to parliamentary material should only be permitted where such material clearly discloses the mischief aimed at or the legislative intention lying behind the ambiguous or obscure words. In the case of statements made in Parliament, as at present advised I cannot foresee that any statement other than the statement of the minister or other promoter of the Bill is likely to meet these criteria. . .

. . . my main reason for reaching this conclusion is based on principle. Statute law consists of the words that Parliament has enacted. It is for the courts to construe those words and it is the court's duty in so doing to give effect to the intention of Parliament in using those words. It is an inescapable fact that, despite all the care taken in passing legislation, some statutory provisions when applied to the circumstances under consideration in any specific case are found to be ambiguous. One of the reasons for such ambiguity is that the members of the legislature in enacting the statutory provision may have been told what result those words are intended to achieve. Faced with a given set of words which are capable of conveying that meaning it is not surprising if the words are accepted as having that meaning. Parliament never intends to enact an ambiguity. Contrast with that the position of the courts. The courts are faced simply with a set of words which are in fact capable of bearing two meanings. The courts are ignorant of the underlying parliamentary purpose. Unless something in other parts of the legislation discloses such purpose, the courts are forced to adopt one of the two possible meanings using highly technical rules of construction. In many, I suspect most, cases references to parliamentary materials will not throw any light on the matter. But in a few cases it may emerge that the very question was considered by Parliament in passing the legislation. Why in such a case should the courts blind themselves to a clear indication of what Parliament intended in using those words? The court cannot attach a meaning to words which they cannot bear, but if the words are capable of bearing more than one meaning why should not Parliament's true intention be enforced rather than thwarted?

. . . I therefore reach the conclusion . . . that the exclusionary rule should be relaxed so as to permit reference to parliamentary materials where: (a) legislation is ambiguous or obscure, or leads to an absurdity; (b) the material relied on consists of one or more statements by a minister or other promoter of the Bill together if necessary with such other parliamentary material as is necessary to understand such statements and their effect; (c) the statements relied on are clear.

(Adapted from The All England Law Reports.)

According to the cases above, what are the arguments for and against allowing the courts to refer to *Hansard*?	Arguments for?	Arguments against?
Following *Pepper v Hart*, when can the courts refer to *Hansard*?		

Explanatory Notes

- The Law Commission, in a 1969 report, recommended that an explanatory memorandum be attached to legislation for the guidance of the courts. This would be a combination of three existing documents: the preamble; the explanatory document prepared for MPs; and the detailed briefings prepared for ministers.

- Although this recommendation has never been fully implemented, the **explanatory notes** have, since 1999, been expanded and published alongside the Act.

Explanatory Notes to Public Acts

With effect from the first Public General Act of 1999, all new Public Acts which result from Bills introduced into either House of Parliament by a Government Minister . . . are to be accompanied by Explanatory Notes. The text of the Explanatory Notes will be produced by the Government Department responsible for the subject matter of the Act. The purpose of these Explanatory Notes is to make the Act of Parliament accessible to readers who are not legally qualified and who have no specialised knowledge of the matters dealt with. They are intended to allow the reader to grasp what the Act sets out to achieve and place its effect in context.

(Adapted from The HMSO website.)

Helping the reader of Bills and Acts

Christopher Jenkins summarises the background to explanatory notes, designed to improve the accessibility of statutes.

So where does this leave users of legislation? There is no doubt that they deserve help in reading legislation, because of the constraints under which legislation is drafted. The means of helping them can be made available and, from the beginning of the current Parliamentary session, they are being made available. As a result of a recommendation made by the House of Lords Select Committee on Modernisation, and adopted by both Houses, explanatory notes are being prepared for all government Bills.

The new notes replace both the previous (usually brief) Explanatory and Financial Memoranda published with Bills, and the notes on clauses which departments generally distributed to MPs and peers. They are published alongside Bills. They are prepared when the Bill is first introduced and revised when it moves to the second House and again when it receives Royal Assent. They are available both in printed form and on the Internet.

The notes do not form part of the Bill and do not claim to be authoritative. They are produced by the government department responsible for the Bill and do not receive Parliament's approval. This means that there is freedom to use techniques which cannot generally be used in Bills. . . The notes can explain the background to a measure; they can summarise its principal provisions; they can give worked examples; they can explain difficult concepts by setting them out in different ways. . .

. . . Two aspects of the notes will be particularly important in ensuring that they will be useful. First, they must be written in clear and simple English, using as few technical terms as possible (and then only with adequate explanation). Secondly, they must be neutral in political tone rather than argumentative: they are there to explain the effect of the enactment, not to justify it. They are not propaganda. They are not the law. They are simply aids to understanding. . .

Christopher Jenkins C.B. Q.C. is First Parliamentary Counsel, 36 Whitehall, London SW1A 2AY.

(Adapted from The New Law Journal, May 28, 1999, p.798.)

Do you think the publication of the new Explanatory Notes will lead to more effective interpretation of legislation?—give your reasons.

Activity ❷

You have been asked to give a short **presentation** to a group of potential law students about aids to statutory interpretation. Using the material in the extracts above, and any other relevant information you can find (*e.g.* from the HMSO website), prepare and deliver this presentation. Make sure that your presentation covers:

- Internal (or intrinsic) aids.

- External (or extrinsic) aids.

- Recent developments (*e.g.* relating to Explanatory Notes).

and that it includes at least **one image**.
You must also produce a **one-page handout** for the audience, giving the main points of your presentation and where they can find further information. Your handout, in addition to the text, must include at least **one image**.

(Evidence: Communications: 3.1b, C3.2, C3.3)

Activity ❸

Using the information you have gathered for Activities 1 and 2, and any further information you have gained as a result of the debate, prepare an **extended document** (e.g. an article of approximately 1000 words for a broadsheet newspaper) that outlines why judges have to interpret legislation, how they do this, and what needs to be done to help them do it more effectively. This document must include at least one **image**.

(Evidence: Communications: C3.2, C3.3)

5 | Precedent

? Issues to Explore

? Why is meant by judicial precedent?

? What is the court hierarchy in England and Wales?

? How are court judgements reported?

? What is the difference between the *ratio decidendi* and *obiter dicta*?

? How can precedents be altered or avoided?

? How effectively does the system achieve a balance between certainty and flexibility in precedent?

? What are the limitations on judicial law-making within the law-making partnership between Parliament and the courts?

Definition:

JUDICIAL PRECEDENT:	Judicial precedent refers to the rules of law developed over time by the courts through the decisions they reach in individual cases.

- The basis of the doctrine of precedent is the principle of *stare decisis* (or, more accurately, *stare rationibus decidendis*). This means that a later court is bound to apply the same reasoning as an earlier court where the two cases raise substantially the same question of principle. Where there is no existing precedent to follow or modify, and no relevant legislation, then the court's decision on the point of law involved will establish an **original precedent**.

- In order to operate a system of binding precedent, a legal system must have three essential elements—a **court hierarchy**, an accurate system of **law reporting**, and a set of principles to identify the **binding element** in a decision.

The court hierarchy

The court structure in England and Wales

The Court Service carries out the administrative and support tasks for the Court of Appeal; the High Court, the Crown Court; the county courts; the Probate Service; and certain tribunals. The structure of the courts in England and Wales is set out below.

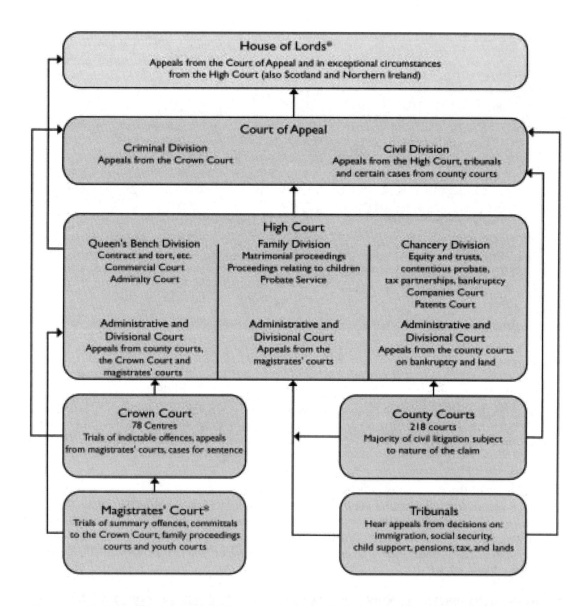

House of Lords*
Appeals from the Court of Appeal and in exceptional circumstances from the High Court (also Scotland and Northern Ireland)

Court of Appeal

Criminal Division
Appeals from the Crown Court

Civil Division
Appeals from the High Court, tribunals and certain cases from county courts

High Court

Queen's Bench Division
Contract and tort, etc.
Commercial Court
Admiralty Court

Family Division
Matrimonial proceedings
Proceedings relating to children
Probate Service

Chancery Division
Equity and trusts,
contentious probate,
tax partnerships, bankruptcy
Companies Court
Patents Court

Administrative and Divisional Court
Appeals from county courts, the Crown Court and magistrates' courts

Administrative and Divisional Court
Appeals from the magistrates' courts

Administrative and Divisional Court
Appeals from the county courts on bankruptcy and land

Crown Court
78 Centres
Trials of indictable offences, appeals from magistrates' courts, cases for sentence

County Courts
218 courts
Majority of civil litigation subject to nature of the claim

Magistrates' Court*
Trials of summary offences, committals to the Crown Court, family proceedings courts and youth courts

Tribunals
Hear appeals from decisions on: immigration, social security, child support, pensions, tax, and lands

(Adapted from The Court Service website.)

> **Briefly explain how the court hierarchy relates to the operation of precedent.**

Law reporting

The history of The Incorporated Council of Law Reporting for England & Wales

While Sir James Burrow may be the father of the modern headnote, the father of **The Law Reports** was certainly W.T.S. Daniel Q.C. His **History and Origin of The Law Reports** shows the efforts that were made in the last century to cure the ills that had arisen in the system of law reporting and produce a more suitable one. In 1863 Daniel proposed a Council of Law Reporting to act gratuitously and be responsible for the appointment of editors and reporters and to undertake the management and direction of the printing and sale of the reports. Editors and reporters would be expected to devote their whole time to the discharge of their duties and salaries should be sufficient to secure the services of men duly qualified by learning and experience. Daniel's scheme was approved in substance and the first meeting of the Council was held on February 25, 1865.

In 1865 the reporters began their work in Westminster Hall, the home of the superior Courts, in Lincoln's Inn Old Hall and the Rolls in Chancery Lane. The present Royal Court of Justice was not opened until 1883. The first volumes of the Law Reports appeared in 1866 by which time there were over 400 subscribers at five guineas a year. In 1870 the Council was incorporated under the Companies Act with the object of

"The preparation and publication, in a convenient form, at a moderate price, and under gratuitous professional control, of reports of judicial decisions of the superior and appellate courts in England."

While **The Law Reports** were to be run as a private enterprise without State aid or interference, it was not intended to be profit making except in so far as it was necessary to make it self-supporting. In fact, in 1970 the Council was registered as a Charity. The Council now consists of members nominated by each of the four Inns of Court and by the General Council of the Bar. The two law officers and the President of The Law Society are *ex officio* members. An executive committee sits once or twice a year and the full council meets only once a year.

Criteria for law reporting

W.T.S. Daniel Q.C. who proposed the Council of Law Reporting in 1863 attached to the outline of his scheme a paper by Nathaniel Lindley, who subsequently became Master of the Rolls in 1897 and then sat as a Lord of Appeal in Ordinary in the House of Lords. That paper set out what was required for a good law report. He started by saying that care should be taken to exclude from the reports those cases which passed without discussion and which were valueless as precedents, and those which were substantially repetitions of what was reported already. On the other hand, he said care should be taken to include:

1. All cases which introduce, or appear to introduce, a new principle or a new rule.

2. All cases which materially modify an existing principle or rule.

3. All cases which settle, or materially tend to settle, a question upon which the law is doubtful.

4. All cases which for any reason are peculiarly instructive.

Daniel then said that reports should be accurate, contain everything material and useful and be as concise as was consistent with those objectives. In particular they should show the parties, the nature of the pleadings, the essential facts, the points contended for by counsel and the grounds on which the judgment was based, as well as the judgment, decree, or order actually pronounced. These guidelines are still followed today.

(Adapted from The Incorporated Council of Law Reporting website.)

Briefly explain the importance of law reporting to precedent and identify where law reports can be found.

Ratio decidendi and *obiter dicta*

- The ***ratio decidendi*** and ***obiter dicta*** are the two most important elements in a court judgement that relate to the operation of precedent.

	What is it?	Is it binding or persuasive on fut... courts?
Ratio decidendi		
Obiter dicta		

The Judicial Committee of the Privy Council

The Judicial Committee of the Privy Council is the court of final appeal for those Commonwealth countries which have retained the appeal to Her Majesty in Council or, in the case of Republics, to the Judicial Committee.

It also has certain domestic jurisdiction within the United Kingdom, including the function of being the court of final appeal for determining "devolution issues" under the United Kingdom devolution statutes of 1998.

Five judges normally sit to hear appeals (except appeals from United Kingdom professional bodies) and three for other matters. The Judicial Committee deals with about 65–75 appeals a year. The court sits in Downing Street.

(Adapted from The Privy Council Office website.)

Briefly describe the different forms of persuasive precedent.

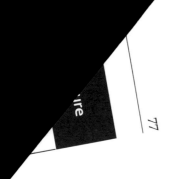

ty ❶

been asked to give a short **presentation** to a group of potential
nts about judicial precedents. Using the material in the extracts
d any other relevant information you can find (e.g. from the
re and deliver this presentation. In preparing this activity, you
' *A Level and AS Level Law: a Study Guide*. Make sure that

- The principle of *stare decisis*.
- The English court hierarchy.
- Law reporting.
- The binding element in a judgment.

and that it includes at least **one image**.
You must also produce a **one-page handout** for the audience, giving the main points of your
presentation and where they can find further information. Your handout, in addition to the
text, must include at least **one image**.

(Evidence: Communications: 3.1b, C3.2, C3.3)

Precedent in action

- Precedent has to balance the competing but equally legitimate aims of **flexibility** and
  certainty. The law needs to be flexible in order to develop and evolve to meet changing
  times and demands. However, it must also be sufficiently certain to allow people to plan
  their affairs and lawyers to advise their clients.

- Flexibility is achieved through the ability of the courts to **overrule**, **distinguish** and
  depart from previous precedents.

- In the judgment (below) from Lord Lane in *R v R (Rape—Marital exemption)*, we can see
  very clearly how precedent can operate to develop rules of law over time. Read the
  judgment carefully, making notes on the key points and cases that Lord Lane discusses.

R v R (rape: marital exemption) [1991] 2 All E.R. 257

COURT OF APPEAL, CRIMINAL DIVISION
LORD LANE C.J., SIR STEPHEN BROWN P, WATKINS, NEILL AND RUSSELL L.JJ.
FEBRUARY 27, MARCH 14, 1991

*Criminal law—rape—husband and wife—marital exemption—whether law of rape subject to marital
exemption—whether husband can be convicted of rape if he has sexual intercourse with wife without
her consent.*

The husband and wife were married in 1984 but separated in October 1989 when the wife left the matrimonial home with their child and went to her parents' home. Two days later the husband telephoned the wife to say that he was going to see about a divorce. The following month the husband broke into the parents' home and either forced the wife to have sexual intercourse or attempted to do so. He was charged with rape and assault occasioning actual bodily harm.

In the course of his trial the judge was asked to give a ruling on whether the husband could be convicted of the rape of his wife. The judge ruled that a wife could unilaterally withdraw her implied consent to sexual intercourse by a withdrawal from cohabitation accompanied by a clear indication that her consent to sexual intercourse had been terminated and accordingly left the charge of rape to the jury. The husband then pleaded guilty to attempted rape and assault occasioning actual bodily harm and was sentenced to three years' imprisonment. He appealed.

LORD LANE C.J.:

. . . The argument before us has . . . raised the question whether there is any basis for the principle, long-supposed to be part of the common law, that a wife does by the fact of marriage give any implied consent in advance for the husband to have sexual intercourse with her, and, secondly, the question whether, assuming that that principle at one time existed, it still represents the law in either a qualified or unqualified form.

Any consideration of this branch of the law must start with the pronouncement by Sir Matthew Hale in his *History of the Pleas of the Crown*, p.629: "But the husband cannot be guilty of a rape committed by himself upon his lawful wife, for by their mutual matrimonial consent and contract the wife hath given up herself in this kind unto her husband, which she cannot retract." That was published in 1736 . . . Hale . . . held the office of Chief Justice for five years, and there can be little doubt that what he wrote was an accurate expression of the common law as it then stood. . .

It is of interest to note that immediately before the passage we have cited, Hale C.J. says that the wider defence based on cohabitation stated by Bracton was no longer the law. Hale C.J. explained the change in the law on the basis that, though "unlawful cohabitation" might be evidence of consent, "it is not necessary that it should be so, for the woman may forsake that unlawful course of life".

It seems clear from the passage we have cited . . . that he founded the proposition that a husband could not be guilty of rape upon his lawful wife on the grounds: (a) that on marriage a wife "gave" her body to her husband and (b) that on marriage she gave her irrevocable consent to sexual intercourse.

The theory that on marriage a wife gave her body to her husband was accepted in matrimonial cases decided in the ecclesiastical courts. Thus in *Popkin v Popkin* (1794) . . . Sir William Scott stated: "The husband has a right to the person of his wife", though he added the important qualification, "but not if her health is endangered".

These concepts of the relationship between husband and wife appear to have persisted for a long time and may help to explain why Hale C.J.'s statement that a husband could not be guilty of rape on his wife was accepted as an enduring principle of the common law.

The first edition of *Archbold Pleading and Evidence in Criminal Cases* (1822), p.259 stated simply: "A husband also cannot be guilty of rape upon his wife."

However, in *R v Clarence* (1888) . . . Wills J. said: "If intercourse under the circumstances now in question constitute an assault on the part of the man, it must constitute rape, unless, indeed, as between married persons rape is impossible, a proposition to which I certainly am not prepared to assent, and for which there seems to me to be no sufficient authority."

Field J. in the course of his judgment said: "But it is argued that here there is no offence, because the wife of the prisoner consented to the act, and I entertain no doubt that, if that was so, there was neither assault nor unlawful infliction of harm. Then, did the wife of the prisoner consent? The ground for holding that she did so, put forward in argument, was the consent to marital intercourse which is imposed upon every wife by the marriage contract, and a passage from Hale's *Pleas of the Crown* was cited, in which it is said that a husband cannot be guilty of rape upon his wife, 'for by their mutual matrimonial consent and contract the wife hath given up herself in this kind to her husband, which she cannot retract.' The authority of Hale, C.J., on such a matter is undoubtedly as high as any can be, but no other authority is cited by him for this proposition, and I should hesitate before I adopted it. There may, I think, be many cases in which a wife may lawfully refuse intercourse, and in which, if the husband imposed it by violence, he might be held guilty of a crime."

Apart from those *dicta* in *R v Clarence*, no one seems to have questioned Hale C.J.'s proposition until Byrne J. in *R v Clarke* [1949] held that the husband's immunity was lost where the justices had made an order providing that the wife should no longer be bound to cohabit with the defendant. In the course of his ruling Byrne J. said: "As a general proposition it can be stated that a husband cannot be guilty of a rape on his wife. No doubt, the reason for that is that on marriage the wife consents to the husband's exercising the marital right of intercourse during such time as the ordinary relations created by the marriage contract subsist between them."

However, in *R v Miller* [1954] Lynskey J., having examined the authorities, ruled that Hale C.J.'s proposition was correct and that the husband had no case to answer on a charge of rape although the wife had before the act of intercourse presented a petition for divorce, which had not reached the stage of a decree nisi.

In *R v O'Brien* [1974] Park J. ruled that a decree nisi effectively terminated a marriage and upon its pronouncement the consent to marital intercourse given by a wife at the time of marriage was revoked: Between the pronouncement of a decree nisi and the obtaining of a decree absolute a marriage subsists as a mere technicality. There can be no question that by a decree nisi a wife's implied consent to marital intercourse is revoked. Accordingly, a husband commits the offence of rape if he has sexual intercourse with her thereafter without her consent.

In *R v Steele* (1976) 65 Cr App R 22 this court held that, where a husband and wife are living apart and there is in existence an undertaking given by the husband to the court not to molest the wife, that is in effect equivalent to the granting of an injunction and eliminates the wife's implied consent to sexual intercourse. In the course of delivering the judgment of that court, having referred to the cases already mentioned here, I said: "Here there has been no decree of the court, here there has been no direct order of the court compelling the husband to stay away from his wife. There has been an undertaking by the husband not to molest his wife. The question which the court has to decide is this. Have the parties made it clear, by agreement between themselves, or has the court made it clear by an order or something equivalent to an order, that the wife's consent to sexual intercourse with her husband implicit in the act of marriage, no longer exists?"

I then went on to set out, *obiter*, a number of matters which would not be sufficient to remove the husband's immunity, having the judgment of Lynskey J. in *R v Miller* in mind.

R v Roberts [1986] Crim LR 188 was another decision of this court. The husband had been restrained from molesting or going near his wife for two months an ouster order was made ordering him out of the matrimonial home. On the same day a formal deed of separation was entered into; there was no non-cohabitation or non-molestation clause. The trial judge had rejected a submission that the wife's implied consent to intercourse with her husband revived when the injunction ran out in August 1984. It was held that the lack of a non-molestation clause in the deed of separation could not possibly have operated to revive the consent of the wife, which had been terminated.

It is against that brief historical background that we turn to consider the submissions of the appellant advanced by Mr Buchanan in a carefully researched argument that the husband's immunity was not lost by what had happened between his wife and himself and that accordingly he was not liable to be tried or convicted for rape.

In the course of his ruling upon the submission the learned judge, Owen J., having set out the authorities, reached a conclusion in the following terms: "what, in law, will suffice to revoke that consent which the wife gives to sexual intercourse upon marriage and which the law implies from the facts of marriage?. . . I accept that it is not for me to make the law. However, it is for me to state the common law as I believe it to be. If that requires me to indicate a set of circumstances which have not so far been considered as sufficient to negative consent as in fact so doing, then I must do so. I cannot believe that it is a part of the common law of this country that where there has been withdrawal of either party from cohabitation, accompanied by a clear indication that consent to sexual intercourse has been terminated, that that does not amount to a revocation of that implicit consent."

Ever since the decision of Byrne J. in *R v Clarke* in 1949, courts have been paying lip service to Hale C.J.'s proposition, whilst at the same time increasing the number of exceptions, the number of situations to which it does not apply. This is a legitimate use of the flexibility of the common law which can and should adapt itself to changing social attitudes.

There comes a time when the changes are so great that it is no longer enough to create further exceptions restricting the effect of the proposition, a time when the proposition itself requires examination to see whether its terms are in accord with what is generally regarded today as acceptable behaviour . . . the idea that a wife by marriage consents in advance to her husband having sexual intercourse with her whatever her state of health or however proper her objections (if that is what Hale C.J. meant) is no longer acceptable. It can never have been other than a fiction, and fiction is a poor basis for the criminal law. The extent to which events have overtaken Hale C.J.'s proposition is well illustrated by his last four words, "which she cannot retract".

It seems to us that where the common law rule no longer even remotely represents what is the true position of a wife in present-day society, the duty of the court is to take steps to alter the rule if it can legitimately do so in the light of any relevant parliamentary enactment. . . We take the view that the time has now arrived when the law should declare that a rapist remains a rapist subject to the criminal law, irrespective of his relationship with his victim.

The remaining and no less difficult question is whether, despite that view, this is an area where the court should step aside to leave the matter to the parliamentary process. This is not the creation of a new offence, it is the removal of a common law fiction which has become anachronistic and offensive and we consider that it is our duty having reached that conclusion to act upon it.

Had our decision been otherwise and had we been of the opinion that Hale C.J.'s proposition was still effective, we would nevertheless have ruled that where, as in the instant case, a wife withdraws from cohabitation in such a way as to make it clear to the husband that so far as she is concerned the marriage is at an end, the husband's immunity is lost. The appeal fails and is dismissed.

Notes:

(Adapted from The All England Law Reports.)

- In *R v R*, we can see a series of cases which distinguished from Hale C.J.'s original proposition, which Lord Lane views as "a legitimate use of the flexibility of the common law which can and should adapt itself to changing social attitudes". But the Court of Appeal has also recognised that this flexibility can be misused, as we see in the statements by **Lord Denning**, below.

Lewis v Averay [1971] 3 All E.R. 907

COURT OF APPEAL, CIVIL DIVISION
LORD DENNING MR, PHILLIMORE AND MEGAW L.JJ.
JULY 23, 1971

LORD DENNING M.R.:

There are two cases in our books which cannot, to my mind, be reconciled the one with the other. One of them is *Phillips v Brooks*, where a jeweller had a ring for sale. The other is *Ingram v Little*, where two ladies had a car for sale. In each case the story is very similar to the present. A plausible rogue comes along. The rogue says that he likes the ring, or the car, as the case may be. He asks the price. The seller names it. The rogue says that he is prepared to buy it at that price. He pulls out a cheque book. He writes or prepares to write, a cheque for the price. The seller hesitates. He has never met this man before. He does not want to hand over the ring or the car not knowing whether the cheque will be met. The rogue notices the seller's hesitation. He is quick with his next move. He says to the jeweller, in *Phillips v Brooks*: "I am Sir George Bullough of 11 St James' Square"; or to the ladies in *Ingram v Little*: "I am P. G. M. Hutchinson of Stanstead House, Stanstead Road, Caterham"; or to Mr Lewis in the present case: "I am Richard Greene, the film actor of the Robin Hood series". Each seller checks up the information. The jeweller looks up the directory and finds there is a "Sir George Bullough at 11 St James's Square". The ladies check up too. They look at the telephone directory and find there is a "P. G. M. Hutchinson of Stanstead House, Stanstead Road, Caterham". Mr Lewis checks up too. He examines the official pass of the Pinewood Studios and finds that it is a pass for "Richard A. Green" to the Pinewood Studios with this man's photograph on it. In each case the seller feels that this is sufficient confirmation of the man's identity. So he accepts the cheque signed by the rogue and lets him have the ring, in the one case, and the car and log book in the other two cases. The rogue goes off and sells the goods to a third person who buys them in entire good faith and pays the price to the rogue. The rogue disappears. The original seller presents the cheque. It is dishonoured. Who is entitled to the goods? The original seller or the ultimate buyer? The courts have given different answers.

In *Phillips v Brooks Ltd* the ultimate buyer was held to be entitled to the ring. In *Ingram v Little* the original seller was held to be entitled to the car. In the present case the deputy county court judge has held the original seller entitled.

It seems to me that the material facts in each case are quite indistinguishable the one from the other. In each case there was, to all outward appearance, a contract; but there was a mistake by the seller as to the identity of the buyer. This mistake was fundamental. In each case it led to the handing over of the goods. Without it the seller would not have parted with them.

This case therefore raises the question: what is the effect of a mistake by one party as to the identity of the other? It has sometimes been said that, if a party makes a mistake as to the identity of the person with whom he is contracting, there is no contract, or, if there is a contract, it is a nullity and void, so that no property can pass under it. . .

For instance, in *Ingram v Little* the majority of the court suggested that the difference between *Phillips v Brooks* and *Ingram v Little* was that in *Phillips v Brooks* the contract of sale was concluded (so as to pass the property to the rogue) before the rogue made the fraudulent misrepresentation, whereas in *Ingram v Little* the rogue made the fraudulent misrepresentation before the contract was concluded. My own view is that in each case the property in the goods did not pass until the seller let the rogue have the goods.

Again it has been suggested that a mistake as to the identity of a person is one thing; and a mistake as to his attributes is another. A mistake as to identity, it is said, avoids a contract; whereas a mistake as to attributes does not. But this is a distinction without a difference. A man's very name is one of his attributes. It is also a key to his identity. If then, he gives a false name, is it a mistake as to his identity or a mistake as to his attributes? These fine distinctions do no good to the law.

(Adapted from The All England Law Reports.)

Precedent in the House of Lords

- Until 1966, the **House of Lords** was bound by its own previous decisions (*London Tramways v London County Council* [1898]). This created a block at the top of the system of precedent, and meant that outdated, incorrect or unacceptable decisions could only be rectified by legislation. Therefore, in **1966**, the Lord Chancellor issued a **Practice Statement** that stated that while the House of Lords would regard its own previous decisions as normally binding, it would depart from them when it appeared right to do so.

Practice Statement: Judicial Decision as Authority: House of Lords [1966] 3 All E.R. 77

LORD GARDINER L.C.:

Their lordships regard the use of precedent as an indispensable foundation upon which to decide what is the law and its application to individual cases. It provides at least some degree of certainty upon which individuals can rely in the conduct of their affairs, as well as a basis for orderly development of legal rules.

Their lordships nevertheless recognise that too rigid adherence to precedent may lead to injustice in a particular case and also unduly restrict the proper development of the law. They propose therefore to modify their present practice and, while treating former decisions of this House as normally binding, to depart from a previous decision when it appears right to do so.

In this connection they will bear in mind the danger of disturbing retrospectively the basis on which contracts, settlements of property and fiscal arrangements have been entered into and also the especial need for certainty as to the criminal law.

This announcement is not intended to affect the use of precedent elsewhere than in this House.

(Adapted from The All England Law Reports.)

What does the Practice Statement tell us about. . .	
The advantages of precedent?	
The disadvantages of precedent?	
When the House of Lords can depart from its own previous decisions?	
The criteria the House should take into account in exercising this discretion?	

Precedent in the Court of Appeal

- The **Court of Appeal (Civil Division)** is normally bound by its own previous decisions, subject to exceptions established in *Young v Bristol Aeroplane Co Ltd* **[1944]**.

Young v Bristol Aeroplane Co. Ltd **[1944] 2 All E.R. 293**

COURT OF APPEAL
LORD GREENE M.R., SCOTT, MACKINNON AND LUXMOORE L.JJ., LORD GODDARD AND DU PARCQ L.J.
JULY 28, 1944

LORD GREENE M.R.:

. . . this court is bound to follow previous decisions of its own. . . The only exceptions to this rule . . . are . . . (i) The court is entitled and bound to decide which of two conflicting decisions of its own it will follow. (ii) The court is bound to refuse to follow a decision of its own which, though not expressly overruled, cannot in its opinion stand with a decision of the House of Lords. (iii) The court is not bound to follow a decision of its own if it is satisfied that the decision was given *per incuriam*. . .

(Adapted from The All England Law Reports.)

Morelle Ltd v Wakeling **[1955] 1 All E.R. 708**

COURT OF APPEAL
SIR RAYMOND EVERSHED M.R., DENNING, JENKINS, MORRIS AND ROMER L.JJ.
FEBRUARY 14, 15, 16, MARCH 3, 1955

SIR RAYMOND EVERSHED M.R.:

. . . As a general rule the only cases in which decisions should be held to have been given *per incuriam* are those of decisions given in ignorance or forgetfulness of some inconsistent statutory provision or of some authority binding on the court concerned: so that in such cases some part of the decision or some step in the reasoning on which it is based is found, on that account, to be demonstrably wrong.

(Adapted from The All England Law Reports.)

In what circumstances can the Court of Appeal (Civil Division) depart from its own previous decisions?

- The **Court of Appeal (Criminal Division)** is similarly bound by its own previous decisions subject to the *Bristol Aeroplane* exceptions and to that established in *R v Taylor* **[1950]**.

R v Taylor [1950] 2 All E.R. 170

COURT OF CRIMINAL APPEAL
LORD GODDARD C.J., HUMPHREYS, STABLE, CASSELS, HALLETT, MORRIS AND PARKER J.J.
MAY 22, 1950

LORD GODDARD C.J.:

. . . I should like to say one word about the re-consideration of a case by this court. A court of appeal usually considers itself bound by its own decisions. . . For instance, the Court of Appeal in civil matters considers itself bound by its own decisions. . . In civil matters it is essential in order to preserve the rule of *stare decisis* that that should be so, but this court has to deal with the liberty of the subject and if, on re-consideration, in the opinion of a full court the law has been either mis-applied or misunderstood and a man has been sentenced for an offence, it will be the duty of the court to consider whether he has been properly convicted. The practice observed in civil cases ought not to be applied in such a case. . .

(Adapted from The All England Law Reports.)

In what additional circumstances can the Court of Appeal (Criminal Division) depart from its own previous decisions? Why?

- The question has also arisen as to whether the Court of Appeal should have the same discretion to depart as the House of Lords enjoys under the Practice Statement.

Davis v Johnson [1978] 1 All E.R. 841

COURT OF APPEAL, CIVIL DIVISION
LORD DENNING M.R., SIR GEORGE BAKER P., GOFF, SHAW AND CUMMING-BRUCE L.JJ.
NOVEMBER 17, 18, 21, 22, 28, 1977

LORD DENNING M.R.:

. . . On principle, it seems to me that, whilst this court should regard itself as normally bound by a previous decision of the court, nevertheless it should be at liberty to depart from it if it is convinced that the previous decision was wrong. What is the argument to the contrary? It is said that, if an error has been made, this court has no option but to continue the error and leave it to be corrected by the House of Lords. The answer is this: the House of Lords may never have an opportunity to correct the error; and thus it may be perpetuated indefinitely, perhaps for ever. . . Even if . . . there is an appeal to the House of Lords, it usually takes 12 months or more for the House to reach its decision. What then is the position of the lower courts meanwhile? They are in a dilemma. Either they have to apply the erroneous decision of the Court of Appeal, or they have to adjourn all fresh cases to await the decision of the House of Lords. That has often happened. So justice is delayed, and often denied, by the lapse of time before the error is corrected.

(Adapted from The All England Law Reports.)

Davis v Johnson [1978] 1 All E.R. 1132

HOUSE OF LORDS
LORD DIPLOCK, VISCOUNT DILHORNE, LORD KILBRANDON, LORD SALMON AND LORD SCARMAN
JANUARY 16, 17, MARCH 9, 1978

LORD DIPLOCK:

. . . In an appellate court of last resort a balance must be struck between the need on the one side for the legal certainty resulting from the binding effect of previous decisions and on the other side the avoidance of undue restriction on the proper development of the law. In the case of an intermediate appellate court, however, the second [consideration] can be taken care of by appeal to a superior appellate court, if reasonable means of access to it are available; while the risk to the first [consideration], legal certainty, if the court is not bound by its own previous decisions grows ever greater with increasing membership and the number of three-judge divisions in which it sits. . . So the balance does not lie in the same place as in the case of a court of last resort. That is why Lord Gardiner L.C.'s announcement about the future attitude towards precedent of the House of Lords in its judicial capacity concluded with the words: "This announcement is not intended to affect the use of precedent elsewhere than in this House."

(Adapted from The All England Law Reports.)

Do you think the Court of Appeal should have the same discretion as the House of Lords to depart from its own previous decisions?	
Arguments for	**Arguments against**

Evaluating precedent

- From the reading and work you have been doing on the doctrine of **judicial precedent**, what do you think are its **benefits** and **drawbacks**?

Advantages of precedent	**Disadvantages of precedent**

Activity ❷

Working in **pairs** or **small groups** and using information you may find, e.g. in books, journals, newspapers or on the internet, prepare the case for or against the involvement of judges in law-making. In preparing this activity, you should also read **Chapter 41** of **A Level and AS Level Law: a Study Guide**. You might also find it helpful to complete the **table** below. You should then **debate** this issue as a whole class.

(Evidence: Communications: C3.1a, C3.2)

Should judges make law?	
Arguments for	Arguments against

Activity ❸

Using the information you have gathered for Activities 1 and 2, and any further information you have gained as a result of the debate, prepare an **extended document** (e.g. an article of approximately 1000 words for a broadsheet newspaper) that outlines the main arguments for and against the involvement of judges in law-making. This document must include at least one **image**.

(Evidence: Communications: C3.2, C3.3)

SECTION TWO: DISPUTE SOLVING

6   Police Powers

? Issues to Explore

? What powers of stop and search do the police have?

? What powers of arrest and detention do the police have?

? What protections exist for the suspect?

? Does the law strike the right balance between police powers and the rights of the individual?

Definition:

POLICE POWERS:	The powers the police have to stop, search, arrest and detain suspects in the course of their duties and investigations.

- The role of the police in a democratic society is a sensitive one, balancing society's interest in the prevention of crime and the prosecution of offenders with the liberties of the individual.

- The **Royal Commission on Criminal Procedure (the Philips Commission)** stated in 1981 that **"a balance must be found between the interests of the community in bringing offenders to justice and the rights and liberties of persons suspected or accused of crime"**.

- Consequently, police powers exist within a legislative framework, principally the **Police and Criminal Evidence Act 1984** (and accompanying **Codes of Practice**) and the **Criminal Justice and Public Order Act 1994,** designed to ensure that individual civil liberties are protected and respected.

Rice v Connolly [1966] 2 All E.R. 649

QUEEN'S BENCH DIVISION
LORD PARKER C.J., MARSHALL AND JAMES J.J.
MAY 3, 1966

Criminal law—obstructing constable when in the execution of his duty—refusal to answer questions—whether wilful obstruction.

The appellant was seen by police officers in the early hours of the morning behaving suspiciously in an area where on the same night breaking offences had taken place. On being questioned he refused to say where he was going or where he had come from. He refused to give his full name and address, though he did give a name and the name of a road, which were not untrue. He refused to accompany the police to a police box for identification purposes, saying, "If you want me, you will have to arrest me". He was arrested and charged with wilfully obstructing the police. On appeal it was conceded that "wilfully" imported something done without lawful excuse.

Held—Although every citizen had a moral or social duty to assist the police, there was no relevant legal duty to that effect in the circumstances of the present case, and the appellant had been entitled to decline to answer the questions put to him and (prior to his arrest) to accompany the police officer on request to the police box to establish identity; accordingly, in the circumstances, "wilful obstruction" by the appellant was not established, although he had been obstructive, because no obstruction without lawful excuse had been established.

(Adapted from The All England Law Reports.)	
Summary of facts	
Ratio decidendi	

Ricketts v Cox [1982] 74 Cr.App.R. 298

QUEEN'S BENCH DIVISION

The police were looking for a group of youths responsible for a serious assault. They approached Ricketts and Blake. The latter refused to give names or information and were abusive to the police. One of the police then took Blake's arm, at which Blake punched him. Blake was arrested (for assault), and Ricketts intervened to prevent his arrest: he was then himself arrested and charged with obstruction. The case against Blake was dismissed by the Sheffield magistrates (because they ruled that the policeman was wrong to take his arm before arresting him, so that Blake was technically acting in self-defence to an assault by the police). But Ricketts was convicted of obstruction. He appealed by way of case stated (*i.e.* on a matter of law) to the Divisional Court, but lost his appeal.

Held—distinguishing *Rice v Connolly*, that the totality of their behaviour and attitude at this stage amounted to an obstruction of the police officers in the execution of their duties and either or both the defendants could then have been charged with obstruction of the police in the execution of their duty.

(Adapted from The Criminal Appeal Reports.)

Summary of facts	
Ratio decidendi	

Police Reform Act 2002

Section 50 Persons acting in an anti-social manner

(1) If a constable in uniform has reason to believe that a person has been acting, or is acting, in an anti-social manner (within the meaning of s.1 of the Crime and Disorder Act 1998 (c. 37) (anti-social behaviour orders)), he may require that person to give his name and address to the constable.

(2) Any person who—

    (a) fails to give his name and address when required to do so under subs.(1), or

    (b) gives a false or inaccurate name or address in response to a requirement under that subsection,

is guilty of an offence and shall be liable, on summary conviction, to a fine not exceeding level 3 on the standard scale.

Do people have to answer police questions in the street?	
Can a refusal to answer questions amount to obstructing the police?	
Are people obliged to give their name and address to the police?	

Kenlin v Gardiner [1966] 3 All E.R. 931

QUEEN'S BENCH DIVISION
LORD PARKER C.J., WINN L.J. AND WIDGERY J.
NOVEMBER 1, 1966

Police—constable—assault on, in execution of duty—police officers in plain clothes detaining boys in order to put questions to them—technical assault by police officers as they were not effecting arrest of the boys—assault by boys on police officers—genuine misunderstanding on both sides—self-defence.

The appellants, both schoolboys, aged 14, were seen by two police officers in plain clothes going from house to house in a street. The officers became genuinely suspicious of their conduct, which, however, was in fact quite innocent. One of the officers went up to the boys and said "We are police officers, here is my warrant card. What are you calling at the houses for?" The boys, apparently, did not appreciate from the warrant card that the respondents were police officers and were frightened at being accosted by strange men. Accordingly, instead of replying, one of them tried to run away, was caught hold of by one of the respondents and struggled violently, hitting and kicking him. The other appellant started to run off, was caught and he too struggled and hit the officer. Both appellants were charged with assaulting the police in the execution of their duty. The magistrates found that the boys had technically assaulted the respondents and convicted them, but granted them an absolute discharge.

Held—The police officers' acts in catching hold of the appellants were not done in the course of arresting either of the appellants, but for the purpose of detaining them in order to put questions to them, and thus the acts were technically assaults; accordingly the justification of self-defence was open to the appellants in answer to charges based on such assaults, and, as it had not been found that the force used by the appellants in self-defence had been excessive, the convictions of the appellants would be quashed.

(Adapted from The All England Law Reports.)

Summary of facts	
Ratio decidendi	

Donnelly v Jackman [1970] 1 All E.R. 987

QUEEN'S BENCH DIVISION
LORD PARKER C.J., ASHWORTH AND TALBOT J.J.
JANUARY 27, 1970

Police—constable—assault on, in execution of duty—duty—scope—attempt to stop suspect to make enquiries—no charge or arrest at that time—constable touched suspect on shoulder—suspect struck constable—alleged assault on constable in execution of duty.

The appellant was walking along the pavement when a police officer in uniform came up to him with a view to making enquiries about an offence which the officer had cause to believe that the appellant might have committed. The appellant ignored the officer's repeated requests to stop and speak to him. At one stage the officer tapped the appellant on the shoulder, and shortly after the appellant tapped the officer on the chest. It became apparent that the appellant had no intention of stopping. The officer then again touched the appellant on the shoulder with the intention of stopping him (but neither then nor previously had the officer any intention to arrest the appellant), whereupon the appellant struck the officer with some force. The appellant was charged with and convicted of assaulting the officer in the execution of his duty.

Held—The touching of the appellant's shoulder was a trivial interference with his liberty and did not amount to a course of conduct sufficient to be outside the course of the officer's duties; accordingly the appeal would be dismissed.

(Adapted from The All England Law Reports.)

Summary of facts	
Ratio decidendi	
Can the police detain someone without arresting them?	

Police powers of stop and search

Stop!

Sarah Wallace outlines the main stop and search powers:

- the new Code A;
- grounds for exercising the powers; and
- obligations imposed on the police.

Lawyers hear frequent complaints from clients relating to the stop and search regime. One-off or repeated stop and searches arouse strong feelings of anger, victimisation, resentment, embarrassment, nervousness, and lack of trust in the police. Many complain about the attitude of the police, *e.g.* provocative language to provoke a reaction in the detainee that could lead to arrest and a failure to provide reasons for the stop. This article aims to serve as a reminder of the main stop and search powers that the police have.

Overview

The stop and search powers of persons and vehicles, together with the powers to enter and search premises, make arrests, detain, question, and charge are largely contained within the Police and Criminal Evidence Act 1984 ("PACE"). There are other statutory provisions relating to stop and search for other offences (*e.g.* drugs and terrorism).

Statutory powers

There are provisions in a number of different statutes that give police the power to stop and search a person or vehicle before or without making an arrest. For example, s.1 of PACE confers a power for constables to stop and search persons and vehicles for stolen goods, articles for use in certain Theft Act offences, offensive weapons and bladed articles. Most of the statutory powers require the officer to have "reasonable grounds to suspect" that a prohibited article or evidence relating to a particular offence will be found.

Code A

The new Code A of the Code of Practice for the exercise of statutory stop and search powers came into force on April 1, 2003. It governs the exercise of statutory powers to search persons and vehicles before or without arrest. The first principle in para.1.1 is: "Powers to stop and search must be used fairly, responsibly, with respect for people being searched and without unlawful discrimination . . . The Race Relations (Amendment) Act 2000 makes it unlawful for police officers to discriminate on the grounds of race, colour or ethnic origin when using their powers". The other principles governing stop and search are set out in paras 1.1 to 1.5. Paragraph 1.5 is a significant amendment. It now expressly states that no stop and search is to be carried out where no legal power exists. Non-observance of the Code does not of itself give rise to any criminal or civil liability (s.67(10) PACE). But compliance with or breach of the Codes may be relevant to decisions about the admissibility of evidence.

Stop and search under s.1 of PACE

Section 1 of PACE covers situations in which a suspect is thought to have offensive weapons or bladed or pointed articles in his possession, or evidence relating to specified Theft Act offences. The evidence of "prohibited articles" could be stolen property or equipment used to commit one of the specified Theft Act offences. A constable whether in uniform or plain clothes may search any person or vehicle for stolen or prohibited articles (ss. 1(2), (7), (8), (9)). A constable who discovers such an article may seize it (s.1(6)). Powers to stop, search and seize are essentially for use in *public places, i.e.* places to which the public has access but which is *not a dwelling* (s.1(1)(b)).

Reasonable grounds for suspicion

"Reasonable grounds for suspicion" is an important phrase within PACE and the Codes. It also appears in the definition of other stop and search powers in other legislation. Looking just at s.1 of PACE, a constable cannot exercise the powers of stop and search under s.1 unless he has "reasonable grounds for suspicion" that he will find "stolen or prohibited articles" (s.1(3)). Reasonable grounds for suspicion is not defined in PACE. For the purposes of stop and search powers, Code A provides some guidance at paras 2.1–2.11. The test is partly subjective (a police officer must have formed genuine suspicion that he will find stolen or prohibited articles) and partly objective, in that there have to be reasonable grounds for forming such a suspicion (*i.e.* a reasonable man having regard to all the circumstances would regard them as giving rise to reasonable grounds for suspicion). The grounds must be based on objective factors rather than hunch or intuition, and ideally a range of objective factors. Reasonable suspicion cannot be supported on the basis of personal factors alone without reliable supporting intelligence or information or some specific behaviour by the person concerned. A person's race, age, appearance or the fact that the person is known to have a previous conviction cannot be used alone or in combination with each other as a reason for searching that person. Reasonable suspicion cannot be based on stereotypical images of certain groups. A person's actions together with all the surrounding relevant circumstances may give rise to reasonable grounds for suspicion that an offence has been committed or that evidence of the commission of the offence may exist on a person or in a car. An officer who has reasonable grounds for suspicion may detain the person concerned in order to carry out the search. Before carrying out a search the officer may ask questions about the person's behaviour or presence in circumstances which gave rise to the suspicion. As a result of questioning the detained person, the reasonable grounds for suspicion necessary to detain that person may be confirmed or, because of a satisfactory explanation, eliminated. Questioning may also reveal reasonable grounds to suspect the possession of a different kind of unlawful article from that originally suspected. Reasonable grounds for suspicion however cannot be provided retrospectively by such questioning during a person's detention or by refusal to answer any questions put. There is no power to stop or detain in order to find grounds for a search. However police officers have many "encounters" with the public which do not involve detaining people against their will. If reasonable grounds emerge during such an encounter, the officer may search the person, even though no grounds existed when the encounter began (Code A para.2.11). Code A provides at para.1.5 that an officer must not search even with consent where no power to search applies. This is a revision to the previous Code which provided for voluntary (non-statutory) stop and search providing the person consented. Now, even if a person is prepared to submit to a search voluntarily, he must not be searched unless the necessary legal power exists (unless they are entering sports grounds or other premises where a search is "carried out with their consent given as condition of entry"). In practice however the police will have many "encounters" with members of the public which do not involve detaining them against their will. If reasonable grounds for suspicion that a person has an unlawful item on them (or in their car) arise then the officer may go on to carry out a "lawful search" under the relevant statutory provision. The Code does not affect the ability of an officer to speak to or question a person without detaining him or exercising any element of compulsion. This is based on the principle that there is a civic duty to help police officers prevent and discover crime. A person's unwillingness to reply does not alter this entitlement of the police but in the absence of a power to arrest or to detain in order to search the person is free to leave at will and cannot be compelled to remain with the officer. Often a brief conversation or exchange will be desirable as a means to avoid a necessary search or to explain the grounds for the stop/search. Where a person is lawfully detained for a search but no search takes place then the detention in the first place is not unlawful.

Searches not requiring reasonable suspicion

Code A paras 2.12—2.29 cover the statutory powers to stop and search where reasonable suspicion is not required. This article just considers s.60(1) of the Criminal Justice and Public Order Act 1994 (CJPOA) which gives powers to the police to stop and search where they *reasonably believe* that incidents involving serious violence might take place, or that persons are carrying dangerous instruments. The purpose is to prevent serious violence or the widespread carrying of weapons without good reason which might lead to persons being seriously injured by disarming potential offenders in circumstances where other powers would not be sufficient. The unusual feature of the power to stop and search if authorised under s.60 of the CJPOA is that there is no need for a constable to have reasonable grounds to suspect that a person is carrying a weapon or dangerous implement. Authority for such searches must be given in writing by an officer of the rank of inspector or above. Authorisations require a reasonable belief on the part of the inspector which must have an objective basis (*e.g.* intelligence, history of antagonism between groups). Under s.60(4) a constable has the power to stop and search any pedestrian/or stop any vehicle, for a dangerous instruments or an offensive weapon—notwithstanding that he has no grounds for suspecting that the person or vehicle is carrying offensive weapons or dangerous instruments (s.60(5)). Dangerous instruments are articles which have a blade or are sharply pointed. Offensive weapon bears the same meaning as under s.1(9) of PACE.

Conduct of police during searches

Section 117 of PACE confers a power on a constable to use *reasonable force if necessary* to exercise a power under PACE (see further Code A, paras. 3.1–3.11).

Duties of disclosure and information giving prior to search

Sections 2 and 3 of PACE contain disclosure and information giving provisions relating to the stop and search powers conferred by s.1 (or any other power to search a person or vehicle without first making an arrest). Paragraphs 3.8 to 3.11 of Code A provide guidance on the information giving steps that an officer should observe prior to a search. Section 2 of PACE imposes a duty on a constable whether in uniform or not to take reasonable steps before he commences the search to bring to the attention of the appropriate person the matters outlined in s.2. Code A, para. 3.8 provides that before any search an officer must take all reasonable steps to provide the information set out in that paragraph. Failure by an officer to take reasonable steps to give the person the information required by s.2 (and the Codes) will render the search unlawful and take the police officer outside of the execution of his duty.

An otherwise lawful search will turn into a trespass and deprive officers who face resistance from the person they are attempting to search of the protection afforded by the offence of assaulting a constable acting in the execution of his duty. An unlawful search is not cured (and rendered lawful) by either the fact that the search was reasonable or that the person consented to it. It does not however necessarily follow however that evidence found following an unlawful search will be found to be inadmissible in any subsequent trial.

Record keeping of the stop and search

Section 3 of PACE provides a duty to make records of searches. Code A, paras 4.1 and 4.2 provide that a record must be made at the time of the search unless there are exceptional circumstances that would make this wholly impracticable (*e.g.* situations involving public disorder or the officer's presence is urgently required elsewhere). If a record is not made at the time it must be made as soon as practicable thereafter. A copy of the record made at the time must be given immediately to the person searched. Paragraph 4.3 sets out the information which must always be included in the record of a search even if the person does not wish to provide any personal details. A person who was searched is entitled to a copy of the record if he asks for one before the expiry of 12 months from the date of the search. Paragraph 4.7 extends the duty to record from stop and search to encounters which do not involve a search. Where officers detain with a view to a search but which is not carried out because grounds for reasonable suspicion are eliminated as a result of questioning, a record must still be made as above.

Monitoring and supervising of stop and search powers

Code A requires officers to monitor the use of stop and search powers and consider Whether there is any evidence that they are being exercised on the basis of stereotyped images or inappropriate generalisations. Senior officers with area or force-wide responsibilities must also monitor the broader use of stop and search powers. Supervision and monitoring needs to be supported by compilation of statistics, and apparent disproportionate use of powers by particular officers or groups of officers or in relation to specific sections of the community should be identified and investigated.

Conclusions and recommendations

Some of the revisions of Code A appear to be a small step in the direction to increase public trust and confidence; improve officer practice and behaviour, and provide for monitoring and accountability. People should be encouraged to be aware of their rights. Basic practical tips are:

- ask for a full explanation for the stop and search;

- be courteous and polite—do not rise to provocative/offensive behaviour by PCs;
- get PC's name/number/station; and
- ensure that a written record of the stop and search is provided at the time and if not, obtain from police station.

Where individuals are concerned about the propriety of stop and search and the conduct of PCs, they should be encouraged to obtain the police written records, make a record of their recollection and consider making a complaint. Evidence obtained in breach of the code may be excluded by a trial judge under s.76 (confessions) or s.78 (exclusion of unfair evidence) or at common law.

(Adapted from The New Law Journal, 30 May 2003, p.813.)

Explain the power of stop and search under s.1 of PACE	
Explain the power of stop and search under s.60 of the CJPOA	
What safeguards exist for the suspect being stopped and searched?	

Final Report into Stop & Search

By Marian FitzGerald (December 1999)

Executive Summary

What do searches contribute to tackling crime?

The study shows that there is a strong consensus about the need for the power in principle to tackle crime. Public perceptions of the legitimate use of the power may go well beyond the strict terms of s.1 of PACE; and many people (in all ethnic groups) would like to see it exercised more widely. In practice, the power contributes to tackling crime in three main ways:

- It contributes directly to the detection and prevention of crime through arrests from searches. Searches have at times contributed to up to 12 per cent of arrests overall in the MPS. However, searches account for nearly all arrests for "going equipped" and offensive weapon (*i.e.* to commit property crimes, including burglaries, thefts of and from cars, etc.).

- Searches contribute more indirectly to the detection and prevention of crime through the intelligence they produce. At local area level, information from the search records is entered onto a central database which, as the report illustrates, is of particular value to Intelligence Unit personnel and crime analysts.

- The power can also have a more general impact on the prevention of crime. Independent analyses conducted for this report show a significant statistical relationship between the fall in searches at the beginning of 1999 and the rise in recorded crime in London. This corroborates qualitative evidence provided by the report which is based not only on the perceptions of police officers but also of young people actually or potentially involved in crime.

Why are searches such a source of tension?

Unlike many other forms of police interaction with suspects, PACE searches take place in public. So their direct impact is not limited to the person (or group) searched, it may also affect bystanders' perceptions of the police.

Survey evidence shows that being searched adds considerably to people's dissatisfaction if they are stopped by the police. Equally important, though, are whether the police are polite and whether they give an adequate explanation for their actions.

Discussions with groups of boys aged 15 and 16 in three areas of London confirmed these findings; and they were further corroborated by other material, including interviews with police officers themselves. The problem was not simply one of officers behaving aggressively—or, as one of the boys put it, "treating us like dirt"—although this was clearly a significant cause of tension. The way in which some officers responded to provocation was clearly an important issue. Ironically, others displayed skills which made all the difference to defusing aggression and calming tense situations.

General concerns

- The manner in which some officers use the power causes unnecessary bad feeling—whether or not they have the reasonable grounds for a search required by PACE. Clearly this problem extends beyond the issue of searches; but searches conducted in this way may have a profound impact in particular on young people who have had little other contact with the police and on members of the public who observe such searches.

- Where people already have criminal records—or are believed to be associating with criminals—they may be targeted for searching as a way of gaining intelligence and/or simply in order to disrupt their activities. These are not legitimate grounds for PACE searches and could be construed as harassment. Ironically, intelligence from other sources are insufficiently co-ordinated and used to brief officers to ensure that the search power is used to best effect.

- The power may be used more generally—and equally unjustifiably in terms of PACE—for purposes of social control.

A new approach

Placing further restrictions on the use of the power and attempting to refine legal definitions may have little impact on the problems identified and are likely to prove counter-productive in the current climate. A more positive approach is required which encourages officers to use the power professionally and to do so within a clearly defined framework linked specifically to public concerns and police objectives. Thus, at borough level:

- Local commanders should conduct an audit of their use of the power—with particular reference to the extent to which this relates to patterns of reported crime and calls from members of the public.

- They should share the results of the audit with other agencies in local crime partnerships.

- The partnership should jointly agree a plan for the use of the power in the context of local crime strategies.

- The plan should be widely publicised, along with clear information targeted especially at young people about the circumstances in which they are liable to be stopped and searched and what they can expect to happen if they are.

(Adapted from The Metropolitan Police website.)

Stop and search figures show strong race bias

Black people are eight times more likely to be stopped by police than white people, a significant rise on two years ago, Home Office figures showed today. Of the 714,000 stop and searches recorded in England and Wales during 2001/2002, 12 per cent were of black people, 6 per cent Asians and 1 per cent other ethnic minorities.

The figures show the over representation of blacks has increased since the aftermath of the 1999 Stephen Lawrence inquiry, when they were five times more likely to be stopped than whites. Compared with 2000/2001, the number of stops and searches conducted by the Metropolitan police rose 8 per cent for whites, 30 per cent for blacks and 40 per cent for Asians. The rest of England and Wales showed 2 per cent fewer whites were stopped and searched, while there was a 6 per cent rise for blacks and a 16 per cent rise for Asians. Asians are now three times more likely to be stopped and searched than white people, the Home Office figures showed. Black people were also four times more likely to be arrested than whites or other ethnic minority groups.

Ravi Chand, the president of the National Black Police Association, said: "It's been alarming levels for the last number of years, and very little seems to have been done to address the real concerns the black community have. The figures indicate to us at this stage that the biggest drop in stop and search is for white [people]," he told the BBC Radio 4 Today programme.

Home Office minister John Denham said a new government unit being set up to examine why the figures are disproportionate would "flush out" racism and discrimination in the criminal justice system. He also announced that officers in Merseyside, Nottingham, Sussex, West Midlands, West Yorkshire, North Wales and the Metropolitan police will begin issuing certificates to every person they stop in the street from April next year even if they do not search them. The procedure was recommended in the Lawrence inquiry to help avoid disproportionate stopping of blacks and Asians. But he warned against people jumping to the conclusion that the figures showed there was racism within the police or indicated levels of criminality in particular communities.

(Adapted from the Guardian, November 7, 2002.)

Black people 27 times more likely to be stopped

by Vikram Dodd

Afro-Caribbean people are more than 27 times more likely than white people to be stopped and searched under a special police power designed to tackle ravers and football hooligans, according to research seen by The Guardian. The use of the power has increased dramatically, and it has been branded "a new sus law", a reference to hated police powers used in the 1970s to target black people without reason.

The power allows stop and searches without an officer having reasonable grounds of suspicion. It is contained under s.60 of the Crime, Justice and Public Order Act 1994, and was introduced to tackle noisy ravers and football hooligans, who are mostly white. As tomorrow's tenth anniversary of the murder of Stephen Lawrence focuses attention on policing and race, a leading academic says the findings show increased police discrimination when officers operate with little legal constraint and do not have to justify their actions. The level of the disproportionate use of s.60 powers against ethnic minority people is even higher than for the more commonly used search powers governed by the Police and Criminal Evidence Act (PACE). For the latter, police need to have reasonable suspicion and Afro-Caribbean people are eight times more likely to be stopped under PACE.

The s.60 power is supposed to be used in only limited circumstances, and allows police to stop people if they believe there is a serious risk of violence. According to research by the criminologist Ben Bowling, the power is 18 times more likely to be used against Asians than whites, and 27.5 times more likely to be used against Afro-Caribbeans. The Home Office said it knew of no research into the use of the power.

Professor Bowling, of King's College, London, said his findings show what police will do when they have the least guidelines and scrutiny. "Wherever officers have the broadest discretion is where you find the greatest disproportionality and discrimination. Under s.60, police have the widest discretion, using their own beliefs about who is involved in crime, using their own stereotypes about who's worth stopping, that's where the problems in police culture affect the decisions that are taken."

In London, its usage more than doubled between 2000/1 to 2001/2 to 6,000 cases. West Midlands police used the power 5,520 times, almost as much as the Met, despite policing a smaller population. Professor Bowling said: "A power that was intended for narrow purposes is being used much more extensively against black and Asian communities. It's a way of getting around the tougher controls on stop and search introduced after the Macpherson report." Trevor Phillips, chairman of the Commission for Racial Equality, has already threatened legal action against the police over the disproportionate use against black and

Asian people of stops under Pace. Mr Phillips said of s.60: "The disproportionality is astonishing and these figures demand explanation. The police need to be transparent about why these powers are being used in this way. No one should pretend it's an accident, it's by design. It may have reasons, but they need to be explained."

(Adapted from the Guardian, April 21, 2003.)

Liberty and the war on terrorism

by Joshua Rozenberg, Legal Editor

When I walk out of my front door this morning, a team of heavily armed police may lawfully stop and search me or the bag I am carrying for bombs, guns, poisons or other articles that could be used for terrorism. If I were to get into my car and drive to work, officers could stop the vehicle and search me, my passengers and my car for similar terrorist-related articles. If I fail to stop, or refuse to take off my hat, coat, jacket, gloves or shoes, I could be imprisoned for six months.

I am not a terrorist, of course, and do not carry anything that could be used in connection with terrorism—except, I suppose, cash and credit cards with which I might buy chemicals. But that makes no difference. The powers to stop and search people and vehicles under s.44 of the Terrorism Act 2000 may be exercised "whether or not the constable has grounds for suspecting the presence of articles of that kind".

For the powers to be available, all that is necessary is for a senior police officer to consider it is "expedient" to authorise them "for the prevention of acts of terrorism". The officer can then allow their use, orally if necessary. The powers will lapse after 48 hours unless confirmed in the meantime by a Cabinet minister, such as the Home Secretary. If confirmed, they can last for up to 28 days. The authorisation must specify the area or place to which the powers apply.

These provisions in the Terrorism Act were clearly designed to by-pass normal safeguards in the Police and Criminal Evidence Act 1984, which says that officers cannot stop and search people or vehicles unless they have reasonable grounds for suspecting that they will find weapons, stolen articles or tools for committing offences. But when Parliament passed the Terrorism Act in 2000, it clearly envisaged that the stop-and-search powers would be used in a specific place for a limited period of time. Otherwise there would have been no need to provide a procedure for urgent oral authorisations and no 28-day limit. Parliament could simply have removed the "reasonable grounds" provision from the 1984 Act.

Shami Chakrabarti, 34, who took over as director of the human rights organisation Liberty last month, says the thinking behind the legislation is that the police would pick up intelligence that a specific place was likely to be attacked by terrorists—the House of Parliament for example. Officers would then throw a cordon round Parliament Square and search everyone caught within it. Miss Chakrabarti, a former Home Office lawyer, would not object to that approach in appropriate cases.

"There may be times when there is a real argument to be made for that kind of policing. I do actually care about national security and my life and my son's life"—she has a toddler aged 17 months. "But it is a draconian power and so you have this supposed safeguard of authorisation by a senior police officer and endorsement by the Home Secretary." In fact, authorisation has been granted across the whole of London for the past two-and-a-half years on what she describes as a "rolling" basis.

Surely the loss of some freedoms is the price we should pay in the fight against terrorism, I suggested to Miss Chakrabarti. She and I, as law-abiding citizens, have nothing to fear if stopped by the police. That is fine if everyone in an area is searched, she replies. But the police cannot check everybody in London. So they exercise discretion in picking targets— demonstrators for example. She argues that in those circumstances they should use the Police and Criminal Evidence Act, with its insistence on reasonable grounds.

The director of Liberty acknowledges that the police have exercised their powers since 2001 with discretion. But, as she says, "if we are not careful we shall find ourselves allowing sweeping authorisations to be made under anti-terror laws that would theoretically allow anybody to be stopped and searched at any time with no suspicion, and to justify that on the basis that we can trust the police. Peaceful protest and the right to be let alone are too precious to be left to a matter of trust."

(Adapted from the Daily Telegraph, October 9, 2003.)

What are the main issues surrounding the use of stop and search?

Activity ❶

You have been asked to give a short **presentation** to a local community youth group about police powers of stop and search. Using the material in the extracts above, and any other relevant information you can find, prepare and deliver this presentation. In preparing this activity, you should also read **Chapter 6** of *A Level and AS Level Law: a Study Guide*. You must also produce a **one-page handout** for the audience, giving the main points of your presentation and where they can find further information. Your handout, in addition to the text, must include at least **one image**.

(Evidence: Communications: 3.1b, C3.2, C3.3)

Activity ❷

Working in **pairs** or **small groups**, and using the information in the articles above, together with any other information you may find (e.g. in books, journals, newspapers or on the internet), prepare a discussion on the issues relating to police powers of stop and search. You should then **debate** this issue as a whole class.

(Evidence: Communications: C3.1a, C3.2)

Activity ❸

Using the information you have gathered for Activity 1 and any further information you have gained as a result of the debate, prepare an **appropriate document** (e.g. an article of approximately 1000 words for a broadsheet newspaper) that outlines the main issues relating to police powers of stop and search. This document must include at least one **image**.

(Evidence: Communications: C3.2, C3.3)

Police powers of arrest and detention

YourRights.org.uk—The *Liberty* Guide to Human Rights

The police may arrest with or without a warrant. There are many powers of arrest under a warrant issued by a justice of the peace or judge, and the rules governing each of them is set out in the statute creating the power. This section deals with police powers of arrest without a warrant.

Arrest at common law for breach of the peace

A breach of the peace is not in itself a criminal offence, but the police and any other person have a power of arrest where there are reasonable grounds for believing a breach of the peace is taking place or is imminent. The Court of Appeal has defined a breach of the peace as being "an act done or threatened to be done which either actually harms a person, or in his presence, his property, or is likely to cause such harm being done".

Summary arrest for arrestable offences

The *Police and Criminal Evidence Act 1984* uses the phrase summary arrest to mean arrest without a warrant and **s.24** lists the arrestable offences for which the police can arrest without a warrant. The following are arrestable offences:

- Offences for which the sentence is fixed by law—including murder—life imprisonment.

- Offences carrying a maximum sentence of imprisonment for five years or more—these include serious offences of violence and dishonesty, but also some relatively minor offences such as shoplifting.

- Various statutory offences, for instance under the Official Secrets legislation, theft, sexual offences, public order and aviation legislation. The list is constantly being extended.

This power of arrest may be carried out by anyone—either a police officer or any other person—a citizen's arrest—in the following circumstances:

- Anyone actually committing or whom he or she reasonably suspects to be committing an arrestable offence.

- Where an arrestable offence has been committed, anyone who is guilty or whom he or she reasonably suspects to be guilty of the offence.

A police officer may arrest in the same circumstances as any person, and also:

- Anyone who is or whom he or she reasonably suspects to be about to commit an arrestable offence.

- Where he or she reasonably suspects an arrestable offence has been committed, anyone whom he or she reasonably suspects to be guilty of the offence.

Arrest subject to conditions

Often, in a minor case, an arrest should be unnecessary. The alleged offender can be summonsed by post to attend court on a particular date and there is no need to go to a police station at all. However, **s.25** of the ***Police and Criminal Evidence Act 1984*** also gives the police a power of arrest for all offences, no matter how trivial, petty or minor, which do not carry a power of arrest under the previously discussed powers. The power of arrest can only be used where:

- A constable has reasonable grounds for suspecting that you have committed or attempted, or are committing or attempting to commit an offence—but not where it is suspected that an offence will be committed in the future.

- It appears to the constable that service of a summons is impracticable or inappropriate because any of the general arrest conditions is satisfied.

Thus, the assumption is that the police should proceed by way of summons for minor offences and the power of arrest ought to be used only if this is impracticable or inappropriate. The impracticability or inappropriateness of the summons must arise from one of the general arrest conditions:

- If your name is unknown to, and cannot be readily ascertained by, the police. You cannot be made to wait while your name is ascertained or confirmed, but might agree to do so to avoid being arrested.

- If the police have reasonable grounds for doubting that you have given your real name.

- If you have failed to furnish a satisfactory address for the service of a summons—that is one at which it appears to the constable, you will be for a sufficiently long period to be served or at which some other specified persons will accept service of a summons.

- If the police have reasonable grounds for doubting whether an address furnished is satisfactory.

- If the police have reasonable grounds for believing that an arrest is necessary to prevent you causing physical injury to yourself or to somebody else, or suffering physical injury, or causing loss of or damage to property—including your own, or committing an offence against public decency, or causing an unlawful obstruction of the highway.

- If the police have reasonable grounds for believing that arrest is necessary to protect a child or other vulnerable person—undefined—from you.

Information to be given on arrest

An arrest is unlawful unless you are told that you are under arrest and the grounds for the arrest at the time. Such an unlawful arrest will become lawful when the police tell you the reason for the arrest. Under **s.28 of the** *Police and Criminal Evidence Act 1984*, this information must be given at the time of the arrest or as soon as possible afterwards. The information need not be given if it was not reasonably practicable to do so because of your escape from arrest before it could be given. If you attend voluntarily at a police station—or any other place with a constable—without having been arrested you are entitled to leave at will unless placed under arrest.

Arrest other than at a police station

Under **s.30** of the *Police and Criminal Evidence Act 1984*, after arrest, a constable must take you to a police station as soon as is practicable—subject to certain exceptions and the power to release you en route. However, a constable may delay taking you to a police station if your presence elsewhere is necessary in order to carry out such investigations as it is reasonable to carry out immediately, such as a search of premises.

Use of force

Under **s.117** of the *Police and Criminal Evidence Act 1984* the police are allowed to use reasonable force when exercising their powers.

(Adapted from YourRights.org.uk—The Liberty Guide to Human Rights website.)

Explain police powers of arrest in relation to each of the following:

Arrest with a warrant	

Arrest for breach of the peace	
Arrest for an arrestable offence (s.24 of PACE)	
Arrest under the general arrest conditions (s.25 of PACE)	
The provisions of s.28, s.30 and s.177 of PACE	

The circumstances in which an arrested person may be kept in police detention are set out in the ***Police and Criminal Evidence Act 1984***. The detention is unlawful unless the provisions of PACE are complied with. A key figure in the scheme is the custody officer, a police officer of at least the rank of sergeant. Normally, the period of detention without charge should not exceed 24 hours, although in some cases the maximum period, with extensions, is as long as 96 hours. The custody officer is responsible for keeping a custody record in which all information required to be logged by PACE and the Codes of Practice is recorded. You or your legal representative are entitled to a copy of this very important document on leaving police detention or appearing before the court. This entitlement lasts for twelve months after release.

On arrival at or after arrest at the police station

As soon as is practicable after your arrival at the police station or answering to bail—or after arrest at the police station, the custody officer must determine whether there is sufficient evidence to charge you with the offence for which the arrest was made. He or she may detain you for as long as is necessary to make such a determination which includes waiting for others arrested with you to be interviewed. If the custody officer decides that there is sufficient evidence to charge you, then you should be charged and must be released unless one of the post-charge detention conditions applies

Detention without charge

If the custody officer decides that there is insufficient evidence to charge you, then you must be released. Under **s.37** of the *Police and Criminal Evidence Act 1984*, if s/he has reasonable grounds for believing that detention without charge is necessary to secure or preserve evidence relating to an offence for which you are under arrest, or to obtain such evidence by questioning you he or she may order further police detention. The grounds for the detention must be recorded in writing on the custody record. You must be told what these grounds are.

Review of detention

Under **s.40** of the *Police and Criminal Evidence Act 1984*, periodic reviews of detention must be carried out for all persons in police custody pending the investigation of an offence. If you have been charged, the review is carried out by the custody officer. If you have not been charged it is carried out by an officer of at least the rank of inspector who has not at any stage been directly involved with the investigation. The general rule is that the first review must be not later than **six hours** after the detention was first authorised, and subsequent reviews must take place at intervals of not more than **nine hours.**

Detention limits and police extensions

Under **s.41** of the *Police and Criminal Evidence Act 1984*, the general rule is that you may not be kept in police detention for more than **24 hours** without being charged. Under **s.42** this period can be extended by a maximum of **12** hours on the authority of an officer of the rank of superintendent or above after giving opportunity for representations to be made. The extension can only be authorised where:

- The officer has reasonable grounds for believing that the offence is a serious arrestable offence.

- The investigation is being conducted diligently and expeditiously.

- Detention without charge is necessary to secure or preserve evidence of an offence for which you are under arrest or to obtain evidence by questioning.

The authorisation cannot last beyond **36 hours** from when the detention clock began.

Detention limits and magistrates' extensions

You must be released by the end of **36 hours** from the starting point, unless an application is made to a Magistrates' Court sitting in private. The application is made on oath by a police officer and supported by written information, which must state the nature of the offence, the general nature of the evidence for the arrest, what enquiries have been made and are proposed, and the reason for believing that continued detention is necessary.

The court may only authorise further detention if:

- the offence is a serious arrestable offence;

- the investigation is being conducted diligently and expeditiously; and

- further detention is necessary to secure or preserve evidence relating to the offence or to obtain such evidence by questioning you.

The court may authorise further detention for up to 36 hours from the time that the application is granted. A further extension of up to 36 hours may be granted if the same procedure is followed. **The total maximum period of detention is 96 hours from the original starting point**—except under the *Terrorism Act 2000* where the maximum is currently seven days.

Detention after charge

After you have been charged, the custody officer must order your release unless one of the following post-charge detention conditions applies:

- Your name or address is unknown or doubted.

- Detention is necessary to prevent your committing an offence—if you were arrested for an imprisonable offence—or from causing physical injury to any other person or damaging property—if you were not arrested for an imprisonable offence.

- Detention is necessary to prevent your failing to appear in court to answer bail.

- Detention is necessary to prevent your interfering with the administration of justice or with the investigation of offences.

- Detention is necessary for your own protection.

(Adapted from YourRights.org.uk—The Liberty Guide to Human Rights website.)

Explain police powers of detention in relation to each of the following:

Detention without charge	

Extension of detention	
Detention following charge	

The rights of suspects at the police station

Introduction

The rights of suspects after arrest are contained principally in the *Police and Criminal Evidence Act 1984* and in the *Code of Practice on the Detention, Treatment and Questioning of Persons*.

Personal searches at the police station

The custody officer is under a duty to list all the property you have with you on your custody record. You may be searched, using reasonable force if necessary if you refuse to co-operate, by a police officer of the same sex. You should be told the reasons for the search. You are allowed to check the list of property and you should sign only if it is correct. Clothes and personal effects—not including cash—may be seized only if the custody officer believes you may use them to cause physical injury to yourself or to somebody else, to damage property, to interfere with evidence, to assist an escape, or if he or she has reasonable grounds for believing that they may be evidence relating to an offence. You should be given the reasons for the seizure.

Strip searches

A strip search may take place if the custody officer considers it necessary, but he or she has no power to authorise an intimate body search. The courts have recognised that strip searches may be deeply humiliating and that the removal of a bra, for instance, would require considerable justification. No person of the opposite sex except for an appropriate adult who has been specifically requested by the person being searched, may be present at such a search, nor anyone whose presence is unnecessary. Except in cases of urgency there must be two people present other than the person being searched, when the search involves exposure of intimate parts of the body. One of these may be the appropriate adult, if relevant. Reasons for a strip search and the results of the search must be recorded on the custody record.

Intimate body searches

An intimate body search consists of the physical examination of any one or more of a person's bodily orifices, including the anus, vagina, ears and nose. The police can only carry out an intimate body search in limited circumstances. They can search you if a police officer of at least the rank of superintendent has reasonable grounds for believing that:

- You may have concealed on you something that you could use to cause physical injury to yourself or to others, and that you might use it while you are in police detention or in the custody of a court.

- You have concealed Class A drugs—such as heroin and cocaine, but not cannabis or amphetamines—on yourself and that you are in possession of the drugs either with intent to supply them to somebody else or with a view to committing a customs offence.

A search for drugs—Class A drugs only—may only be carried out by a registered medical practitioner or a registered nurse. It should only be carried out at a hospital, at a registered medical practitioner's surgery or at some other place used for medical purposes. An intimate search for potentially harmful items should also be carried out by a doctor or nurse, but may be conducted by a police officer if an officer of at least the rank of superintendent believes that it is not practicable for it to be carried out by a doctor or nurse. The search may be carried out at a police station.

The right to legal advice

If you are arrested and held at a police station or other premises you have a statutory right to consult a solicitor—if you wish—in private and free of charge at any time. A duty solicitor scheme is in operation at every police station in England and Wales, so that free telephone advice or a free visit from a solicitor is available. On arrest you should be informed by the custody officer, orally and in writing, of this right, as well as the right to have someone informed of the arrest. You should also be informed of your right to consult the *Codes of Practice*, and that these are continuing rights—if you do not take advantage of them when offered you can do so at any time you are in the police station. The police must remind you of your right to see a solicitor at many points during your detention: for instance, before the beginning or recommencement of any interview or before a review.

Access to legal advice may be delayed by the police, however, if you are detained for a serious arrestable offence, a drug-trafficking offence or certain other specified offences where the police are attempting to recover property and you have not yet been charged with an offence for up to 36 hours from the relevant time or for up to 48 hours in the case of a person detained under the *Prevention of Terrorism legislation*. Delay may be authorised only by an officer of at least the rank of superintendent if he or she has reasonable grounds—which must be recorded in writing—for believing that the exercise of the right to legal advice would lead to any of the following:

- Interference with evidence of a serious arrestable offence.

- Harm to others.

- The alerting of accomplices.

- Hindering the recovery of property.

The right not to be kept incommunicado

If you are detained in a police station or other premises, you are entitled to have one friend, relative or person who is known to you or likely to take an interest in your welfare notified of your whereabouts as soon as possible, at public expense. The right is subject to the same delay as consultation with a solicitor except that it can be authorised by an officer of the rank of inspector or above.

Intimate and non-intimate samples

An intimate sample is a sample of blood, semen or any other tissue, fluid, urine, saliva, pubic hair or a swab taken from a bodily orifice other than the mouth. An intimate sample—other than urine—may only be taken by a registered medical practitioner or nurse and dental impressions by a registered dentist, and only if an officer of at least the rank of superintendent authorises it and you consent to it in writing. The authorisation may only be given if the officer has reasonable grounds for believing that the sample will confirm or disprove your involvement in a recordable offence.

A non-intimate sample is a sample of hair other than pubic hair, a sample taken from a nail or from under a nail, a swab taken from any part of a person's body other than an orifice, and a skin impression, footprint or a similar impression of any part of a person's body other than a part of the hand—except dental impressions. Non-intimate samples may be taken with your written consent or without consent if:

- You are in police detention or being held in custody on the authority of a court and an officer of at least the rank of superintendent authorises it. He or she may do this if there are reasonable grounds for believing the sample will confirm or disprove your involvement in a serious arrestable offence. Reasons for taking the sample must be provided to you and recorded.

- You have been charged with or informed you will be reported with a view to summons for a recordable offence and either have not had a non-intimate sample taken in the course of investigation of the offence or such a sample was taken but it was not suitable or was insufficient for the same means of analysis—often DNA.

- You have been convicted of a recordable offence.

Explain the rights of person detained at the police station in relation to each of the following:	
Personal searches	
The right to legal advice	
The right to inform someone of the detention	
The taking of samples	

Outline the main issues relating to detention and questioning of suspects at the police station

7 Criminal Process

? Issues to Explore

? What are the rules regarding the granting of bail?

? What are the roles of the magistrates' court, the Youth Court, and the Crown Court?

? What are the appeal routes from trials at these different courts?

? How does the system deal with miscarriages of justice?

Definition:

CRIMINAL PROCESS:	The process by which those charged with criminal offences are brought to trial, including the courts involved and opportunities for appeal.

Criminal offences fall into three categories:

- **Summary offences**—these are minor offences that are tried only in magistrates' courts.

- **Indictable offences**—these are serious offences that are only tried in the Crown Court.

- **Either-way offences**—these are intermediate offences, such as theft, that can be tried either summarily in the magistrates' court or on indictment in the Crown Court.

Bail Act 1976

4 General right to bail of accused persons and others

(1) A person to whom this section applies shall be granted bail except as provided in Schedule 1 to this Act.

SCHEDULE 1

PERSONS ENTITLED TO BAIL: SUPPLEMENTARY PROVISIONS

Exceptions to right to bail

2. The defendant need not be granted bail if the court is satisfied that there are substantial grounds for believing that the defendant, if released on bail (whether subject to conditions or not) would:

    (a) fail to surrender to custody, or
    (b) commit an offence while on bail, or
    (c) interfere with witnesses or otherwise obstruct the course of justice, whether in relation to himself or any other person.

2A. The defendant need not be granted bail if:

    (a) the offence is an indictable offence or an offence triable either way; and
    (b) it appears to the court that he was on bail in criminal proceedings on the date of the offence.

3. The defendant need not be granted bail if the court is satisfied that the defendant should be kept in custody for his own protection or, if he is a child or young person, for his own welfare.

Decisions under paragraph 2

9. In taking the decisions required by paragraph 2 [or 2A] of this Part of this Schedule, the court shall have regard to such of the following considerations as appear to it to be relevant, that is to say:

    (a) the nature and seriousness of the offence or default (and the probable method of dealing with the defendant for it),
    (b) the character, antecedents, associations and community ties of the defendant,
    (c) the defendant's record as respects the fulfilment of his obligations under previous grants of bail in criminal proceedings,
    (d) except in the case of a defendant whose case is adjourned for inquiries or a report, the strength of the evidence of his having committed the offence or having defaulted,

as well as to any others which appear to be relevant.

Bail (Amendment) Act 1993

1. Prosecution right of appeal

(1) Where a magistrates' court grants bail to a person who is charged with or convicted of:

    (a) an offence punishable by a term of imprisonment of 5 years or more, or

(b) an offence under section 12 (taking a conveyance without authority) or 12A (aggravated vehicle taking) of the Theft Act 1968,

the prosecution may appeal to a judge of the Crown Court against the granting of bail.

Criminal Justice and Public Order Act 1994

25. No bail for defendants charged with or convicted of homicide or rape after previous conviction of such offences

(1) A person who in any proceedings has been charged with or convicted of an offence to which this section applies in circumstances to which it applies shall be granted bail in those proceedings only if the court or, as the case may be, the constable considering the grant of bail is satisfied that there are exceptional circumstances which justify it.

(2) This section applies, subject to subsection (3) below, to the following offences, that is to say:

    (a) murder;
    (b) attempted murder;
    (c) manslaughter;
    (d) rape; or
    (e) attempted rape.

(3) This section applies to a person charged with or convicted of any such offence only if he has been previously convicted by or before a court in any part of the United Kingdom of any such offence or of culpable homicide and, in the case of a previous conviction of manslaughter or of culpable homicide, if he was then sentenced to imprisonment or, if he was then a child or young person, to long-term detention. . .

Section 4 of the Bail Act 1976 creates a general presumption in favour of bail—so when can bail be refused?

In deciding whether bail can be refused, what other factors can the court consider?	
When can the prosecution appeal against a grant of bail?	
In what circumstances is the general presumption in the '76 Act reversed by the CJPOA '94?	

Activity ❶

You have been asked to give a short **presentation** to a group of potential magistrates about granting bail. Using the material in the extracts above, and any other relevant information you can find, prepare and deliver this presentation. In preparing this activity, you should also read **Chapter 7** of *A Level and AS Level Law: a Study Guide*. You must also produce a **one-page handout** for the audience, giving the main points of your presentation and where they can find further information. Your handout, in addition to the text, must include at least **one image**.

(**Evidence: Communications: 3.1b, C3.2, C3.3**)

The Magistrates' Court

The magistrates' courts are a key part of the criminal justice system—virtually all criminal cases start in a magistrates' court and over 95 per cent of cases are also completed there. In addition, magistrates' courts deal with many civil cases, mostly family matters plus liquor licensing and betting and gaming work.

Cases in the magistrates' courts are usually heard by panels of three lay magistrates (Justices of the Peace), of which there are around 30,000 in England and Wales. They are unpaid, but do receive a contribution to necessary expenses. They undergo a substantial amount of initial and ongoing training, but are not lawyers. To advise them on points of law and procedure, they have the services of a court clerk. In addition, there are approximately 100 District Judges. District Judges (Magistrates Court) are experienced solicitors or barristers who are appointed by the Lord Chancellor. They sit alone in court and generally deal with the more complex cases.

The Crown Court

The Crown Court deals with more serious criminal cases, such as murder, rape and robbery, which are either committed or transferred from the magistrates' courts. It also hears appeals against decisions of magistrates' courts, and deals with cases sent for sentence from magistrates' courts.

(Adapted from the Court Service website.)

Youth Court

Adult Magistrates' Courts can only undertake trials and sentence people for offences for which the maximum penalty is six months in prison. Magistrates' Courts deal mainly with cases involving people over the age of 18. They can deal with young people, but only if they are being tried with an adult.

The Youth Court is a section of the Magistrates' Court and can be located in the same building. It deals with almost all cases involving young people under the age of 18. This section of the Magistrates' Court is served by Youth Panel Magistrates and District Judges. They have the power to give Detention & Training Orders of up to 24 months, as well as a range of sentences in the community.

Youth Courts are less formal than Magistrates' Courts, are more open and engage more with the young person appearing in court and their family. Youth Courts are essentially private places and members of the public are not allowed in. The victim(s) of the crime, however, has/have the opportunity to attend the hearings of the court if they want to, but they must make a request to the court if they wish to do so. The needs and wishes of victims will always be considered by the court and, through the Youth Offending Team (YOT), they often have the opportunity to have an input into the sentencing process.

(Adapted from the Youth Justice Board website.)

Outline the role of the Magistrates' Court in the criminal process:

Early administrative hearings	

Summary Trial	
Youth Court	
Outline the role of the Crown Court in the criminal process:	
Trial on indictment	
Appeals from Magistrates' Court	

Criminal Cases Review Commission

Introducing the Commission

The Criminal Cases Review Commission is an independent body responsible for investigating suspected miscarriages of criminal justice in England, Wales and Northern Ireland. The Commission has at least 11 Members appointed by Her Majesty the Queen, on the recommendation of the Prime Minister. They are supported by caseworkers and administrative staff. The Commission's principal role is to review the convictions of those who believe they have either been wrongly found guilty of a criminal offence, or wrongly sentenced. The Commission can seek further information relating to a case and carry out its own investigations, or arrange for others to do so. Once the investigations have been completed to the Commission's satisfaction, it decides whether or not to refer the case to the appropriate appeal court.

Background to the Commission

Until March 31, 1997, applications were made to the Home Secretary under s.17 of the Criminal Appeal Act 1968. In Northern Ireland, application was made to the Secretary of State for Northern Ireland under s.14 of the Criminal Appeal (Northern Ireland) Act 1980. The Secretaries of State could refer cases to the Court of Appeal. In practice, this power was exercised in cases where there was new evidence or where some other consideration of substance had emerged after the trial.

On March 14, 1991 the then Home Secretary announced the establishment of a Royal Commission on Criminal Justice to be chaired by Viscount Runciman of Doxford. The Royal Commission was charged with examining the effectiveness of the criminal justice system in securing the conviction of the guilty and the acquittal of the innocent. In making the announcement, the Home Secretary referred to such cases as the Birmingham Six which had raised serious issues of concern to all, and the undermining of public confidence when the arrangements for criminal justice failed.

The Royal Commission's report was presented to Parliament in July 1993. It recommended the establishment of an independent body:

- to consider suspected miscarriages of justice;

- to arrange for their investigation where appropriate; and

- to refer cases to the Court of Appeal where the investigation revealed matters that ought to be considered further by the courts.

The Criminal Appeal Act 1995 was subsequently passed, enabling the establishment of the Criminal Cases Review Commission as an executive Non-Departmental Public Body on January 1, 1997. The Commission started handling casework from March 31, 1997.

The Criminal Cases Review Commission has three further responsibilities:

- The Court of Appeal may ask the Commission to help in settling an issue which it needs to resolve before it can decide a case.

- The Home Secretary can ask the Commission for advice when he is considering advising Her Majesty The Queen to issue a Royal Pardon.

- The Commission can refer cases to the Home Secretary where it feels a Royal Pardon should be considered.

Figures to October 31, 2003

Total applications	6,297
Open	228
Actively being worked on	406
Completed	5,663 (including ineligible)—216 referrals
Heard by Court of Appeal	160 (104 quashed; 50 upheld; 6 reserved)

(Adapted from the Criminal Cases Review Commission website.)

Man wrongly convicted of murder freed after 25 years

Nick Hopkins, crime correspondent

A convicted murderer who has been protesting his innocence from jail for the past 25 years walked free yesterday when the court of appeal accepted "compelling" evidence of police corruption, bullying and non-disclosure of vital evidence. Speaking shortly after being released, Robert Brown, 45, said he had been in "an abyss of hell" since he was arrested for killing 51-year-old Annie Walsh, a woman he maintains he never met.

The court heard that Mr Brown was beaten up by officers from Greater Manchester police. They intimidated him into signing a confession, fabricated two other statements, and withheld an important piece of forensic material from his defence team. Details of widespread corruption within this particular squad were known to the Home Office and Manchester police in 1983, when one of the detectives in the case was sent to jail for perverting the course of justice. But Mr Brown's attempts to have his case referred back to the appeal court were turned down twice in the early 1990s.

Mr Brown, from Glasgow, was 19 when Walsh, a spinster, was found bludgeoned to death in her flat in Charles Barry Crescent, Hulme, Manchester, on January 31, 1977. She had been hit over the head 16 times. Her blood was spattered on the walls, furniture and ceiling. Mr Brown was arrested four months later by detectives from Platt Lane police station; within 36 hours he had signed a confession. There was little corroborating evidence; a witness, Margaret Jones, who claimed to have seen Walsh with a man shortly before she died, attended a series of identity parades, and picked out a 37-year-old man. But no charges were brought against him.

Mr Brown claimed at trial that he had been threatened, intimidated and physically abused by officers, who, he said, had written his confession and manufactured two other statements. In his summing up, the late Mr Justice Milmo told jurors that the case rested on who they believed—Mr Brown or the police. "That is the principal issue with which you will have to deal in your deliberations," he said. But neither he nor the jury knew that one of the central officers in the case, Detective Inspector Jack Butler, was "deeply corrupt", the Court of Appeal heard yesterday. "Not only had he been involved in serious corruption himself, but he had presided over a conspiracy of corrupt officers under his direct control at Platt Lane police station between 1973 and 1979," said Mr Brown's barrister, Ben Emmerson Q.C. "The evidence strongly suggests that these officers had engaged in a pattern of corruption—over a period of years, which both pre-dated and post-dated [Mr Brown's] arrest." Mr Butler, who had been promoted to detective chief inspector, was convicted in 1983 and sentenced to four years in jail, Mr Emmerson said.

The prosecution of Mr Butler and two other officers was based on a report by Superintendent Peter Topping that detailed the culture of corruption in the station. This report was known to Manchester police and the Home Office, but its contents were not disclosed to the defence until last week, 20 years after it was written.

Pressure brought to bear on Mr Brown was psychological as well as physical, the appeal court heard. During questioning by detectives, Mr Brown was shown a bloodied pair of jeans that officers claimed were his and proved he had attacked Walsh. In fact, they belonged to a woman who had just suffered a miscarriage. Mr Emmerson said prosecutors had also failed to tell the defence about a fibre that was found on the coat of the victim which matched a jumper seized from another suspect, Robert Hill. This cast "serious doubt on the reliability" of Mr Brown's supposed confession and would have been an important element of the defence case. Two professors of linguistics had studied Mr Brown's confession statement and concluded it could not have been taken down in dictation, as Mr Butler and two other officers had claimed. "If that is right, then the account of all three officers was false. This shakes the very foundation of the prosecution," said Mr Emmerson. The "stench of corruption" permeated the police inquiry.

Quashing Mr Brown's conviction, Lord Justice Rose said: "This verdict cannot be regarded as safe. We could not possibly be sure on what we have heard that the jury, had they known what we know, would have reached the same verdict. It is, to put it at its lowest, a possibility that they might have reached a quite different verdict."

(Adapted from The Guardian, November 14, 2002.)

Judges quash murder verdict after 24 years

Martin Wainwright

A man with learning difficulties, who was grilled for two days by detectives without being allowed to wash and with only scant food, was cleared yesterday of a murder for which he spent nearly 20 years in jail. The appeal court quashed the 1979 conviction of Anthony Steel, 46, after hearing evidence that he had broken down under questioning far too harsh for such a vulnerable man.

Mr Steel, a gardener, confessed to killing 20-year-old Carol Wilkinson, a Bradford bakery worker, and was convicted of murder. Lord Justice Rix, sitting with Mr Justice Henriques and Mr Justice Treacy in London, yesterday said that new evidence from consultant psychologists had decided the appeal. Doctors called by both sides agreed Mr Steel had been much more suggestible than was realised when he confessed. "They took the view that he is and was mentally handicapped and at the borderline of abnormal suggestibility and compliability," Lord Justice Rix said. "He was therefore a significantly more vulnerable interviewee than could be appreciated at the time." Had the jury in 1979 had access to this view they might have taken a more sceptical view of his confession, made on the third day of his interviews with detectives.

(Adapted from The Guardian, March 1, 2003.)

Why was the CCRC established?	
What is the role of the CCRC?	
How effective has the CCRC been?	

Activity ❷

Working in **pairs** or **small groups**, and using the information in the articles above, together with any other information you may find (e.g. in books, journals, newspapers or on the internet), prepare a discussion on the issues relating to resolving miscarriages of justice. You should then **debate** this issue as a whole class.

(Evidence: Communications: C3.1a, C3.2)

Activity ❸

Using the information you have gathered for Activity 2 and any further information you have gained as a result of the debate, prepare an **appropriate document** (e.g. an article of approximately 1000 words for a broadsheet newspaper) that outlines the main issues relating to miscarriages of justice. This document must include at least one **image**.

(Evidence: Communications: C3.2, C3.3)

8 | Sentencing

? Issues to Explore

? What are the aims of sentencing?

? What are the main options in sentencing adult offenders?

? What are the main options in sentencing young offenders?

? How effective is the criminal justice system in preventing offending and re-offending?

Definition:

SENTENCING LEGISLATION:	The various ways in which a court can deal with someone convicted of a criminal offence.

Criminal sentences fall into three main categories:

- **Custodial**—these are sentences that involve depriving the offender of their liberty—*e.g.* by sending them to prison.

- **Community**—these are sentences that involve punishing the offender in the community—*e.g.* through an unpaid work requirement.

- **Fines**—these are sentences that involve imposing a financial penalty on the offender.

The Aims of Sentencing

Criminal Justice Act 2003

142 Purposes of sentencing

(1) Any court dealing with an offender in respect of his offence must have regard to the following purposes of sentencing:

(a) the punishment of offenders,

(b) the reduction of crime (including its reduction by deterrence),

(c) the reform and rehabilitation of offenders,

(d) the protection of the public, and

(e) the making of reparation by offenders to persons affected by their offences.

Custodial Sentences

Criminal Justice Act 2003

152 General restrictions on imposing discretionary custodial sentences

(2) The court must not pass a custodial sentence unless it is of the opinion that the offence, or the combination of the offence and one or more offences associated with it, was so serious that neither a fine alone nor a community sentence can be justified for the offence.

(3) Nothing in subsection (2) prevents the court from passing a custodial sentence on the offender if:

(a) he fails to express his willingness to comply with a requirement which is proposed by the court to be included in a community order and which requires an expression of such willingness, or

(b) he fails to comply with an order under section 161(2) (pre-sentence drug testing).

153 Length of discretionary custodial sentences: general provision

(2) . . . the custodial sentence must be for the shortest term (not exceeding the permitted maximum) that in the opinion of the court is commensurate with the seriousness of the offence, or the combination of the offence and one or more offences associated with it.

R v Cunningham [1993] 2 All E.R. 15

COURT OF APPEAL, CRIMINAL DIVISION
LORD TAYLOR OF GOSFORTH C.J., POTTS AND JUDGE J.J.
NOVEMBER 23, 27, 1992

LORD TAYLOR OF GOSFORTH C.J.

. . .The purposes of a custodial sentence must primarily be to punish and to deter. Accordingly, the phrase "commensurate with the seriousness of the offence" must mean commensurate with the punishment and deterrence which the seriousness of the offence requires.

  In *A-G's Reference (No.9 of 1989)* . . . Lord Lane C.J. said: "Businesses such as small post offices coupled with sweetie-shops—that is exactly what these premises were—are particularly susceptible to attack. They are easy targets for people who wish to enrich themselves at other people's expense. That means that in so far as is possible the courts must provide such protection as they can for those who carry out the public service of operating those post offices and sweetie-shops, which fulfil a very important public function in the suburbs of our large cities. The only way in which the court can do that is to make it clear that if people do commit this sort of offence, then, if they are discovered and brought to justice, inevitably a severe sentence containing a deterrent element will be imposed upon them in order so far as possible to persuade other like-minded robbers, greedy persons, that it is not worth the candle." Although those remarks were made before the 1991 Act, we consider they still hold good. The sentence commensurate with the seriousness of an offence of this kind will be substantial to reflect the need both for punishment and for deterrence. . .

Prevalence of this kind of offence was also mentioned by the learned judge. Is that a legitimate factor in determining the length of the custodial sentence to be passed? Again, our answer is Yes. The seriousness of an offence is clearly affected by how many people it harms and to what extent. For example, a violent sexual attack on a woman in a public place gravely harms her. But, if such attacks are prevalent in a neighbourhood, each offence affects not only the immediate victim but women generally in that area, putting them in fear and limiting their freedom of movement. Accordingly, in such circumstances, the sentence commensurate with the seriousness of the offence may need to be higher there than elsewhere. Again, and for similar reasons, a bomb hoax may at one time not have been so serious as it is when a campaign of actual bombings mixed with hoaxes is in progress.

(Adapted from The All England Law Reports.)

In what general circumstances can a court impose a custodial sentence?	
When imposing a custodial sentence, how should the court determine the length of the sentence?	

Minimum, mandatory, indeterminate and extended sentences

Powers of Criminal Courts (Sentencing) Act 2000

110 Minimum of seven years for third class A drug trafficking offence

(1) This section applies where:

(a) a person is convicted of a class A drug trafficking offence committed after 30th September 1997;

(b) at the time when that offence was committed, he was 18 or over and had been convicted in any part of the United Kingdom of two other class A drug trafficking offences; and

(c) one of those other offences was committed after he had been convicted of the other.

(2) The court shall impose *an appropriate custodial sentence [a sentence of imprisonment]* for a term of at least seven years except where the court is of the opinion that there are particular circumstances which:

(a) relate to any of the offences or to the offender; and

(b) would make it unjust to do so in all the circumstances.

111 Minimum of three years for third domestic burglary

(1) This section applies where:

(a) a person is convicted of a domestic burglary committed after 30th November 1999;

(b) at the time when that burglary was committed, he was 18 or over and had been convicted in England and Wales of two other domestic burglaries; and

(c) one of those other burglaries was committed after he had been convicted of the other, and both of them were committed after 30th November 1999.

(2) The court shall impose *an appropriate custodial sentence [a sentence of imprisonment]* for a term of at least three years except where the court is of the opinion that there are particular circumstances which:

(a) relate to any of the offences or to the offender; and

(b) would make it unjust to do so in all the circumstances.

Criminal Justice Act 2003

287 Minimum sentence for certain firearms offences

After section 51 of the Firearms Act 1968 (c.27) there is inserted the following
Section: "**51A Minimum sentence for certain offences under s.5** . . .

(2) The court shall impose an appropriate custodial sentence (or order for detention) for a term of at least the required minimum term (with or without a fine) unless the court is of the

opinion that there are exceptional circumstances relating to the offence or to the offender which justify its not doing so.

(5) In this section "the required minimum term" means:

    (i) in the case of an offender who was aged 18 or over when he committed the offence, five years, and

    (ii) in the case of an offender who was under 18 at that time, three years . . .

R v Offen [2001] 2 All E.R. 154

COURT OF APPEAL, CRIMINAL DIVISION
LORD WOOLF C.J., STEEL AND RICHARDS J.J.
OCTOBER 17, NOVEMBER 9, 2000

LORD WOOLF C.J.

. . . The question of whether circumstances are appropriately regarded as exceptional must surely be influenced by the context in which the question is being asked. The policy and intention of Parliament was to protect the public against a person who had committed two serious offences. It therefore can be assumed the section was not intended to apply to someone in relation to whom it was established there would be no need for protection in the future. In other words, if the facts showed the statutory assumption was misplaced, then this, in the statutory context was not the normal situation and in consequence, for the purposes of the section, the position was exceptional.

(Adapted from The All England Law Reports.)

Criminal Justice Act 2003

225 Life sentence or imprisonment for public protection for serious offences

(1) This section applies where:

    (a) a person aged 18 or over is convicted of a serious offence committed after the commencement of this section, and

    (b) the court is of the opinion that there is a significant risk to members of the public of serious harm occasioned by the commission by him of further specified offences.

(2) If:

    (a) the offence is one in respect of which the offender would apart from this section be liable to imprisonment for life, and

    (b) the court considers that the seriousness of the offence, or of the offence and one or more offences associated with it, is such as to justify the imposition of a sentence of imprisonment for life, the court must impose a sentence of imprisonment for life.

(3) In a case not falling within subsection (2), the court must impose a sentence of imprisonment for public protection.

(4) A sentence of imprisonment for public protection is a sentence of imprisonment for an indeterminate period. . .

227 Extended sentence for certain violent or sexual offences: persons 18 or over

(1) This section applies where:

(a) a person aged 18 or over is convicted of a specified offence, other than a serious offence, committed after the commencement of this section, and
(b) the court considers that there is a significant risk to members of the public of serious harm occasioned by the commission by the offender of further specified offences.

(2) The court must impose on the offender an extended sentence of imprisonment, that is to say, a sentence of imprisonment the term of which is equal to the aggregate of:

(a) the appropriate custodial term, and
(b) a further period ("the extension period") for which the offender is to be subject to a licence and which is of such length as the court considers necessary for the purpose of protecting members of the public from serious harm occasioned by the commission by him of further specified offences.

(3) In subsection (2) "the appropriate custodial term" means a term of imprisonment (not exceeding the maximum term permitted for the offence) which:

(a) is the term that would (apart from this section) be imposed in compliance with section 153(2), or
(b) where the term that would be so imposed is a term of less than 12 months, is a term of 12 months.

(4) The extension period must not exceed:

(a) five years in the case of a specified violent offence, and
(b) eight years in the case of a specified sexual offence.

(5) The term of an extended sentence of imprisonment passed under this section in respect of an offence must not exceed the maximum term permitted for the offence.

In what circumstances must the court impose a minimum sentence?	
What circumstances must the court impose a life sentence?	
In what circumstances must the court pass an indeterminate sentence?	
What circumstances must the court impose an extended sentence?	

Custody plus, custody minus (suspended sentences), and intermittent custody

Criminal Justice Act 2003

181 Prison sentences of less than 12 months

(1) Any power of a court to impose a sentence of imprisonment for a term of less than 12 months on an offender may be exercised only in accordance with the following provisions of this section unless the court makes an intermittent custody order (as defined by section 183).

(2) The term of the sentence:

    (a) must be expressed in weeks,
    (b) must be at least 28 weeks,
    (c) must not be more than 51 weeks in respect of any one offence, and
    (d) must not exceed the maximum term permitted for the offence.

(3) The court, when passing sentence, must:

    (a) specify a period (in this Chapter referred to as "the custodial period") at the end of which the offender is to be released on a licence, and
    (b) by order require the licence to be granted subject to conditions requiring the offender's compliance during the remainder of the term (in this Chapter referred to as "the licence period") or any part of it with one or more requirements falling within section 182(1) and specified in the order.

(4) In this Part "custody plus order" means an order under subsection (3)(b).

(5) The custodial period:

    (a) must be at least 2 weeks, and
    (b) in respect of any one offence, must not be more than 13 weeks.

(6) In determining the term of the sentence and the length of the custodial period, the court must ensure that the licence period is at least 26 weeks in length.

182 Licence conditions

(1) The requirements falling within this subsection are:

    (a) an unpaid work requirement (as defined by section 199),
    (b) an activity requirement (as defined by section 201),
    (c) a programme requirement (as defined by section 202),
    (d) a prohibited activity requirement (as defined by section 203),
    (e) a curfew requirement (as defined by section 204),
    (f) an exclusion requirement (as defined by section 205),
    (g) a supervision requirement (as defined by section 213), and
    (h) in a case where the offender is aged under 25, an attendance centre requirement (as defined by section 214).

183 Intermittent custody

(1) A court may, when passing a sentence of imprisonment for a term complying with subsection (4):
    (a) specify the number of days that the offender must serve in prison under the sentence before being released on licence for the remainder of the term, and
    (b) by order:

    (i) specify periods during which the offender is to be released temporarily on licence before he has served that number of days in prison, and

    (ii) require any licence to be granted subject to conditions requiring the offender's compliance during the licence periods with one or more requirements falling within section 182(1) and specified in the order.

(2) In this Part "intermittent custody order" means an order under subsection (1)(b).

(4) The term of the sentence:

    (a) must be expressed in weeks,
    (b) must be at least 28 weeks,
    (c) must not be more than 51 weeks in respect of any one offence, and
    (d) must not exceed the maximum term permitted for the offence.

(5) The number of custodial days:

    (a) must be at least 14, and
    (b) in respect of any one offence, must not be more than 90.

(6) A court may not exercise its powers under subsection (1) unless the offender has expressed his willingness to serve the custodial part of the proposed sentence intermittently, during the parts of the sentence that are not to be licence periods.

189 Suspended sentences of imprisonment

(1) A court which passes a sentence of imprisonment for a term of at least 28 weeks but not more than 51 weeks in accordance with section 181 may:

    (a) order the offender to comply during a period specified for the purposes of this paragraph in the order (in this Chapter referred to as "the supervision period") with one or more requirements falling within section 190(1) and specified in the order, and
    (b) order that the sentence of imprisonment is not to take effect unless either:
        (i) during the supervision period the offender fails to comply with a requirement imposed under paragraph (a), or
        (ii) during a period specified in the order for the purposes of this sub-paragraph (in this Chapter referred to as "the operational period") the offender commits in the United Kingdom another offence (whether or not punishable with imprisonment), and (in either case) a court having power to do so subsequently orders under paragraph 8 of Schedule 12 that the original sentence is to take effect.

(3) The supervision period and the operational period must each be a period of not less than six months and not more than two years beginning with the date of the order.

Explain what is meant by "custody plus" sentences	
Explain what is meant by "intermittent custody"	
Explain what is meant by a "suspended sentence" ("custody minus")	

Community sentences

Criminal Justice Act 2003

147 Meaning of "community sentence", etc.

(1) In this Part "community sentence" means a sentence which consists of or includes:

    (a) a community order (as defined by section 177), or
    (b) one or more youth community orders.

(2) In this Chapter "youth community order" means:

    (a) a curfew order as defined by section 163 of the Sentencing Act,
    (b) an exclusion order under section 40A(1) of that Act,
    (c) an attendance centre order as defined by section 163 of that Act,
    (d) a supervision order under section 63(1) of that Act, or
    (e) an action plan order under section 69(1) of that Act.

148 Restrictions on imposing community sentences

(1) A court must not pass a community sentence on an offender unless it is of the opinion that the offence, or the combination of the offence and one or more offences associated with it, was serious enough to warrant such a sentence.

(2) Where a court passes a community sentence which consists of or includes a community order:

    (a) the particular requirement or requirements forming part of the community order must be such as, in the opinion of the court, is, or taken together are, the most suitable for the offender, and

    (b) the restrictions on liberty imposed by the order must be such as in the opinion of the court are commensurate with the seriousness of the offence, or the combination of the offence and one or more offences associated with it.

177 Community orders

(1) Where a person aged 16 or over is convicted of an offence, the court by or before which he is convicted may make an order (in this Part referred to as a "community order") imposing on him any one or more of the following requirements:

    (a) an unpaid work requirement (as defined by section 199),
    (b) an activity requirement (as defined by section 201),
    (c) a programme requirement (as defined by section 202),
    (d) a prohibited activity requirement (as defined by section 203),
    (e) a curfew requirement (as defined by section 204),
    (f) an exclusion requirement (as defined by section 205),
    (g) a residence requirement (as defined by section 206),
    (h) a mental health treatment requirement (as defined by section 207),
    (i) a drug rehabilitation requirement (as defined by section 209),
    (j) an alcohol treatment requirement (as defined by section 212),
    (k) a supervision requirement (as defined by section 213), and
    (l) in a case where the offender is aged under 25, an attendance centre requirement (as defined by section 214).

In what circumstances can a court impose a community sentence?

Fines

Criminal Justice Act 2003

164 Fixing of fines

(1) Before fixing the amount of any fine to be imposed on an offender who is an individual, a court must inquire into his financial circumstances.

(2) The amount of any fine fixed by a court must be such as, in the opinion of the court, reflects the seriousness of the offence.

(3) In fixing the amount of any fine to be imposed on an offender (whether an individual or other person), a court must take into account the circumstances of the case including, among other things, the financial circumstances of the offender so far as they are known, or appear, to the court.

How should a court proceed in setting the amount of any fine to be imposed on the offender?

Sentencing young offenders

Youth or Crown Court

When a young person is charged with an offence, they will appear before the Youth Court. If the case cannot be dealt with immediately, the court will make a decision as to whether the young person will be bailed or remanded into custody. If a young person pleads not guilty, a date will be set for the trial when the magistrates will hear all the evidence and decide whether or not the young person is guilty. If the decision is guilty, they will then decide on the most appropriate sentence. If the case is very serious, the Youth Court will send the case to the Crown Court for trial and/or sentence.

Youth Court

The Youth Court is a section of the Magistrates' Court and can be located in the same building. It deals with almost all cases involving young people under the age of 18. This section of the Magistrates' Court is served by Youth Panel Magistrates and District Judges. They have the power to give Detention & Training Orders of up to 24 months, as well as a range of sentences in the community.

Youth Courts are less formal than Magistrates' Courts, are more open and engage more with the young person appearing in court and their family. Youth Courts are essentially private places and members of the public are not allowed in. The victim(s) of the crime, however, has/have the opportunity to attend the hearings of the court if they want to, but they must make a request to the court if they wish to do so. The needs and wishes of victims will always be considered by the court and, through the Youth Offending Team (YOT), they often have the opportunity to have an input into the sentencing process.

Youth Offending Teams

The Youth Offending Teams (YOT) are key to the success of the Youth Justice System. There is a YOT in every local authority in England and Wales. They are made up of representatives from the police, Probation Service, social services, health, education, drugs and alcohol misuse and housing officers. Each YOT is managed by a YOT Manager who is responsible for co-ordinating the work of the youth justice services. Because the YOT incorporates representatives from a wide range of services, it can respond to the needs of young offenders in a comprehensive way. The YOT identifies the needs of each young offender by assessing them with a national assessment. It identifies the specific problems that make the young person offend as well as measuring the risk they pose to others. This enables the YOT to identify suitable programmes to address the needs of the young person with the intention of preventing further offending.

Pre-court orders

When young people first get into trouble, behave anti-socially or commit minor offences, they can be dealt with outside of the court system. If children are behaving anti-socially, the police and local authority can use a variety of pre-court orders including:

- **Acceptable Behaviour Contracts**—An Acceptable Behaviour Contract is given when a local authority and Youth Offending Team (YOT) identify a young person who is behaving anti-socially at a low level. With the young person and their parents/carers, they agree a contract under which the young person agrees to stop the patterns of behaviour that are causing nuisance to the local community and undertake activities to address their offending behaviour. they breach the terms of the contract, the local authority can use this to get an Anti-Social Behaviour Order applied to the young person.

- **Anti-Social Behaviour Orders**—An Anti-Social Behaviour Order can be applied for by the police and/or a local authority. The order can be used with anyone who is over 10 years of age who is behaving in a manner that causes distress or harassment to someone or some people who do not live in their own household. An Anti-Social Behaviour Order stops the young person from going to particular places or doing particular things. If they do not comply with the order, they can be prosecuted.

- **Local Child Curfews**—Under a Local Child Curfew, all children under 10 years of age must be in their homes by a certain time in the evening. Children found outside their homes after the curfew can be the subject of a Child Safety Order. A local authority can apply to the Home Secretary for a Local Child Curfew where children are causing alarm or distress to others living in a particular area. A Local Child Curfew can last for up to 90 days and only applies to children under 10 years of age.

- **Child Safety Orders**—This order only applies to children under 10 years of age. It can be applied to a child who has committed an offence, has breached a Child Curfew or has caused harassment, distress or alarm to others. Under a Child Safety Order, a social worker or officer from the Youth Offending Team (YOT) supervises the child. If the order is not complied with, the child can be the subject of a care order.

If they have committed a first or second minor offence, a system of Reprimands and Final Warnings can be used by the police. A Reprimand is a formal verbal warning given by a police officer to a young person who admits they are guilty of a minor first offence.

Sometimes the young person can be referred to the Youth Offending Team (YOT) to take part in a voluntary programme to help them address their offending behaviour. A Final Warning is a formal verbal warning given by a police officer to a young person who admits their guilt for a first or second offence. Unlike a Reprimand, however, the young person is also assessed to determine the causes of their offending behaviour and a programme of activities is identified to address them.

The purpose of these pre-court orders is to stop young people getting sucked into the Youth Justice System too early, whilst still offering them the help and support they need to stop offending.

(Adapted from The Youth Justice Board website.)

Where are young people accused of criminal offences tried?

What measures can be taken to prevent young people ending up in court?

Detention and Training Order

The Detention and Training Order (DTO) sentences a young person to custody. It can be given to 12- to 17-year-olds. The length of the sentence can be between four months and two years. The first half of the sentence is spent in custody whilst the second half is spent in the community under the supervision of the Youth Offending Team. The court can require the young person to be on an Intensive Supervision and Surveillance Programme (ISSP) as a condition of the community period of the sentence. A DTO is only given by the courts to young people who represent a high level of risk, have a significant offending history or are persistent offenders and where no other sentence will manage their risks effectively. The seriousness of the offence is always taken into account when a young person is sentenced to a DTO.

Supervision Order

A Supervision Order can last up to three years. A range of conditions can be attached to a Supervision Order when the sentence is used for more serious offences. These are called "specified activities" and can last for up to 90 days. Examples of "specified activities" might be participation in an Intensive Supervision and Surveillance Programme (ISSP), drug treatment (for young people aged 16+), curfews or residence requirements which might require a young person to live in local authority accommodation for the period of the sentence. A young person receiving a Supervision Order is also required to take part in activities set by the Youth Offending Team (YOT) which could include repairing the harm done by their offence either to the victim or the community and programmes to address their offending behaviour such as anger management.

Community Rehabilitation Order

This sentence is only available to courts for young people aged 16–17. It is equivalent to a Supervision Order, but for this specific age range. It is supervised by a Youth Offending Team (YOT) and can include activities such as repairing the harm caused by their offence, programmes to address offending behaviour or an Intensive Supervision & Surveillance Programme (ISSP).

Community Punishment Order

This sentence is only available to courts for young people aged 16–17. It requires a young person to complete unpaid community work for a period of 40–240 hours. Examples of the type of activities involved are carpentry, conservation, decorating, working with the elderly or vulnerable. The sentence is supervised by the Probation Service Community Service Team.

Community Rehabilitation & Punishment Order

This sentence is only available to courts for young people aged 16–17. It involves elements of both the Community Punishment Order and the Community Rehabilitation Order. It can last for 12 months to three years. The unpaid community work can last between 40–100 hours.

Action Plan Order

An Action Plan Order is an intensive, community-based programme lasting three months. The order is supervised by the Youth Offending Team (YOT). The programme developed by the YOT is specifically tailored to the risks and needs of the young person. It can include repairing the harm done to the victim of the offence or the community, education and training, attending an Attendance Centre or a variety of other programmes to address a young person's offending behaviour.

Attendance Centre Order

An Attendance Centre Order sentences a young person to attend an Attendance Centre. Attendance Centres are normally run by the police. The regime typically involves discipline, physical training and social skills. The order can last up to 36 hours depending on the age of the offender and the seriousness of the offence.

Referral Order

All young people who plead guilty to a first offence in court must receive a Referral Order, unless they are given an absolute discharge, or the offence is so serious that a custodial sentence is required. Once a Referral Order is made, the young person is required to attend a Youth Offender Panel which is made up of a Youth Offending Team (YOT) officer and two volunteers from the local community. The Panel with the young person, their parents/carers and the victim (where appropriate) agree a contract lasting between three and 12 months. The contract can include attending programmes to address offending behaviour, repairing the harm done by their offence or a variety of other actions. The conviction is spent once the contract has been completed.

Reparation Order

Reparation Orders are designed to help young offenders understand the consequences of their offending and take responsibility for their behaviour. They require the young person to repair the harm caused by their offence either directly to the victim (this can involve victim/offender mediation if both parties agree) or indirectly to the community. Examples of this might be cleaning up graffiti or undertaking community work. The order is overseen by the Youth Offending Team (YOT).

Curfew Order

This sentence requires a young person to remain for set periods of time at a specified place. The time period can be between 2–12 hours a day and the sentence can last no more than six months for those 16 years of age and above, or three months for those under 16 years of age.

Parenting Order

Parenting Orders can be given to the parents/carers of young people who offend, truant or who have received a Child Safety Order, Anti-Social Behaviour Order or Sex Offender Order. It lasts for three months, but can be extended to 12 months. It does not result in the parent/carer getting a criminal record. A parent/carer who receives a Parenting Order will be required to attend counselling or guidance sessions. They may also have conditions imposed on them such as attending their child's school, ensuring their child does not visit a particular place unsupervised or ensuring their child is at home at particular times. A failure to fulfil the conditions can be treated as a criminal offence and the parent/carer can be prosecuted.

Drug Treatment & Testing Order

The Drug Treatment & Testing Order is used for young offenders who have drug misuse issues that require treatment. It can only be used with young people who are 16 years of age or older and the young person must agree to comply with the order before it can be made. The order lasts between six months and three years. Under the order, the young person receives regular drug testing and treatment in the community. The young person receiving the order is supervised by the Probation Service.

(Adapted from The Youth Justice Board website.)

Summarise the various sentences than can be used when dealing with young offenders.

The effectiveness of the criminal justice system

What is the justice gap?

In 2000–2001, 5.17 million crimes were recorded, but only 19.8 per cent of them resulted in an offender being brought to justice. This is the justice gap, the difference between the number of offences recorded and the number of offences for which an offender receives either a caution, a conviction or has the offence taken into consideration by the court. Between these two points, cases fall out of the system at every stage (this process is sometimes described as "attrition").

How does the justice gap vary by offence type?

Nineteen point eight per cent of all offences were brought to justice in 2000–01. But the proportion of recorded offences which are brought to justice varies significantly by offence type, largely because of the differing detection rates between crimes. These variations reflect the relative ease of detection of different crimes types. The table below gives some examples of the variations in the percentage of crimes brought to justice for different categories of offence:

Offence type	Per cent of offences brought to Justice
Violence against the person	35.5
Sex offences	37.0
Burglary	8.9
Robbery	11.2
Theft & handling of stolen goods	17.7
Criminal damage	9.7

Why does this matter?

Better performance is absolutely vital, because it will help to reduce crime and demonstrate that the criminal justice system is effective:

- **The current size of the justice gap is unacceptable**—In 80 per cent of crimes recorded by the police, the offender goes unpunished. The size of the justice gap is a vital benchmark of the success of the criminal justice system. We must improve on this.

- **The more offences brought to justice, the less crime**—catching and punishing offenders is more effective in reducing crime than the severity of punishment. Evidence from Home Office research, awaiting publication, shows that increasing the frequency of an offender being caught and convicted is the most effective single way of shortening their criminal career. There is also evidence from other countries that there is a correlation between increased chances of offenders being caught and decreasing crime.

(Adapted from the "Narrowing the Justice Gap" Framework document, on the Criminal Justice System website.)

Summary

The problem

1. Prison sentences are not succeeding in turning the majority of offenders away from crime. Of those prisoners released in 1997, **58 per cent** were convicted of another crime within two years. **Thirty-six per cent** were back inside on another prison sentence. The system struggles particularly to reform younger offenders. Male prisoners between the ages of 18 and 20 were reconvicted at a rate of **72 per cent** over the same period; **47 per cent** received another prison sentence.

2. Despite falling in the 1980s, the reconviction rate rose again in the 1990s and has remained obstinately high in recent years. The factors behind this are complex, but it is possible to single out a number of changes over that period which may have contributed: these include an erosion in post-release support for short-term prisoners—those sentenced to less than 12 months; a change in benefit rules for prisoners; and the sharp rise in social exclusion, in areas such as child poverty, drug use, school exclusion, and inequality.

3. In fact, the headline reconviction figure masks a far greater problem for public safety. We know, for instance, that of those reconvicted in the two years following release, each will actually have received **three further convictions** on average. For each reconviction, it is estimated that **five** recorded offences are committed. At a conservative estimate, released prisoners are responsible for at least **one million** crimes *per* year—**18 per cent** of recorded, notifiable crimes. This takes no account of the amount of unrecorded crime that ex-prisoners, reconvicted or otherwise, will have committed.

The cost

4. Many of the costs of re-offending by ex-prisoners are not quantifiable, but can be devastating and long-term, and are frequently felt by the most vulnerable in society. Most obviously, there is the impact on victims, many of whom will be repeat victims, and on their families; also on communities, predominantly the most disadvantaged. In turn, where re-offenders are caught and imprisoned, a heavy toll is taken on their families and on their own lives.

5. The financial cost of re-offending by ex-prisoners, calculated from the overall costs of crime, is staggering and widely felt. In terms of the cost to the criminal justice system of dealing with the consequences of crime, recorded crime alone committed by ex-prisoners comes to at least **£11 billion** *per* year.

6. An ex-prisoner's path back to prison is extremely costly for the criminal justice system. A re-offending ex-prisoner is likely to be responsible for crime costing the criminal justice system an average of **£65,000**. Prolific offenders will cost even more. When re-offending

leads to a further prison sentence, the costs soar. The average cost of a prison sentence imposed at a crown court is roughly £30,500, made up of court and other legal costs. The costs of actually keeping prisoners within prison vary significantly, but average £37,500 *per year*.

7. Yet these costs are only a fraction of the overall cost of re-offending. First, recorded crime accounts for between only a quarter and a tenth of total crime, and ex-prisoners are likely to be prolific offenders. They may, therefore, be responsible for a large proportion of unrecorded crime and its costs as well. Secondly, there are high financial costs to: the police and the criminal justice system more widely; the victims of the crimes; other public agencies who also have to pick up the pieces; the national economy through loss of income; the communities in which they live; and, of course, prisoners themselves and their families.

The causes

8. There is now considerable evidence of the factors that influence re-offending. Building on criminological and social research, the Social Exclusion Unit (SEU) has identified nine key factors:

- education;
- employment;
- drug and alcohol misuse;
- mental and physical health;
- attitudes and self-control;
- institutionalisation and life-skills;
- housing;
- financial support and debt; and
- family networks.

9. The evidence shows that these factors can have a huge impact on the likelihood of a prisoner re-offending. For example, being in employment reduces the risk of re-offending by between a third and a half; having stable accommodation reduces the risk by a fifth.

10. The challenge of turning a convicted offender away from crime is often considerable. Many prisoners have poor skills and little experience of employment, few positive social networks, severe housing problems, and all of this is often severely complicated by drug, alcohol and mental health problems.

11. Many prisoners have experienced a lifetime of social exclusion. Compared with the general population, prisoners are **13** times as likely to have been in care as a child, **13** times as likely to be unemployed, **10** times as likely to have been a regular truant, **two-and-a-half times** as likely to have had a family member convicted of a criminal offence, **six** times as likely to have been a young father, and **15** times as likely to be HIV positive.

12. Many prisoners' basic skills are very poor. **Eighty per cent** have the writing skills, **65 per cent** the numeracy skills and **50 per cent** the reading skills at or below the level of an 11-year-old child. **Sixty to 70 per cent** of prisoners were using drugs before imprisonment. Over **70 per cent** suffer from at least two mental disorders. **Twenty per cent** of male and **37 per cent** of female sentenced prisoners have attempted suicide in the past. The position

is often even worse for 18–20-year-olds, whose basic skills, unemployment rate and school exclusion background are all over **a third** worse than those of older prisoners.

13. Despite high levels of need, many prisoners have effectively been excluded from access to services in the past. It is estimated that around **half** of prisoners had no GP before they came into custody; prisoners are over **twenty** times more likely than the general population to have been excluded from school; and one prison drugs project found that although **70 per cent** of those entering the prison had a drug misuse problem, **80 per cent** of these had never had any contact with drug treatment services.

14. There is a considerable risk that a prison sentence might actually make the factors associated with re-offending worse. For example, **a third** lose their house while in prison, **two-thirds** lose their job, **over a fifth** face increased financial problems and **over two-fifths** lose contact with their family. There are also real dangers of mental and physical health deteriorating further, of life and thinking skills being eroded, and of prisoners being introduced to drugs. By aggravating the factors associated with re-offending, prison sentences can prove counter-productive as a contribution to crime reduction and public safety.

What can be done?

15. There is increasing evidence of what works in tackling the problems of offenders, and in reducing re-offending. The following are some examples of the good practice that the SEU has identified during its visits and consultation:

   • offending behaviour programmes can reduce reconviction rates by up to **14 per cent**. They aim to change the way offenders think, to bring home the effect of their behaviour on themselves and others, and to teach positive techniques to avoid the situations that lead to offending;

   • the RAPT Alcohol and Drug Addiction Recovery Project has shown that of the two-thirds of prisoners who complete its programme, reconviction rates are **11 per cent** lower than would normally be expected;

   • at HMP Norwich, the Anglia Care Trust negotiated with landlords to help prisoners retain or terminate their tenancies. They advised prisoners on finance and debt management issues during and after their sentence. More than **50 per cent** of prisoners retained their tenancy with no added debt and only **5 per cent** left prison with nowhere to go;

   • at HMP Reading, the Lattice Foundation train young offenders in forklift truck driving. Participants attend a day-release course, leading to a nationally accredited qualification. Over **70 per cent** of participants have found employment on release, and only around **6 per cent** are known to have re-offended. The scheme has been further developed to include training as groundwork engineers for the gas industry; and

   • at HMP Leeds, the education department has adapted existing courses to deliver basic and key skills qualifications. Despite an annual turnover of 6,000 prisoners and an average stay of only 12 weeks, all prisoners receive targeted education and training, including testing for dyslexia.

16. These examples show that prison sentences can provide a real opportunity for constructive work. It is clear from the profile of the prison population, that a sentence can be

the first time many have been in sustained contact with public services. In many cases, the task is not to resettle prisoners in society, but *settle* them for the first time.

(Adapted from "Reducing re-offending by ex-prisoners", a report by the Social Exclusion Unit, from the Social Exclusion Unit website.)

Lord Woolf, The Lord Chief Justice of England and Wales, The 2002 Rose Lecture, "Achieving Criminal Justice" Manchester Town Hall, October 29, 2002

. . . Punishment

I turn to the question of punishment. There have been at least three recent reports which are relevant to sentencing, each of which makes extremely depressive reading. By far the most important, is the Halliday Report, *Making Punishments Work: Report of a Review of Sentencing Framework for England & Wales*—July 2001, to which I already referred. The second, is the report of the Social Exclusion Unit for the Cabinet Office and, finally, there is the report of the Public Accounts Committee. Each report describes a situation which makes it clear that our present sentencing policy is not working. It is clearly failing to deliver what should be the primary role of the criminal justice system—the protection of the public.

Let me remind you of some of the worrying facts! The cost to the criminal justice system of dealing with the consequences of recorded crime is at least £11 billion *per* year. There are, as I speak, over 72,000 prisoners within the prison system. An increase of approximately 30,000 over 10 years. The position in relation to the female prison population is particularly disturbing. The numbers have increased by over 20 per cent in the last year alone.

The average cost of a prison place is £36,651 per year. Overcrowding is excessive despite a building program (since 1995) which has cost £1.28 billion producing 12,000 extra places. Because the system is overcrowded 1,000 prisoners are once more being kept in police cells, the costs of which amount to no less than £300 per night (providing an interesting perspective on the cost of a room in a hotel in Manchester).

Almost three-fifths of all prisoners in England and Wales are reconvicted within two years of their release. For younger prisoners and those serving short prison sentences, the reconviction rates are even higher. The expense caused by reoffending by ex-prisoners is staggering. A reoffending ex-prisoner is likely to be responsible for crime costing the criminal justice system £65,000. These costs are large enough in themselves but they are likely to be a fraction of the actual overall expense caused by reoffending. This is because recorded crime accounts for between only one-quarter and one-tenth of the total crime. Seventy-five per cent of prisoners leave prison without a job, 30 per cent leave prison homeless, 50 per cent of prisoners have poor literary skills, 65 per cent have poor numeracy skills and are usually unemployable. Those re-convicted will have received a further three convictions within two years, 70 per cent of prisoners are not released to education, training or employment.

The shortcomings are particularly unfortunate because there is now clear statistical evidence that if prisoners have a home and a job to go to on their release it is very much less likely that they will reoffend. It is also extremely depressing that these shortcomings should arise at the point at which the prison service has developed considerable skill in education, training and tackling offending behaviour in order to reduce the likelihood of a prisoner reoffending after release. Unfortunately, the combination of overcrowding, the lack of resources and an inability to release a prisoner back into the community with the necessary support, means that, all too often, either the education and training is not provided or, if it is, it is wasted because of lack of continuity.

The problem of overcrowding in prisons is a cancer eating at the ability of the prison service to deliver. It is exacerbated by a large number of prisoners who should not be there. The most significant groups being those who are sentenced to less than 12 months' imprisonment. It is now accepted on all sides that prisons can do nothing for prisoners who are sentenced to less than 12 months. In many of those cases, the prisoners could have been punished in the community. If prison was what was called for, the most appropriate sentence would be one of no longer than one month, to give the offender the experience of the "clang of the prison door". . .

With goodwill on all sides, I am confident that by working together we can dramatically improve the way in which we handle the criminal process. The problems which confront us in dealing with offenders after they have pleaded guilty or have been convicted is much more intractable and requires a fundamentally different approach. The present situation to which I referred earlier is simply unacceptable.

Part of the difficulty is that sentencing is a highly political subject. It is also of immense importance to the public since, while criminals should be brought to justice, it is also essential that the sentence passed by the court reduces the likelihood of the offender reoffending. In addition, hopefully, the sentence will deter others from offending. Failing this, the prosecution of the offenders to conviction achieves little, if any, protection for the public.

I recognise that what I am about to say is capable of being labelled soft or liberal. In fact it is neither soft nor liberal, but realistic common sense. The lesson of the statistics on reconviction rates to which I have referred, is that the effectiveness of the criminal justice system has to be judged by the extent to which it can reduce the pattern of reoffending. This should be at the centre of the system. It should influence the decision as to whether to prosecute, it should influence the charges which are brought, it should influence what happens during the period that the offender is being punished and it should influence the provision which is made for the offender when released from punishment.

The fact that the situation is so unsatisfactory is surprising. We have, in relation to many areas of offending, identified constructive ways in which to tackle offending behaviour on the part of a substantial number of those who are convicted of criminal conduct. I have already referred to positive effects of education, training and providing accommodation and employment on release. In addition, the probation service can today play a much greater role in assessing the risk of reoffending. We also have a prison service that is capable, if given the opportunity, of not only warehousing prisoners but of sending them back into the community better equipped to avoid reoffending.

What has gone wrong is overcrowding. I have no doubt that it is a central problem that makes progress virtually impossible. The number of prisoners at any one time is not decisive, though at all times the prison population should be kept at a minimum. What is decisive is the capacity of the prisons. The prison estate has a finite capacity. If you insist on trying to take in through the front door more prisoners than a prison can hold without letting the necessary number out of the back door, a prison will simply explode. This is what happened during the Strangeways series of riots. It is also possibly what happened at Lincoln last week. Mr Narey, the excellent Director-General of the prison service attributes the problem to mischief-makers. However I am sceptical as to whether mischief-makers can result in the loss of a prison if they are not able to make mischief in fertile ground.

If the number of prisoners that the courts are sending to prison is in excess of the number that the prisons can both accommodate and deal with constructively, then you have only three choices: (1) you build more prisons to accommodate the number of prisoners being sent to prison, or (2) you reduce the number of prisoners being sent to prison (or you both build more prisons and reduce the number of prisoners), or (3) you continue to send more prisoners to prison than the prisons can accommodate and accept the consequences. There is I suggest no further option.

In this country, so far we have adopted the third alternative. We need to cease doing this. The cost of the present policy is growing astronomically and, although it is said that more prison accommodation is to be built, at best this will only keep up with the expected inflation in the prison population if our policies do not change. We are already imprisoning more people than any other country in Western Europe apart from Turkey. In addition, quite apart from the cost, it is difficult to find sites for new prisons. A continuation in the growth of the prison population is forecast by the Government, and, if as could well happen, the prison population rises over the next 10 years as fast as it has over the last 10 years, we could be faced with having to accommodate 100,000 prisoners, an unacceptable number.

The increased size of the prison population over the last 20 years is not due to the number of people being sentenced or an increase in the gravity of the offences. It is due to a widening of the custodial "net" both by an increase in the number of offences deemed to require imprisonment and by a lengthening of the period of sentences.

So far neither the Government or Parliament has indicated what should be the maximum size of the prison population. Instead the response of ministers of this and the previous administrations to questions referring to the size of the prison population is to respond that it is judges who send prisoners to prison not the government, suggesting that the size of the prison population is all the judges' fault.

On the judges' behalf, I am prepared to accept some blame. (You cannot say I'm not objective!). Judges on occasions impose imprisonment when they should not have done so and impose higher sentences then they should. However, there are relatively few cases where the sentences imposed are higher than the going rate (the going rate being the sentence which is appropriate for the criminal conduct of the particular offender). If it is the going rate that is the problem, why do the judges not reduce the going rate? In order to answer that question it is necessary to understand how the present going rate has become increasingly punitive over recent years. The going rate is at least in part the result of guideline judgments given by the Court of Appeal over the years. Broadly speaking the judgments seek to provide a sentencing bracket for each offence by inserting that offence at the appropriate level having regard to its seriousness in relation to the pattern of sentences as a whole.

There is a continuous upward pressure, and very rarely any downward pressure, on the level of sentences. The upward pressure comes from public opinion and the media, the government of the day and Parliament. I suspect that usually when, in response to a sensational crime, Parliament, at the behest of the Government, increases the maximum sentence for that crime, it is not appreciated that this has an effect on the going rate for all sentences for that crime and indirectly for other crimes as well. When the maximum sentence is increased, the judges, as the guideline judgments show, take that as an indication that Parliament wishes all sentences for that offence to be increased. This increase then has an indirect effect on other offences because of the need to keep sentencing for different, but similar, offences in proportion with each other. Thus, when Parliament increased the maximum sentence for cases of death by dangerous driving, sentences for all such cases were pushed up and there was a knock-on effect on sentences for dangerous driving cases without death as an aggravating factor.

In addition, Parliament has, also at the behest of the Government, increased the proportion of the sentence served in prison and the period during which an offender can be recalled to prison. It has also provided for extended sentences and mandatory terms both of which have an upward effect on the prison population.

In addition, the fact that the attorney general can and does appeal against unduly low sentences has a direct and indirect upward effect. Directly on the sentence which is the subject of the appeal, and indirectly on other sentences for the same and similar offences. The increasing number of guideline judgments and Attorney General's appeals also have a damping effect on the sentencing judges' discretion to extend leniency because of the particular circumstances of a case.

If sentences have increased in this way, should not the judges now decrease all sentences because of the conditions in our prisons? (In Germany the judges in one Lander reduced all sentences by 10 per cent.) Our judges, when sentencing in individual cases, can and should take into account the situation within the prisons, but it is questionable whether action reducing sentences across the board can be taken by anyone other than Parliament.

Parliament could take action when establishing the new Sentencing Advisory Council. The Council's task will be to create a new code of sentencing guidelines. The Council will consist of sentencers at all levels. It will be independent and the holder of my office will preside. A judge in passing sentence will be expected to take its guidance into account. The legislation establishing the Council should, in my judgement, make clear the Council's remit. It should require the Council, when setting guidelines, to devise guidelines that take into account the facilities and resources that are available for dealing with offenders both in the community and in the prisons. It should also state that the Council should not make guidelines which will result in the prisons being overcrowded. If the Council was required to produce guidelines that would result in a match between the number of prisoners and the size of the prison accommodation, this could be done.

An illustration of the changes that the Council could promote is provided by what is happening in the Youth Justice System. The Youth Justice Board has the principle statutory aim of preventing (rather than punishing) offending. This does not mean that there is no need to punish. It means that it should be recognised that punishment is only part of what is to be achieved. The punishment should be constructed to make it clear that crime does not pay, but it must also be constructive and result in the offender, at the end of his punishment, being less likely rather than more likely to re-offend. The remit of the Board should be extended to a wider range of offenders. Lord Warner in the recent annual review (2001/2002) explains what has been achieved:

> "the local engines for driving the majority of the reforms to the youth justice system have been the new multi-agency Youth Offender Teams (YOT)—bringing together police, social services, education, health and probation to deliver a wider range of programs that tackle offending behaviour at the different stages of its development".

I agree with him that YOTs are a success and entitled to considerable credit for what they are achieving. And I echo his call for the Crown Courts to consider more carefully whether use of custody is necessary.

In New York, they have been piloting with equal success, community courts such as the Red Hook Community Justice Center that are also known as problem-solving courts. At Red Hook they seek to solve the neighbourhood problems like drugs, crime, domestic violence and landlord and tenant disputes by using a single judge who has an array of sanctions and services at his disposal, including community restitution projects on-site training, drug treatment and mental health counselling. But the courts reach goes beyond what happens in the court. It reaches out into the community and engages the community in achieving Justice.

I found my visit inspiring and was particularly impressed how the outlook of the community towards its court had been transformed by its problem solving approach. The tackling of the problems of minor offenders prevents them becoming serious criminals.

On a smaller scale, Drug Treatment and Testing orders in this jurisdiction are intended to achieve what is being achieved at Red Hook. The order was introduced in October 2000 and already the reports are encouraging. The distinctive feature of the orders is the continued involvement of the sentencing judge through review hearings. The judge tracks the offender's progress. It is found that the involvement of the judges maintains the motivation of those who are the subject of the orders. They respond to both the deterrent effect and the approbation they receive when they make good progress. The involvement of the judge is not only good for the offenders, it is good for the judges themselves. Their involvement means that they obtain valuable experience as to how to use the orders most effectively. They appreciate that the programs are long-term and that progress can be slow with an ever-present danger of relapse. When an offender fails, it does not mean that the program should be abandoned. It is often more effective to return an offender to the order so that they can renew their attempt to break their addiction. Encouragingly, the number of orders terminated for failure to comply with the requirements is now running at 29 per cent . . .

We have tried a more punitive approach and that has failed. There is an opportunity now for a different approach, a holistic approach, which recognises that all parts of the justice system need to pull together.

(Adapted from The Department for Constitutional Affairs website.)

How effective is the Criminal Justice System in preventing offending and reoffending?	
What are the main reasons for this poor performance?	
Do you think the sentencing measures in the Criminal Justice Act 2003 will improve the situation?	

Activity ❶

You have been asked to give a short **presentation** to a group of potential magistrates about the aims of sentencing. Using the material in the extracts above, and any other relevant information you can find, prepare and deliver this presentation. You should ensure that you illustrate the aims by reference to different sentencing options, and distinguish between adult and young offenders. In preparing this activity, you should also read **Chapter 20** of **A Level and AS Level Law: a Study Guide**. You must also produce a **one-page handout** for the audience, giving the main points of your presentation and where they can find further information. Your handout, in addition to the text, must include at least **one image**.

(Evidence: Communications: 3.1b, C3.2, C3.3)

Activity ❷

Working in **pairs** or **small groups**, and using the information in the extracts above, together with any other information you may find (e.g. in books, journals, newspapers or on the internet), prepare a discussion on the issues relating to the effectiveness of the criminal justice system. You should then **debate** this issue as a whole class.

(Evidence: Communications: C3.1a, C3.2)

Activity ❸

Using the information you have gathered for Activity 2 and any further information you have gained as a result of the debate, prepare an **appropriate document** (e.g. an article of approximately 1000 words for a broadsheet newspaper) that outlines the main issues relating to the effectiveness of the criminal justice system. This document must include at least one **image**.

(Evidence: Communications: C3.2, C3.3)

9 | Civil Process

? Issues to Explore

? What are the roles of the various civil courts?

? The Woolf reforms and the "three-track" system.

? What are the appeal routes in civil cases?

? How effective have the Woolf reforms been to civil justice?

Definition:

CIVIL PROCESS:	The process by which civil claims, such as those for negligence or breach of contract, are brought to trial, including the courts involved and opportunities for appeal.

- Courts exercising civil jurisdiction include the Magistrates' Court, the County Court, the High Court, the Court of Appeal (Civil Division), and the House of Lords.

- Following Lord Woolf's 1996 report "Access to Justice", a streamlined "three-track" system for civil claims was introduced in April 1999, with the "overriding objective" of justice, efficiency and proportionality.

- The Woolf reforms simplified the civil process by introducing a single set of Civil Procedure Rules, by modernising terminology (*e.g.* "plaintiff" became "claimant", and "writ" became "claim form"), by encouraging early settlement (through pre-action protocols) and alternative dispute resolution (ADR), and by introducing a streamlined "three-track system" for civil litigation with improved case management.

Making a claim

If someone owes you money and you cannot settle things in any other way, you may decide to issue a claim through the county court. People also issue claims for other reasons, including: bad workmanship; damage to their property; road traffic accidents; personal injury; goods not supplied; and faulty goods.

County courts deal with all these types of claim, and can be referred to as the **Small Claims Court**, which is a special procedure used within the county court to handle smaller claims.

The system for handling smaller claims is designed to be quick, cheap and easy to use. But it will usually only apply to claims for £5,000 or less (or £1,000 or less if the claim is for personal injury or housing disrepair), against a person, firm or company in England and Wales.

Where do I start my claim?

You can "issue" (start) a claim in any County Court in England and Wales. Although the procedures and forms are the same, you can only issue a claim in the High Court if your claim is for more than £15,000. Most "litigants" (people involved in court actions) acting for themselves will choose to issue in a county court. You can also visit *www.moneyclaim.gov.uk* for a simple, convenient and secure way of making a claim online.

What happens next?

Whether your claim has been issued online or through the county court a copy of the claim form and a "response pack" will be posted to the defendant. The response pack contains the forms which the defendant can use to reply to your claim. These are: an admission form; a defence form; and an acknowledgment of service.

What can the defendant do when the claim form is received?

The defendant can: do nothing, that is, not reply to your claim at all; admit that the whole or part of your claim, is owed; dispute ("defend") the whole or part of your claim.

(Adapted from the Court Service website.)

The small claims track

The small claims track provides a simple and informal way of resolving disputes. You should be able to do this without a solicitor. This guidance tells you about the sort of cases that are likely to be allocated to it and about how cases in the small claims track will be handled.

If a claim is disputed ("defended") you will be sent a copy of the defendant's defence and an allocation questionnaire. The information you provide in the questionnaire will help the judge decide which is the most appropriate track for your case. If you feel that your case is one that should be dealt with as a small claim in the small claims track, you should indicate this in the questionnaire. However, you must understand that, even though your view and that of the defendant will be taken into account, it is for the judge to decide.

As well as your view and that of the defendant, the judge will take into account:

- **The amount in dispute**—the amount in dispute should not be more than £5,000.

- **The type of claim**—these will usually be consumer claims (*e.g.* goods sold, faulty goods or workmanship), accident claims, disputes about ownership of goods, and disputes between landlords and tenants about repairs, deposits, rent arrears, and so on, **but not possession.**

- **The amount and type of preparation needed to be able to deal with the case justly**—the judge will have in mind that this procedure is intended to be simple enough for people to conduct their own cases without a solicitor's help, if they wish. The claim should require only minimal preparation for the final hearing, for example, cases in the small claims track will not normally involve a lot of witnesses or difficult points of law.

If your claim is for less than £5,000, but includes a claim for personal injury, or for housing disrepair to residential premises and damages arising from the disrepair, your case will not be allocated to the small claims track unless the amounts claimed in respect of personal injury, disrepair and damages are each no more than £1,000.

Can I ask for my claim to be dealt with in the small claims track if the amount in dispute is over £5,000?

Yes, but the defendant must agree with your suggestion and the judge must be satisfied that the claim is straightforward enough for the small claims procedure.

What will happen at the hearing?

The judge can adopt any method of conducting the hearing which is fair. Generally, however:

- the hearing will be informal;

- the strict rules of evidence will not apply;

- the judge need not take evidence on "oath" (make you swear or affirm) that you are telling the truth;

- the judge can limit the time you and the defendant have to cross examine (put questions to) each other, or your witnesses; and

- can also limit cross examination to a particular subject or issue.

At the end of the hearing the judge will tell you the decision reached (the judgment) and give brief reasons for it.

(Adapted from the Court Service website.).

The fast track and the multi track

What does the judge take into account when deciding whether a claim should be allocated to the fast track?

As well as your views, and those of the defendant, the judge will take into account:

- the amount in dispute—this would normally be more than £5,000 but not more than £15,000 for allocation to the fast track; and

- timetable and evidence needed—the judge will bear in mind that cases allocated to the fast track will generally require only limited "disclosure", a period of no more than around 30 weeks to prepare for the trial, written expert evidence only, if it is needed at all, and a trial lasting no more than one day (five hours).

If the judge feels that your claim could not be dealt with justly in the fast track, *e.g.* because of the amount in dispute is more than £15,000, it requires more disclosure than the fast track allows and requires oral expert evidence at trial, your claim may be allocated to the multi-track. The maximum time allowed for a fast track trial will be one day (five hours).

The standard directions and a typical timetable for a fast track case might be for:

- disclosure (followed by inspection)—four weeks after allocation;

- exchange of witness statements—10 weeks;

- exchange of expert reports (where experts have been allowed)—14 weeks;

- court to send out listing questionnaires—20 weeks;

- return listing questionnaires—22 weeks; and

- trial—around 30 weeks.

You should note that there is no standard procedure for multi-track cases. Each claim will be case managed according to its individual need. The judge may use standard directions, case management conferences or a pre-trial review, or any combination of these.

What is a case management conference?

A case management conference is an informal meeting of all the parties and the judge to review the progress of a case. If the judge decides to hold a case management conference, you will be told when and where to attend. Matters which may be considered at a case management conference include:

- reviewing the steps which you and the defendant have taken to prepare the case;

- making sure that you and the defendant have followed, or are following, any directions which the judge has given;

- giving any other directions to ensure you and the defendant understand each other's case;

- noting any agreement between you and the defendant on any part of the case;

- setting a timetable for any other steps which the judge considers necessary; and

- monitoring costs.

What is a pre-trial review?

The purpose of a pre-trial review is to decide:

- a timetable for the trial itself;

- who will give evidence at the trial and in what order;

- the content of the "trial bundle" (all the papers required for the trial) and the date by which it has to be "lodged" (delivered) at the court; and

- the "trial estimate" (time to be allowed for the trial).

(Adapted from the Court Service website.)

Explain the various elements involved in making a civil claim.

Explain how the small claims track works.

Explain how the fast track and multi track work.

Activity ❶

You have been asked to give a short **presentation** to a local community group about making a civil claim. Using the material in the extracts above, and any other relevant information you can find, prepare and deliver this presentation. In preparing this activity, you should also read **Chapter 8 of A Level and AS Level Law: a Study Guide**. You must also produce a **one-page handout** for the audience, giving the main points of your presentation and where they can find further information. Your handout, in addition to the text, must include at least **one image**.

(Evidence: Communications: 3.1b, C3.2, C3.3)

Appeals in civil cases

Tanfern Ltd v Cameron-MacDonald [2000] 2 All E.R. 801

COURT OF APPEAL, CIVIL DIVISION
LORD WOOLF M.R., PETER GIBSON AND BROOKE L.JJ,
MAY 12, 2000

Practice—appeal—new provisions governing civil appeals in private law matters—explanation and guidance.

BROOKE L.J.:

Appeal to next level in judicial hierarchy: the general rule

15. As a general rule, appeal lies to the next level of judge in the court hierarchy. Thus in the county court appeal lies from a district judge to a circuit judge, and from a circuit judge to a High Court judge; and in the High Court appeals lie from . . . a High Court judge to the Court of Appeal . . .

Permission to appeal: the general rule

20. As a general rule permission is required for an appeal . . . Permission may be granted either by the lower court at the hearing at which the decision to be appealed was made, or by the appeal court . . .
21. Permission to appeal will only be given where the court considers that an appeal would have a real prospect of success or that there is some other compelling reason why the appeal should be heard . . . Lord Woolf MR has explained that the use of the word "real" means that the prospect of success must be realistic rather than fanciful . . .

The appellate approach: the general rule

30. As a general rule, every appeal will be limited to a review of the decision of the lower court . . . The appeal court will only allow an appeal where the decision of the lower court was wrong, or where it was unjust because of a serious procedural or other irregularity in the proceedings in the lower court . . .

Second appeals

41. Parliament . . . has now made it clear that it is only in an exceptional case that a second appeal may be sanctioned. Section 55(1) of the 1999 Act provides that: "Where an appeal is made to a county court or the High Court in relation to any matter, and on hearing the appeal the court makes a decision in relation to that matter, no appeal may be made to the Court of Appeal from that decision unless the Court of Appeal considers that—(a) the appeal would raise an *important* point of principle or practice, or (b) there is some other *compelling* reason for the Court of Appeal to hear it." (My emphasis.)

42. This reform introduces a major change to our appeal procedures. It will no longer be possible to pursue a second appeal to the Court of Appeal merely because the appeal is "properly arguable'" or 'because it has a real prospect of success'.

(Adapted from The All England Law Reports.)

Briefly outline the rules relating to appeals in civil cases

The Woolf reforms to civil justice

ACCESS TO JUSTICE Final Report By The Right Honourable the Lord Woolf, Master of the Rolls (JULY 1996)

Overview

The Principles

1. In my interim report I identified a number of principles which the civil justice system should meet in order to ensure access to justice. The system should:

(a) be *just* in the results it delivers;

(b) be *fair* in the way it treats litigants;

(c) offer appropriate procedures at a reasonable *cost*;

(d) deal with cases with reasonable *speed*;

(e) be *understandable* to those who use it;

(f) be *responsive* to the needs of those who use it;

(g) provide as much *certainty* as the nature of particular cases allows; and

(h) be *effective*: adequately resourced and organised.

The problems

2. The defects I identified in our present system were that it is too expensive in that the costs often exceed the value of the claim; too slow in bringing cases to a conclusion and too unequal: there is a lack of equality between the powerful, wealthy litigant and the under resourced litigant. It is too uncertain: the difficulty of forecasting what litigation will cost and how long it will last induces the fear of the unknown; and it is incomprehensible to many litigants. Above all it is too fragmented in the way it is organised since there is no one with clear overall responsibility for the administration of civil justice; and too adversarial as cases are run by the parties, not by the courts and the rules of court, all too often, are ignored by the parties and not enforced by the court.

The basic reforms

3. The interim report set out a blueprint for reform based on a system where the courts with the assistance of litigants would be responsible for the management of cases. I recommended that the courts should have the final responsibility for determining what procedures were suitable for each case; setting realistic timetables; and ensuring that the procedures and timetables were complied with. Defended cases would be allocated to one of three tracks:

(a) an expanded small claims jurisdiction;

(b) a new fast track for straightforward cases, with strictly limited procedures, fixed timetables and fixed costs; and

(c) a new multi-track for other cases, providing individual hands on management by judicial teams for the heaviest cases, and standard or tailor made directions where these are appropriate.

The new landscape

9. The new landscape will have the following features.

- Litigation will be avoided wherever possible through, for example, ADR and pre-action protocols.

- Litigation will be less adversarial and more co-operative.

- Litigation will be less complex.

- The timescale of litigation will be shorter and more certain.

- The cost of litigation will be more affordable, more predictable, and more proportionate to the value and complexity of individual cases.

- Parties of limited financial means will be able to conduct litigation on a more equal footing.

- Judges will be deployed effectively so that they can manage litigation in accordance with the new rules and protocols.

(Adapted from the Department for Constitutional Affairs website.)

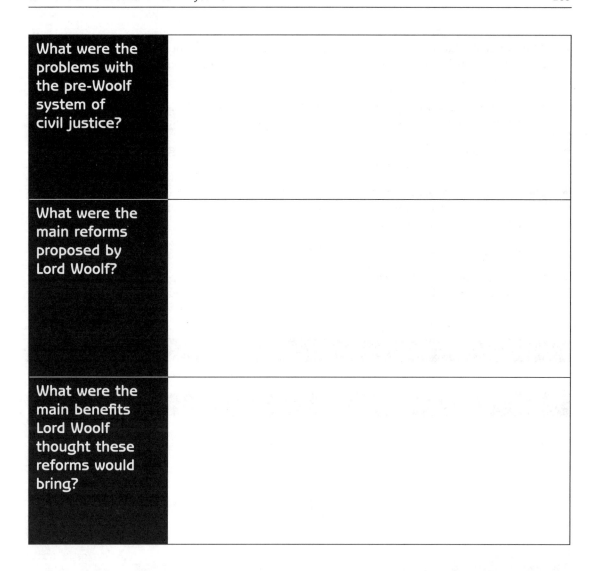

What were the problems with the pre-Woolf system of civil justice?	
What were the main reforms proposed by Lord Woolf?	
What were the main benefits Lord Woolf thought these reforms would bring?	

Further Findings—A continuing evaluation of the Civil Justice Reforms (August 2002)

Key Findings:

- Overall there has been a drop in the number of claims issued, in particular in the types of claim most affected by the new Civil Procedure Rules introduced in April 1999.

- Evidence suggests that pre-action protocols are working well to promote settlement and a culture of openness and co-operation.

- There is evidence to show that settlements at the door of the court are now fewer and that settlements before the hearing day have increased.

- After a substantial rise in the first year following the introduction of the Civil Procedure Rules, there has been a levelling off in the number of cases in which Alternative Dispute Resolution is used.

- The use of single joint experts appears to have worked well. It is likely that their use has contributed to a less adversarial culture and helped achieve earlier settlements.

- Case Management Conferences are a key factor in making litigation less complex, and appear to have been a success.

- The time between issue and hearing for those cases that go to trial has fallen. The time between issue and hearing for small claims has risen since the introduction of the Civil Procedure Rules but may now be falling.

- The number of appeals in the course of proceedings appears to have fallen sharply.

- It is still too early to provide a definitive view on costs. The picture remains relatively unclear with statistics difficult to obtain and conflicting anecdotal evidence. Where there is evidence of increased costs, the causes are difficult to isolate.

(Adapted from the Department for Constitutional Affairs website.)

How effective have the Woolf reforms been?

Activity ❷

Working in **pairs** or **small groups**, and using the information in the articles above, together with any other information you may find (e.g. in books, journals, newspapers or on the internet), prepare a discussion on the issues relating to the reform of civil justice. You should then **debate** this issue as a whole class.

(Evidence: Communications: C3.1a, C3.2)

Activity ❸

Using the information you have gathered for Activity 2 and any further information you have gained as a result of the debate, prepare an **appropriate document** (e.g. an article of approximately 1000 words for a broadsheet newspaper) that outlines the main issues relating to the reform of civil justice. This document must include at least one **image**.

(Evidence: Communications: C3.2, C3.3)

10 Alternative Dispute Resolution

? Issues to Explore

? What is the role of negotiation in resolving legal disputes?

? What is the role of mediation and conciliation in resolving legal disputes?

? What is the role of arbitration in resolving legal disputes?

? What is the role of tribunals in resolving legal disputes?

Definition:

ALTERNATIVE DISPUTE RESOLUTION:	The various processes by which civil disputes can be resolved without going through the traditional court system.

- Many disputes are resolved informally (*e.g.* through negotiation, concession and compromise). However, where an informal approach is unsuccessful or inappropriate, formal mechanisms must be available to ensure the dispute is resolved fairly. The traditional formal mechanism is the court system. However, for a variety of reasons, the courts themselves are not always the most suitable or appropriate method. Therefore, a range of alternative mechanisms has been developed to supplement and complement the work of the courts.

- The main alternative mechanisms are tribunals, arbitration, mediation and conciliation.

Alternatives to court

Dealing with problems without going to court

Going to court to solve a problem can be expensive, stressful and time-consuming. But there are other ways of dealing with many types of complaint.

What alternatives are there to court?

Until recently, if you had a legal problem, you would normally have to go to court or a tribunal in what is often called "litigation". This is still a common way of sorting out such problems. But going to court can be expensive and off-putting. Now there are more alternative ways of sorting out complaints and legal problems. Together they are often called "alternative dispute resolution" (ADR) and include things like arbitration, mediation and ombudsmen schemes. With most types of problem, courts encourage people to try these sorts of schemes first before they resort to the courts.

Negotiation

This involves dealing directly with the person or organisation you have a problem with. You can do this yourself, or you can get a representative (such as an adviser or solicitor) to do it for you. Negotiation is usually a good first step. It starts with you approaching the other side with details of your complaint and suggestions for how it can be sorted out. The other side does not need to agree to take part before you or your representative approach them.

The process is not binding, although both sides can agree to make a negotiated agreement into a legally-binding contract or order. This would mean that you could then take the other side to court if they didn't do what they had agreed to.

Most disagreements can be solved through negotiation. A common example is settlement discussions between solicitors. More than nine out of ten legal claims are settled without needing a trial. Negotiation is different from conciliation and mediation in that the person negotiating for you: acts for you, and represents your interests; is not independent; and may also advise you about the best course of action.

Mediation and conciliation

These involve an independent mediator (someone who doesn't take sides and who will not gain or lose anything by the outcome). They will help you and the other person or company find a solution to the problem. You and your opponent, not the mediator, decide what will happen and the terms of any agreement you make. The process is voluntary, however, so you cannot force the person or organisation you have a problem with to take part.

Mediation and conciliation themselves are non-binding, but they can be made binding if there is a signed mediated agreement. This means that the courts can make either side do what they agreed to in the agreement. However, people tend to keep to mediated agreements because they have come up with the terms of their agreement themselves. But what is said in a mediation session is confidential, so it cannot be used in court later.

When can I use mediation or conciliation?

- relationship and family problems;

- problems with neighbours; and

- problems at work.

Arbitration

This is sometimes described as a "private version" of going to court. It involves an independent arbitrator who is impartial (someone who doesn't take sides, and who won't gain or lose anything by the outcome). They will hear both sides of the disagreement and make a decision to solve the problem.

You and the other person or company must both agree to go to arbitration. The process is confidential and so is any amount of compensation that the arbitrator awards. Sometimes the arbitrator makes their decision based on papers that each person gives them to support their case. At other times they hold a hearing where both sides can present their cases. However, this is usually less formal than a court hearing.

Arbitration is binding, so you cannot take your case to court after the arbitrator has made a decision unless the arbitrator has made obvious legal mistake or behaved improperly.

When can I use arbitration?

Arbitration can be used for a range of problems. One area where it is often used is to deal with problems with goods and services.

Problems with goods and services

Trade associations for different companies often have arbitration schemes. Some of them run their own schemes, but others are run by an independent organisation called the Chartered Institute of Arbitrators (CIArb). One example is the Association of British Travel Agents (ABTA), which can arbitrate on, for example, a disagreement about holidays. If you have a complaint with a business, and they are a member of a trade association, ask the trade association whether they have an arbitration scheme to deal with your problem. You can also contact the Chartered Institute of Arbitrators to see which organisations they run arbitration schemes for.

(Adapted from the Legal Services Commission website.)

What are the problems people may face trying to settle a dispute by going to court?

How can negotiation be used to settle disputes?

How can mediation and conciliation be used to settle disputes?

How can arbitration be used to settle disputes?

Activity ❶

You have been asked to give a short **presentation** to a local community group about resolving disputes through mediation. Using the material in the extracts above, and any other relevant information you can find, prepare and deliver this presentation. In preparing this activity, you should also read **Chapter 9** of *A Level and AS Level Law: a Study Guide*. You must also produce a **one-page handout** for the audience, giving the main points of your presentation and where they can find further information. Your handout, in addition to the text, must include at least **one image**.

(Evidence: Communications: 3.1b, C3.2, C3.3)

Tribunals for Users—One System, One Service: Report of the Review of Tribunals by Sir Andrew Leggatt (March 2001)

An overview

The review

In the 44 years since tribunals were last reviewed, their numbers have increased considerably and their work has become more complex. Together they constitute a substantial part of the system of justice in England and Wales. But too often their methods are old-fashioned and they are daunting to users. The object of this review is to recommend a system that is independent, coherent, professional, cost-effective and user-friendly. Together tribunals must form a system and provide a service fit for the users for whom they were intended.

Tribunals now

There are 70 different administrative tribunals in England and Wales, leaving aside regulatory bodies. Between them they deal with nearly one million cases a year, and they employ about 3,500 people. But of these 70 tribunals only 20 each hear more than 500 cases a year and many are defunct. Their quality varies from excellent to inadequate.

Independence

The Franks Committee said that tribunals should be independent, accessible, prompt, expert, informal, and cheap. The most important of these qualities is independence.

A tribunals service

There is only one way to achieve independence and coherence: to have all the tribunals supported by a Tribunals Service, that is, a common administrative service. It would raise their status, while preserving their distinctness from the courts.

Helping users

It should never be forgotten that tribunals exist for users, and not the other way round. No matter how good tribunals may be, they do not fulfil their function unless they are accessible by the people who want to use them, and unless the users receive the help they need to prepare and present their cases. Working where possible with user groups, tribunals should do all they can to render themselves understandable, unthreatening, and useful to users, who should be able to obtain all the information they need about venues, timetables, and sources of professional advice.

Legal representation

Tribunals are intended to provide a simple, accessible system of justice where users can represent themselves. So it is discouraging to note the growing perception that they cannot. Every effort should be made to reduce the number of cases in which legal representation is needed. Logically that can only be done by seeking to ensure: (a) that decision-makers give comprehensible decisions, (b) that the Tribunals Service provides users with all requisite information, (c) that voluntary and other advice groups are funded so that they can offer legal advice, and (d) that the tribunal chairmen are trained to afford such assistance as they legitimately can by ensuring that the proceedings are intelligible and by enabling users to present their cases. But however good the support, there will always be a residual category of complex cases in which legal representation is imperative. Voluntary and community bodies should be funded so that they can provide it. Only as a last resort should it be provided by legal aid.

Divisions

Within the System the tribunals should be grouped by subject-matter into Divisions in a structure that is at once apparent to a user, and into which any new tribunal may be expected to fit. For the first-tier tribunals the Divisions are: education, financial, health and social services, immigration, land and valuation, social security and pensions, transport, regulatory and employment. To entertain appeals from the tribunals in each Division there should be a corresponding appellate tribunal; and the appellate tribunals should be grouped together in an appellate Division.

The council on tribunals

The Council should act as the hub of the wheel that is the Tribunals System. Its functions should include taking evidence from user groups, from the Tribunals Service, from the departments, and from the Judicial Studies Board about how well the system is working.

A new culture

In a Tribunals System properly so-called there should be a new culture, starting with improved recognition of just how daunting the tribunal experience usually is for first-time users, as most are. Administrators should strive to improve the speedy and efficient throughput of cases from dissatisfaction with an initial adjudication by department or agency to the conclusion of the ultimate appeal. That should be achieved by skilful listing, by enlightened case management, by keeping users informed in all their dealings with the tribunal, by ensuring that standards are met, and by learning lessons by taking heed of complaints. Speed should not be an end in itself. It should follow from obedience to the watchwords which should inform every tribunal: informality, simplicity, efficiency, and proportionality.

(Adapted from the Tribunals Review website.)

What were the problems with the tribunal system identified by Leggatt?

What were the main proposals put forward in the Leggatt Review?

Government announces modernised tribunals service in the greatest shake-up for 40 years

A new, unified Tribunals Service was announced today by Lord Irvine, the Lord Chancellor, as part of the Government's programme to modernise the justice system and improve the delivery of legal services to the customer. The Government's proposals will be the biggest change to the tribunal system in over 40 years. They are part of a larger Government strategy of modernisation which has included reforms in the civil and criminal justice systems.

The Government's announcement today will form the foundation for policy proposals to be outlined in a forthcoming White Paper which will: increase accessibility to tribunals; raise customer service standards; and improve administration.

Lord Irvine said, "I want to ensure that the three great pillars of the justice system are reformed and the reforms are brought into effect successfully and efficiently. We have substantially reformed the civil justice pillar and are embarking on major reform of the criminal pillar; the third is the administrative justice pillar, tribunals justice . . . A unified tribunal service will have at its core the top 10 non-devolved tribunals which currently exist throughout departments in Whitehall. By combining the administration we will deliver a more efficient and effective service to the users of tribunals. . . The new Service will be established as a distinct part of the justice system, accountable to the Lord Chancellor. The Service will bring together the 10 largest tribunals from across central Government, with smaller tribunals joining as appropriate."

Lord Newton of Braintree OBE DL, Chairman of the Council on Tribunals, said, "The Council sees this as a major step forward, underpinning tribunals' independence and paving the way for further improvements in standards."

The Government will continue to consult and develop proposals around the establishment of a unified tribunal service, and will publish its plans in a White Paper, later in the year. These proposals come following Sir Andrew Leggatt's review of tribunals. Sir Andrew's report *Tribunals for Users—One System, One Service* was published in 2001, the first review of the tribunal system since Sir Oliver Franks' review in 1957.

(Adapted from the Department for Constitutional Affairs website.)

Activity ❷

Working in **pairs** or **small groups**, and using the information in the articles above, together with any other information you may find (e.g. in books, journals, newspapers or on the internet), prepare a discussion on the issues relating to modernising the tribunal system. You should then **debate** this issue as a whole class.

(Evidence: Communications: C3.1a, C3.2)

Activity ❸

Using the information you have gathered for Activity 2 and any further information you have gained as a result of the debate, prepare an **appropriate document** (e.g. an article of approximately 1000 words for a broadsheet newspaper) that outlines the main issues relating to modernising the tribunal system. This document must include at least one **image**.

(Evidence: Communications: C3.2, C3.3)

SECTION THREE: LEGAL PERSONNEL

11 The Legal Profession

? Issues to Explore

? The role, training and work of barristers.

? The role, training and work of solicitors.

? The role, training and work of paralegals.

? The role of the Crown Prosecution Service.

? The social, racial and gender composition of the profession.

? The efficiency of a divided profession.

? The accountability of the profession for the quality of the services it provides.

Definition:

LEGAL PROFESSION:	The various professional groups that exist to provide general or specialist legal advice, representation and other services to the community as a whole.

- The legal profession in England and Wales is divided into two main branches—**barristers** and **solicitors**. In general terms, the **barrister** may be thought of as the **legal consultant** and the **solicitor** as the **legal general practitioner**. Legal work is also performed by a variety of **"paralegals"** such as **legal executives** and **licensed conveyancers**.

The two branches of the legal profession: England and Wales

The legal profession in England and Wales is divided into two branches. *Barristers* are specialist legal advisers and courtroom advocates. At the end of December 2002, there were 10,742 barristers, 1,145 of whom—around 10 per cent—were Queen's Counsel. *Solicitors* provide a wide range of legal services, from general legal advice, through preparing cases for court, to appearing as advocates. All solicitors can appear as advocates in the lower courts, and since 1993 have been able to seek to appear in the higher courts as well. In August 2002, there were 89,045 solicitors, 1,787 of whom had rights to appear in the higher courts and seven—less than 0.5 per cent—were Queen's Counsel.

(Adapted from the Department for Constitutional Affairs website.)

Barristers

What barristers do

Barristers are specialist legal advisers and court room advocates. They are independent and objective and trained to advise clients on the strengths as well as the weaknesses of their case. They have specialist knowledge and experience in and out of court which can make a substantial difference to the outcome of a case.

In several cases early advice could save you the cost and worry of an unnecessary trial. A high proportion of civil cases are settled out of court and instructing a barrister greatly strengthens the client's hand at negotiation. Even at a trial whether in a civil or criminal court, a well argued case will impress a judge. Good cross-examination will impress the jury. A barrister's training in advocacy could make a big difference to the outcome of a case.

How do I get in touch with a barrister?

Normally, barristers can only be approached through a solicitor and you should discuss with your solicitor whether it is important to have a barrister's advice. Solicitors have good working relationships with barristers and are likely to know or be able to find out the most suitable barrister to deal with your case. Assuming that that barrister is available and that there are no conflicts of interest, he or she is under a duty to take your case.

Some professions can instruct barristers directly in matters within their own expertise. For example, an accountant or a tax specialist could approach a barrister for advice directly on a taxation problem or an architect could approach a barrister directly in relation to a planning matter. Barristers could also be instructed on this basis to appear at inquiries or tribunals, but not in the County Court, the High Court or above.

Meeting your barrister

In many cases, barristers are able to give advice on a case simply by looking at the papers. In more complex matters, however, and certainly in ones which will be going to court, it will usually be necessary to have a conference or consultation with the barrister. This can take place either in the barrister's chambers or in a solicitor's office.

Where do barristers practice?

Barristers are individual practitioners who work in groups of offices known as chambers which are situated in cities and towns throughout England and Wales.

(Adapted from The Bar Council website.)

> **Summarise the main characteristics of the barrister's job.**

Initial training

In order to qualify as a barrister a person must:

(a) be a member of an Inn;

(b) satisfy the academic stage of training either by completing a qualifying law degree with at least a lower second class honours, or by completing a non-law degree and passing the CPE. The Academic Stage is the first stage of training for the Bar. It usually consists of a "Qualifying Law Degree" or a degree in another subject supplemented by the Common Professional Examination (CPE) or an approved Post Graduate Diploma in Law (PgDL) course. The Academic Stage is designed to ensure that the student has a basic body of legal knowledge, which can be assumed and built upon at the Vocational Stage;

(c) pass the Bar Vocational Course (BVC) at one of the eight validated institutions. The purpose of the vocational stage is to ensure that students intending to become a barrister acquire the skills, knowledge of procedure and evidence, attitudes and competence to prepare them for the more specialised training in the twelve months of pupillage which follow; and

(d) serve one year in pupillage either in chambers or employment. Pupillage is the final stage of the route to qualification at the Bar, in which the pupil gains practical training under the supervision of an experienced barrister. Pupillage is divided into two parts: the non-practising six months during which pupils shadow their pupil master and the second practising six months when pupils, with their pupil masters permission, can undertake to supply legal services and exercise rights of audience.

Continuing professional development

On completion of the academic and vocational stages of training, barristers have acquired the essential knowledge and skills to enable them to supply legal services to clients at a competent and professional level. However, the education and training received prior to qualification cannot equip a barrister with all the relevant knowledge and skills that will be required throughout the development of his or her career.

In order to maintain and enhance the quality of legal services that they offer, barristers need to update and develop specialist areas of knowledge and ensure that their skills are regularly refreshed. Furthermore, in the face of increasing competition in the market for legal services, barristers must have sufficient flexibility to adapt to the changing demands of clients, the profession and their own career.

The Bar Council introduced the New Practitioners' Programme on October 1, 1997 for barristers in their first three years of independent practice. This was extended on October 1, 1998 to barristers entering employed practice with the intention of exercising rights of audience. A continuing professional development (CPD) scheme was introduced for established practitioners from January 1, 2001. Under this scheme established practitioners are required to undertake continuing professional development throughout their careers to refresh their knowledge and skills in specialist areas.

(Adapted from The Bar Council website.)

Summarise the initial and continuing training requirements for barristers.

The issue of Queen's Counsel.

Barrister advocates are divided into junior and Queen's Counsel. The first Queen's Counsel was appointed at the end of the sixteenth century to supplement the advice given to the Crown by the Law Officers. During the seventeenth century, the office "was granted more frequently and came to be seen as a bestowal of rank on an individual rather than as an engagement of forensic assistance for the Crown". Until 1996, only barristers were eligible for appointment as Queen's Counsel, but the right was then extended to solicitors with rights to appear in the higher courts.

Queen's Counsel have traditionally been appointed annually by The Queen on the advice of the Lord Chancellor. Lawyers who wish to be considered are invited to apply to the Lord Chancellor. In the last three years, individuals have had to pay a fee to cover the administrative cost of processing their application. Following wide consultation with the judiciary and the profession, the Lord Chancellor then recommends for appointment those practitioners whom he considers have demonstrated that they meet the criteria to a degree which marks them out as leaders of the profession, that is to a standard comparable with those already appointed Queen's Counsel in the same or comparable practice type (the kind of work which lawyers do varying considerably with the area of law involved). The status of

Q.C. is also awarded on an honorary basis to people who are not practising advocates, but who have made a significant contribution to the law, for example as distinguished academics.

Queen's Counsel tend to specialise in different types of work. First, cases which are legally or factually complex, or of significance, or where the law is not clear may need specialist expertise. Secondly, in some areas of the law at least, Queen's Counsel appear in court more often than junior counsel, and therefore have the chance to develop and practice specialist skills in advocacy. Thirdly, in cases where there is a large amount of material to be managed, a "Silk" may be chosen to lead a team of advocates.

A focus on fewer, more complex cases usually leads to an increased fee rate *per* case. This may explain why appointment as a Q.C. is widely assumed to be an opportunity for practitioners to increase, perhaps substantially, the fees they charge for cases. There is, for example, some anecdotal evidence of practitioners increasing their fees for cases in which they were already appearing at the time of appointment.

(Adapted from the Department for Constitutional Affairs website.)

Explain what is meant by "Queen's Counsel" and its benefits to the barrister.

A Department for Constitutional Affairs Consultation Paper— Constitutional Reform: The Future of Queen's Counsel (July 2003)

Should the rank of Queen's Counsel continue?

In the Public Interest? asked users of advocacy services . . . how useful the Q.C. mark was to them. The following points were made in favour of the current system by barristers and solicitors:

- it provides a body of advocates who are identified as leaders of their profession and so gives a clear mark of distinction as an advocate;

- that mark is internationally recognised, and as such is both an example to other systems, and a very substantial source of foreign earnings, particularly by attracting commercial litigation to the UK;

- it assists solicitors in selecting the quality of legal assistance their client needs, particularly in areas with which the solicitors may be less familiar;

- it allows users to instruct with confidence advocates of whom they have little or no experience;

- it enhances competition in the interests of the consumer, by enabling solicitors to shop around among a number of barristers who have been recognised by the award of Silk;

- it promotes and maintains the level of expertise amongst practitioners, which is important for the court system; and

- it provides a career structure for barristers.

. . . Other respondents, however, did not find the Q.C. mark to be of use. They saw the market in legal advocacy as highly developed and were not convinced that solicitors needed a broad and undifferentiated quality mark to help them decide whom to instruct. Competence, reputation and previous experience were said to be the deciding factors when instructing an advocate in a complex case. Many solicitors thought there were better ways of assessing these qualities than by relying on the Q.C. status alone, and that it was part of their role to find the right advocate for a case. . . Other concerns included:

- the rank of Q.C. is not a reliable guarantee of quality or—in an increasingly specialist market—expertise (particularly as the current system does not include a stage for review and possible removal, or indicate the area of any specialism);

- the rank restricts competition and does not allow market forces freely to determine the allocation of resources. For example, it is suggested that choice is reduced because the system discourages the use of highly competent junior counsel;

- the division of the barristers' profession into only two ranks does not constitute a sufficient career structure, and the emphasis on the attainment of Q.C. places a disproportionate premium on that step;

- the current focus on oral advocacy in court puts at a disadvantage any barrister who specialises in areas of the law where the majority of his or her work is on paper or is directed towards achieving resolution out of court. Solicitors are seen to be similarly disadvantaged.

(Adapted from the Department for Constitutional Affairs website.)

Q.C.s face extinction after 400 years of power and privilege

Lord Chancellor signals end for elite counsel in anti-competition debate

Clare Dyer, legal correspondent

The elite rank of Queen's Counsel, which dates back to the reign of Elizabeth I, is likely to be abolished, the lord chancellor signalled yesterday in a speech to 121 new "silks" who could be the last to win the coveted title of Q.C. Swearing in this year's new Q.C.s at the House of Lords, Lord Irvine said: "If silk goes, that would make you the last in an illustrious line of leading counsel recognised by the state as leaders of the profession."

He stressed that no conclusions had yet been reached, but the writing has been on the wall for the Q.C. system since the office of fair trading branded it anti-competitive two years ago and questioned why the state should be involved in it.

The Lord Chancellor is expected to relinquish his role in the selection process but he made clear yesterday that any alternative system set up by the legal profession to recognise top practitioners would not be allowed to use the title Queen's Counsel. Lord Irvine said next year's competition for the Q.C. title—given to the top 10 per cent of barristers and a few solicitors—would be postponed pending the outcome of a consultation paper to be published before the summer. This would consider whether Q.C.s should still be appointed by the lord chancellor, but the main issue would be "whether the status of Queen's Counsel should continue to exist."

The OFT report into restrictive practices in March 2001 attacked the Q.C. system and the Lord Chancellor's role in it, questioning why the government should be involved in a process that makes it possible for the top 10 per cent of barristers to charge enhanced fees. John Vickers, director general of fair trading, said at the time that the demarcation between Q.C.s and junior barristers affected competition between suppliers "but it is hard to see what benefits it brings to consumers."

The Bar Council claimed the system was a "kitemark of quality" helping solicitors to choose the best barristers for their clients. But the arguments have failed to convince the OFT, or ministers, that there are sufficient public interest benefits to outweigh the anti-competitive effects.

Lord Irvine said the Q.C. selection process was now "better focused, with scrutiny hugely enhanced". But he added: "Still the issues are: first, is the system objectively in the public interest? And second, does it command public confidence?" He said the Director General of Fair Trading had asked whether a quality mark was necessary in a largely referral profession, where solicitors choose the barristers for cases. The principal arguments in favour were that the system provides a body of advocates recognised as leaders of their profession, assists solicitors in selecting the quality of legal assistance their client needs and enhances competition in the interests of the consumer, by enabling solicitors to shop around among silks.

But there were opposing arguments, he said. "Solicitors know who are the experts in their area of practice. Even if there were any doubt, the market now provides a range of reference books and websites—focused and regularly updated—which solicitors, and perhaps in the future members of the public, can use. In addition, many assert that the rank of silk drives up legal costs unjustifiably. It is also argued that the system reduces rather than increases choice in the legal market by discouraging the use of highly competent junior counsel who have not been awarded silk."

(Adapted from The Guardian, April 30, 2003.)

Should Q.C.s be abolished?

Michael Zander Q.C. weighs the opposing arguments.

Thirty-five years ago, in my first book *Lawyers and the Public Interest* (1986), I devoted a chapter to arguing that the title Queen's Counsel be abolished. At that time, no one paid the slightest attention. Today, the issue is not merely live but close to decision. The Government's consultation exercise closed on November 7.

The most important contributions from the "abolitionists" came from the Office of Fair Trading (OFT) and the Law Society. Given the momentum toward abolition, generated by the

Lord Chancellor's extra-ordinary suspension of the whole applications process last April, the Bar is clearly fighting an uphill battle to preserve the title.

All agree that the key issue is whether the public interest justifies the title as a quality mark. The OFT accepts that a quality mark can help ill-informed consumers choose between suppliers of a service but, like the Law Society, it questions whether solicitors are ill-informed. If they want information, there are now a variety of publications—published annually and therefore up-to-date—indicating areas of expertise and experience. The title gives no indication of the specific field of the Q.C.s competence. In fact, it may be positively misleading in that it suggests general expertise across a range of skills, whereas it is largely based on an assessment of skill in advocacy.

The OFT argues that the title fails on the key conditions for a quality mark:

- that it be awarded according to clear, relevant and objective criteria in a transparent way (despite recent reforms, this is still not the case);

- that the mark can be lost as well as won;

- that holding the mark is contingent on high quality of performance that must be appraised on a continuing basis; and

- that it does not distort competition (distortion arises from the advantage to advocates over competitors with over relevant legal skills; from the convention that there is work done by the Q.C.s and work done by juniors; from the fact that Q.C.s enjoy precedence in court; from the perception that the judge may give more weight to arguments advanced by a Q.C. than the same arguments put by a junior; and from the fact that Q.C.s have consistently, over time, been 10 per cent of the practicing Bar, suggesting a quota).

The OFT and the Law Society contend that appointment as a Q.C. involves an immediate step-change in the fees charged—with inflationary effects both for the Q.C. and for any junior instructed with him. The inflationary effect is increased insofar as the title creates pressure on the other side to match one Q.C. by employing another.

The OFT and the Law Society question whether it is right for the Government to have responsibility for conferring a title on some practitioners in a profession, enhancing their earning power and competitive position. The Government's involvement in the process also raises concerns as to the full independence of barristers. There is also the issue of "secret soundings" as a basis for appointments, which was the reason the Law Society gave in 1999 for its dramatic decision to withdraw from the whole process.

For the Bar Council, "The advocate's role is so linked with the administration of justice that the State must have an interest in ensuring that the higher standards of advocacy are maintained. The award of the rank of Q.C. is a public demonstration of such an interest." It also recognises qualities of independence, integrity and honesty. The existing system, it says, has the support of both clients and the judiciary.

Q.C.s are part of the badge by which English law is recognised internationally, bringing significant economic benefit to this country.

To abolish Q.C.s as a state-appointed rank would also "impact substantially on a new generation of women and minority ethnic lawyers poised to become the Q.C.s and judges of tomorrow, who would increase overall confidence in the justice system". This is a strong argument that has only recently come to the fore. (See the letter to *The Times*, November 3, 2003, from three ethnic minority silks—and the reply from an ethnic minority solicitor-advocate, *The Times*, November 14, 2003.)

The Bar argues that far from being anti-competitive, the title actually promotes competition and drives up standards. The OFT's assertion that it enhances earning power and competitive position is not backed by any evidence. Moreover, senior and experienced practitioners in any system would earn more than those with less seniority and experience.

The Bar concedes that changes should be made to modernise the system. Q.C.s should no longer enjoy any privilege of position or precedence in court. There should be a way of revoking the grant of Q.C. in cases of demonstrated lack of integrity or quality of performance, through regular re-appraisal or re-accreditation would be neither practical nor necessary.

As to method of appointment, the Bar suggests that there should be a new independent initial selection panel consisting of a senior retired judge, two barristers, a solicitor, and three lay persons, with appropriate secretariat. The shortlist should go to a judicial panel of senior judges who would put names to the Secretary of State (or Attorney-General) who would have to give reasons for removing a name. The minister would recommend the final list to the Queen.

The Bar makes a powerful case, but I believe the case for abolition is even stronger. Concerns over the selection process and the formal precedence given to silks in court might be handled by a reformed system, but such reform would not address the chief vice of the system—the distorting effect of the title on fees and costs.

Those who instruct barristers will lose little of significance, while those who pay for them will gain. Anyone who has or who aspires to the title, understandably will grieve, and many others, both inside and outside the legal system, will feel some sense of loss. But the administration of justice will basically be unaffected, as when the title of Sergeant was abolished.

Michael Zander Q.C. is Professor Emeritus, LSE

(Adapted from The New Law Journal, November 21, 2003, p.1725.)

Should the rank of Q.C. be retained or abolished?	
Arguments for retention?	
Arguments for abolition?	

Solicitors

The role of the solicitor

A solicitor's role is to provide skilled legal advice and representation to businesses, members of the public, charities, and many other clients.

Most solicitors work in private practice—a partnership of solicitors working as a firm. Others work as employed solicitors for an organisation, such as Shell or BT, local government, the Crown Prosecution Service or other body.

Solicitors and firms specialise as experts in areas of law. These areas can include corporate and commercial law, insurance, shipping, banking, entertainment and media law, among others.

Many solicitors work in small or medium-sized firms, serving the local community and dealing with a variety of legal problems affecting the public. Solicitors are often at the centre of a local business community. This work can include criminal matters, conveyancing (buying and selling houses or land), or personal injury claims, family and child-care law, employment and contract law, making wills and administering estates of people who have died.

Solicitors also work in larger firms, often based in large cities, particularly London. This work tends to relate to large, corporate clients, perhaps on large deals. Such law firms often have multi-national clients, so may have offices in major financial and business centres around the world.

The Law Society regulates and represents the solicitors profession in England and Wales and has a public interest role in working for reform of the law. Solicitors in Scotland and Northern Ireland are represented by the Law Societies in Scotland and Northern Ireland respectively.

(Adapted from The Law Society website.)

Summarise the main characteristics of the solicitor's job.

How to qualify as a solicitor

The quickest and most common route to qualification is by means of a qualifying law degree. . . If you decide to take a degree in a subject other than law, you will have to complete a one year full-time (or two years part-time) course leading to the Common Professional Examination or the post-graduate Diploma in Law. . . The course will give you the basic grounding in law which you need to qualify as a solicitor.

After successful completion of the law degree, or CPE, or Diploma in Law, you will have to undertake the Legal Practice Course, which is the professional training for solicitors. This course takes one academic year, or two years if studied part-time. . . The course teaches the practical application of the law to the needs of clients, and is offered by a number of different colleges and universities.

Having successfully completed the Legal Practice Course, you will enter a two-year training contract with a firm of solicitors or other approved organisation (such as a local authority or the Crown Prosecution Service), gaining practical experience in a variety of areas of law. At this stage, you will be paid a salary and will be a trainee solicitor.

For those who do not wish to take a degree, it is possible to qualify as a solicitor by obtaining employment in a legal office, joining the Institute of Legal Executives and taking the examinations to qualify as a member and subsequently a Fellow of the Institute of Legal Executives. This can be a stepping stone to qualifying as a solicitor.

(Adapted from The Law Society website.)

Summarise the initial and continuing training requirements for solicitors.

Paralegals

Become a Legal Executive

Legal Executives are qualified lawyers, working alongside solicitors and barristers. With a minimum of four GCSEs, graded A to C, one being English. . . you. . . can become a qualified lawyer. . . It takes approximately four years to qualify—you will be working and studying at the same time—earning and learning. . . The first two years are set at A-Level standard and the final two years are set at degree level. ILEX offers the opportunity for you to qualify as a lawyer with or without a degree.

(Adapted from the ILEX website.)

Licensed Conveyancers

The Council for Licensed Conveyancers (CLC) is the regulatory body for Licensed Conveyancers who are qualified specialist property lawyers. All conveyancing—essentially the legal processes involved in transferring buildings and/or land from one owner to another and dealing with the financial transactions—was the sole responsibility of solicitors until 1987. Under current legislation, it is now possible for other people to become conveyancers, known as Licensed Conveyancers. Banks, lenders, property developers and solicitors employ Licensed Conveyancers. Many Licensed conveyancers practise on their own or in partnership. Once the CLC examinations have been successfully completed and the practical training requirements undertaken, an applicant may apply for a licence which would permit them to offer conveyancing services as an employed person. Once they have held an employed licence for a period of three years, they may then apply for a full licence, which would permit them to offer conveyancing services directly to the public as the sole principal, as a partner in a firm of Licensed conveyancers or a director of a recognised body, *i.e.* limited company.

(Adapted from The Council for Licensed Coneyancers website.)

Outline the training and work of legal executives and licensed conveyancers.	
Legal Executives	
Licensed Conveyancers	

The Crown Prosecution Service

The role of the CPS

The Crown Prosecution Service (CPS) is the Government Department responsible for prosecuting people in England and Wales who have been charged by the police with a criminal offence. Created by the Prosecution of Offences Act 1985, we are an independent body that works closely with the police. The head of the Crown Prosecution Service is the Director of Public Prosecutions. . . The Crown Prosecution Service is the principal prosecuting authority in England and Wales. We are responsible for advising the police on cases for possible prosecution, reviewing cases submitted by the police, preparing cases for court and the presentation of cases at court. The role of the Service is to prosecute cases firmly, fairly and effectively when there is sufficient evidence to provide a realistic prospect of conviction and when it is in the public interest to do so.

The principles we follow

The Code for Crown Prosecutors sets out the basic principles to be followed by Crown Prosecutors when they make case decisions. The decision on whether or not to go ahead with a case is based on two tests outlined in the Code.

The evidential test

This is the first stage in the decision to prosecute. Crown Prosecutors must be satisfied that there is enough evidence to provide a "realistic prospect of conviction" against each defendant on each charge. They must consider whether the evidence can be used and is reliable. They must also consider what the defence case may be and how that is likely to affect the prosecution case. A "realistic prospect of conviction" is an objective test. It means that a jury or a bench of magistrates, properly directed in accordance with the law, will be more likely than not to convict the defendant of the charge alleged. (This is a separate test from the one that criminal courts themselves must apply. A jury or magistrates' court should only convict if it is sure of a defendant's guilt.) If the case does not pass the evidential test, it must not go ahead, no matter how important or serious it may be.

The public interest test

If the case does pass the evidential test, Crown Prosecutors must then decide whether a prosecution is needed in the public interest. They must balance factors for and against prosecution carefully and fairly. Some factors may increase the need to prosecute but others may suggest that another course of action would be better. A prosecution will usually take place however, unless there are public interest factors tending against prosecution which clearly outweigh those tending in favour. The CPS will only start or continue a prosecution if a case has passed both tests.

(Adapted from The Crown Prosecution Service website.)

Outline the organisation and role of the Crown Prosecution Service.

Activity ❶

You have been asked to give a short **presentation** to a group of students considering a legal career on the respective roles and training of solicitors and barristers. Using relevant information (e.g. from the Law Society and Bar Council websites), prepare and deliver this presentation. In preparing this activity, you should also read **Chapter 10** of *A Level and AS Level Law: a Study Guide*. You must also produce a **one-page handout** for the audience, giving the main points of your presentation and where they can find further information. Your handout, in addition to the text, must include at least **one image**.

(Evidence: Communications: 3.1b, C3.2, C3.3)

The social composition of the legal profession.

Q: Why is entry to the profession so difficult?

A: The Bar Council has worked to broaden entry into the profession to people of all backgrounds, but the drying up of local authority grants and the proposed top-up-fees threaten that work. Competition law means the Bar Council cannot restrict the numbers training for the Bar, and can only warn of the tough competition that any student will face in seeking qualification. The pupillage application process is being revised to reduce the risk of people paying for the Bar Vocational Course before they know whether they have secured a place in chambers.

As the profession grows, and it becomes increasingly difficult to provide funding for young barristers within chambers, there is a serious risk that the Bar will return to the days when only the rich can afford to practise. We are extremely anxious to prevent that happening. Consequently, we have made compulsory a minimum income during pupillage of £10,000. The profession as a whole already provides almost £12 million each year to support those training to become barristers. A Taskforce led by the DPP has examined ways in which BVC students might be supported. Proposals are the subject of consultation, with a view to firm recommendations being considered by the Council by the end of 2003.

(Adapted from The Bar Council website.)

Top barristers block levy to help students

by Clare Dyer, legal correspondent.

The Bar Council has been forced to abandon a plan to levy its high-earning barristers to support recruits through bar school, because of opposition from commercial practitioners. The decision came as a survey found record earnings for senior barristers, with a quarter of Q.C.s earning more than £281,000 a year. Conversely, the same survey found that 94 per cent of young barristers were in the red, with 57 per cent saying it would take them more than three years to clear their debt. Some said they emerged from their postgraduate year at bar school owing £20,000 or more for fees and living expenses.

The Council, concerned that entrants from poorer families were being discouraged from joining the profession, proposed a sliding scale levy on well-paid barristers to support students in financial difficulties through bar school. The plan has been scuppered by opposition from commercial and chancery barristers, the two best-paid sectors of practice at the bar. . . The Criminal Bar Association, whose members rely largely on the less well-paid publicly funded work, supported the proposal. . .

The survey, by BDO Stoy Hayward, also found that the introduction of a rule obliging chambers to pay pupils at least £10,000 a year from next year was deterring them from recruiting. Some 700 students a year normally secure pupillages, a necessary stage for practice at the bar; the survey suggests that up to 139 pupillages could be lost next year. . .

(Adapted from the Guardian, November 19, 2002.)

Pay survey for solicitors shows women get 15 per cent less

by Robert Verkaik, legal affairs correspondent

Female solicitors earn up to 15 per cent less than their male colleagues, an independent investigation into sexism in the legal profession shows. Half of the young women interviewed said that they believed their promotion prospects were blocked by a glass ceiling.

The authors of the survey, which will be published in the magazine *Legal Business* next week, warned that there was cause for concern in the salary gap between male and female salaries at all levels. Male lawyers with between six and nine years of post-qualification experience earn, on average, £11,000 more than their female counterparts. Male solicitors with up to two years of post-qualification experience can expect to earn on average £47,813. A female solicitor can expect to earn £45,503. Women with between three and five years of post-qualification experience earn about 6 per cent less than men. Men and women with between six and nine years' post-qualification experience had the greatest disparity, with men earning about 15 per cent more than women (£84,023 to £73,036).

Adrian Barham, of the Young Solicitors Group (YSG), said: "We are particularly concerned about the disparity in pay between male and female assistants at the same level of qualification. The fact that this gap widens with the greater level of qualification is even more worrying. The YSG, with the help of the Law Society and the Association of Women Solicitors, is looking at the reasons why more women than men leave the profession and this may well be one factor."

Tom Freeman, editor of *Legal Business,* added: "Given the increasing numbers of women flooding into the profession at junior levels, greater efforts have to be made to keep them on board. Women are getting a raw deal and it gets rawer as time goes on."

The survey also found that the longer assistants stayed in their jobs, the more cynical they became of the prospects of becoming a partner. The Equal Opportunities Commission said that, on average across all occupations, women in Britain earned 18 per cent less than men.

(Adapted from the Independent, November 5, 2003.)

What are the main issues relating to the social, racial and gender composition of the legal profession?

Activity ❷

Working in **pairs** or **small groups**, and using the information in the articles above, together with any other information you may find (e.g. in books, journals, newspapers or on the internet), prepare the case for or against the view that women and people from the ethnic minorities face difficulties in pursuing a legal career. You should then **debate** this issue as a whole class.

(Evidence: Communications: C3.1a, C3.2)

Activity ❸

Using the information you have gathered for Activity 2 and any further information you have gained as a result of the debate, prepare an **appropriate document** (e.g. an article of approximately 1000 words for a broadsheet newspaper) that outlines the main arguments for and against the view that women and people from the ethnic minorities face difficulties in pursuing a legal career. This document must include at least one **image**.

(Evidence: Communications: C3.2, C3.3)

The efficiency of a divided profession?

- The formal division of the profession has been controversial for some years. Both the **Benson Commission** (1979) and **Marre Committee** (1988) argued for retaining the division.

- However, a significant body of opinion continues to argue for fusion into a single profession. While this may have some advantages (*e.g.* some reduction in the cost of legal services) there are also potential disadvantages (for example, a possible decline in the availability of specialists).

- Also, in those jurisdictions (*e.g.* the USA) where there is no formal (*de jure*) division, there still tends to be an informal (*de facto*) distinction between office lawyers and trial lawyers.

- Furthermore, both the **Courts and Legal Services Act 1990** and **Access to Justice Act 1999** have removed many of the distinctions between the two branches, notably regarding advocacy rights, and the Bar Council has recently approved draft proposals to allow direct access by the public to barristers, and it will be some time before the consequences of these reforms can be fully assessed. That said, a report by the Office of Fair Trading in 2001 criticised the structure of the legal profession as anti-competitive and against the interests of consumers.

Why do I need two lawyers?

Most legal cases need a variety of different skills. Solicitors generally deal with the day-to-day preparation of cases and documents. They only involve barristers when they need specialist advice about a difficult area of the law, to draft documents or for "advocacy" (presenting a case in court). Barristers are trained as specialist advisers and advocates and do not have the facilities or expertise to do the work solicitors carry out. While some solicitors do have similar expertise in advocacy, many find it easier to use a barrister (also called counsel) for specialist work. The two roles do not overlap and the two should have a good working relationship. Together the solicitor and barrister form your team.

(Adapted from The Bar Council website.)

What are the arguments in favour of fusion?	
What are the arguments against fusion?	

Given the changes to the profession in recent years, is fusion still a significant debate?

The accountability of the profession

The Office for the Supervision of Solicitors

We were set up by the Law Society of England and Wales to deal with complaints about solicitors and to regulate their work. The Law Society funds our work, but it cannot get involved in individual cases.

Some members of the public, appointed by the Master of the Rolls, are involved in our decision and policy making. The Legal Services Ombudsman monitors the way we work.

We are here to help people who have problems with a solicitor. We do this by:

- monitoring how solicitors deal with complaints about their work; and

- investigating complaints about the quality of solicitors' service and the standard of their professional conduct (behaviour).

Where possible we try to conciliate complaints, in other words help both sides reach agreement. If this is not possible, we can take action such as reducing bills, awarding compensation or disciplining solicitors.

(Adapted from The Law Society website.)

Bar Council complaints system

What can I complain about?—The Bar Council will look into complaints about any aspect of a barrister's professional work. It is sensible to discuss with your solicitor, if you have one, whether he agrees with your complaint and, if so, whether he can resolve it properly. If the Bar Council decides that there is merit in your complaint, it has to decide how serious it is and whether it involves professional misconduct or inadequate professional service or both.

Is there a time limit?—Normally you must complain to us within six months of the complaint arising. We will only look at complaints which arrive later than that date if they are particularly serious or if there is a good reason for the delay.

Does it cost anything?—The Bar Council does not charge for this service.

Professional misconduct—Professional misconduct is a serious error or misbehaviour by a barrister which may well involve some element of dishonesty or serious incompetence. It might include:

- misleading the court;
- failure to keep your affairs confidential;
- leaving a case without good reason at short notice; and
- acting against a client's instructions or best interests.

Depending on how serious it is, the Bar Council has a number of penalties which range from simply giving advice to disbarring the barrister (*i.e.* so that he or she ceases to be a barrister) and include suspension for a period of time, a fine or an order to repay fees.

Inadequate Professional Service— This is defined as service towards the client falling significantly below that which would normally be expected of a barrister. It is not as serious as misconduct but may well have caused significant concern or inconvenience to a client such as:

- delay in dealing with papers;
- poor or inadequate work on a case; and
- serious rudeness to the client.

We can require a barrister to apologise to a client, to repay fees or to pay compensation of up to £5000. We can only do this if the complainant is the barrister's client.

Adapted from The Bar Council website.)

The Legal Services Ombudsman

- If someone is dissatisfied with the way in which their complaint was considered by the relevant professional body, they may approach the **Legal Services Ombudsman** to investigate the way in which the complaint has been dealt with. The Ombudsman is neither a solicitor nor a barrister. If the Ombudsman thinks that the complaint was not investigated properly, she can recommend that the complaint be reconsidered or that compensation be paid by the professional body or the individual practitioner or both.

SUMMARY OF THE TWELFTH ANNUAL REPORT OF THE LEGAL SERVICES OMBUDSMAN

The history of complaint handling within the legal profession reveals a general lack of progress. In particular, the historical perspective provides stark evidence of a consistent pattern of poor performance at the OSS. Even as the OSS once again take welcome steps to reverse this trend, there are reasons to doubt their likely effectiveness.

The performance statistics for the past year made sober reading. The number of complaints received by the Law Society increased significantly, as did the number of complaints referred to the Ombudsman. She was dismayed to see that for every 10 of the Law Society's cases received by the Office more than three had resulted in a recommendation or criticism by her predecessors. Perhaps even more alarming was the realisation that this actually represented an improvement from the previous year.

More work needs to be done in treating the causes of poor service—the way that lawyers behave. Until efforts are really made to tackle these root causes, little progress will be made in improving the quality of service provided by lawyers or the poor perception of lawyers by the general public.

This raises the question of self-regulation: whether the legal professions operate in the public interest; fairly serve the needs of their consumers; and give the public justified cause to have confidence in the integrity of those who provide legal services, and the impartiality of those who regulate them.

The Ombudsman intends to work closely with the Department for Constitutional Affairs and the professional bodies to implement tangible solutions to the fundamental problems that are evident in the current provision of legal services.

(Adapted from The Office of the Legal Services Ombudsman website.)

Bar Council to revamp how it handles complaints

by Clare Dyer, legal correspondent

The Bar Council is to overhaul its complaints regime after independent research showed that 74 per cent of complainants were very dissatisfied with the system, while only 3 per cent of barristers who had complaints made against them were equally dissatisfied. The council is likely to appoint more non-lawyers to the panels hearing complaints after the research by MORI found a widespread feeling among complainants that barristers "protect their own".

The "huge gulf" between barristers' and complainants' views of the system is consistent with research into complaints handling in other sectors, said the MORI report. Around 68 per cent of complaints are dismissed. Fewer than 500 complaints are received annually about the 10,000 barristers in England and Wales. The legal services ombudsman, the independent watchdog on complaints handling by barristers and solicitors, regularly gives the Bar's system a clean bill of health: only two decisions were criticised in 2002 and three recommended for reconsideration.

Complainants' biggest criticism was that the system was too legalistic and dominated by lawyers. Only 25 per cent felt their concerns were understood. MORI suggests bringing in more lay members. "Complainants are so disgruntled that anything which can reduce their resentment must constitute a worthwhile aim, so that the Bar Council may wish to consider how it can better inform and educate this highly disenchanted minority," the report said.

(Adapted from the Guardian, March 31, 2003.)

Law Society may lose power to rule on complaints against solicitors

by Joshua Rozenberg, Legal Editor

Solicitors are likely to lose their powers to decide complaints against themselves following a new way of regulating legal services promised yesterday by Lord Falconer, the Lord Chancellor and Constitution Secretary. The Law Society has always regarded self-regulation as the mark of an independent profession. The task of devising a new regulatory framework has been given to David Clementi, a former deputy chairman of the Bank of England. He will lead an independent review over the next 18 months. Lord Falconer said the current framework was "outdated, inflexible, over-complex and insufficiently accountable or transparent". There are currently 22 overlapping regulators, some controlling the service while others regulate the provider. This led to "confusion and fragmentation" . . . such as when solicitors provide financial advice, they may be answerable to two or more different regulators. Asked whether the Law Society, which represents 90,000 solicitors in England and Wales, will lose its self-regulation powers, Lord Falconer said: "I think there's a significant chance that they will. A case has got to be made which answers the question: is it in the interest of the consumer and the public that lawyers regulate themselves?. . . If you're giving a particular group a monopoly in the provision of services—which in some areas they [lawyers] are given—then that monopoly carries with it a need to provide a service that meets the needs of the consumer. It may be that external regulation will bring more benefits for the consumer."

(Adapted from the Daily Telegraph, July 25, 2003.)

Do you think the legal profession is adequately accountable for the quality of the service it provides? In particular, do you think self-regulation can be justified?

12 The Judiciary

? Issues to Explore

? The different types of judge and the courts in which they sit.

? The appointment of judges.

? The role of the Lord Chancellor.

Definition:

THE JUDICIARY:	The various professional judges that, along with the lay magistracy (see Chapter 13), that are responsible for the administration of civil and criminal justice in England and Wales.

- Most judicial appointees are barristers, and although recent legislation has increased the potential for solicitors and judges, this is likely to remain the case for the foreseeable future. Appointments (excluding senior judicial offices) are made by the Lord Chancellor. For junior judicial posts (District Judge, Recorder and Circuit Judge), appointment is by application and interview (with consideration being given to an assessment exercise including role-play). Applications are invited for appointment as a High Court Judge, although there is no interview and the Lord Chancellor is not restricted to appointing only those who apply. Appointment as Lord Justice of Appeal and Lord of Appeal in Ordinary (Law Lord) is by invitation.

- The senior judicial offices are: **Lord Chancellor**—this is a political appointment, made by the monarch on the advice of the Prime Minister. The Lord Chancellor is the head of the Judiciary; **Lord Chief Justice**—this is the senior full-time judicial appointment. The Lord Chief Justice presides over the Court of Appeal (Criminal Division) and the Queen's Bench Division of the High Court; **Master of the Rolls**—presides over the Court of Appeal (Civil Division); **Vice-Chancellor**—is the head of the Chancery Division of the High Court; **President of the Family Division of the High Court**—presides over the Family Division of the High Court.

Judge	Qualifications	Appointment	Court	Salary (as at April 1, 2003)
Lord of Appeal in Ordinary	Generally appointed from among the experienced judges of the Court of Appeal	By The Queen on the recommendation of the Prime Minister, who receives advice from the Lord Chancellor.	House of Lords	£175,055
Lord Justice of Appeal	The statutory qualification is a 10-year High Court qualification or to be a judge of the High Court. Appointment is usually on promotion from the ranks of experienced High Court Judges.	By The Queen on the recommendation of the Prime Minister, who receives advice from the Lord Chancellor.	Court of Appeal	£166,394
High Court Judge	The statutory qualification is a 10-year High Court qualification or to have been a Circuit Judge for at least two years.	By The Queen on the recommendation of the Lord Chancellor.	High Court	£147,198
Circuit Judge	The statutory qualification is a 10-year Crown Court or 10-year County Court qualification, or to be a Recorder, or to be the holder of one of a number of other judicial offices of at least three years' standing in a full-time capacity.	By The Queen on the recommendation of the Lord Chancellor.	Crown Court County Court	£110,362

Judge	Qualifications	Appointment	Court	Salary (as at April 1, 2003)
Recorder	The statutory qualification for appointment as a Recorder is a 10-year Crown Court or 10-year County Court qualification.	By The Queen on the recommendation of the Lord Chancellor.	Crown Court County Court	
District Judge	The statutory qualification is a seven-year general qualification.	By the Lord Chancellor.	County Court	£88,546 (£92,546 in London)
District Judge (Magistrates' Court)	The statutory qualification is a seven-year general qualification.	By The Queen on the recommendation of the Lord Chancellor.	Magistrates' Court	£88,546 (£92,546 in London)

The training of judges

The Judicial Studies Board

The Judicial Studies Board provides training and instruction for all full-time and part-time judges in the skills necessary to be a judge. It also has an advisory role in the training of lay magistrates and of chairmen and members of tribunals. The Board's area of responsibility is for England and Wales. An essential element of the philosophy of the JSB is that the training of judges and magistrates is under judicial control and directions.

The Judicial Studies Board (JSB) was set up in 1979, following the Bridge Report which identified the most important objective of judicial training as being: *"To convey in a condensed form the lessons, which experienced judges, have acquired from their experience. . .".* This remains the essence of the JSB's role. A circuit judge, currently Judge William Rose, is seconded to the JSB full-time as Director of Studies. The work of the Committees is supplemented by JSB publications.

The JSB has five objectives:

- **Objective 1:** To provide high quality training to full- and part-time judges in the exercise of their jurisdiction in Civil, Criminal and Family Law.

- **Objective 2:** To advise the Lord Chancellor on the policy for and content of training for lay magistrates, and on the efficiency and effectiveness with which Magistrates' Courts Committees deliver such training.

- **Objective 3:** To advise the Lord Chancellor and Government Departments on the appropriate standards for, and content of, training for judicial officers in Tribunals.

- **Objective 4:** To advise the Government on the training requirement of judges, magistrates, and judicial officers in Tribunals if proposed changes to the law, procedure and court organisation are to be effective, and to provide, and advise on the content of, such training.

- **Objective 5:** To promote closer international co-operation over judicial training.

(Adapted from the Judicial Studies Board website.).

Summarise and comment on the training of judges.

Reforming the appointments process?

Top judges still white and male

by Clare Dyer, legal correspondent

The senior judiciary of England and Wales is as white and public school-educated today as it was 10 years ago, despite Labour's five years in power, a survey by the magazine Labour Research reveals today. The proportion of public-school educated judges appointed or promoted since Labour came to power is exactly the same as in the judiciary as a whole—67 per cent. And despite the Lord Chancellor's repeated commitment to a more diverse judiciary, fewer than 1 per cent of judges comes from an ethnic minority. The few ethnic minority judges are all on the lowest tier, the circuit bench. There has never been a black or Asian judge in the high court, court of appeal, or House of Lords.

Women have done slightly better, rising from 6 per cent to 8.9 per cent of the judiciary under Labour. The number of women in the court of appeal has risen from one to three. Unlike the supreme courts of the US and the Commonwealth countries, the UK's highest court, the House of Lords, has never had a woman judge (until the appointment of Lady Hale in October 2003). Canada, by contrast, has had women supreme court judges for 20 years and has a woman as chief justice, the top judicial job.

The findings will add to growing pressure for an independent appointments commission to replace the current system, under which the Lord Chancellor makes appointments after consulting judges and senior legal figures. Critics say this "old boy" system produces clones of those already in place. The independent commission set up by the lord chancellor to monitor the appointments system—headed by Sir Colin Campbell, vice-chancellor of Nottingham University—described the judiciary in its first report in October as "overwhelmingly white, male, and from a narrow social and educational background". The survey was done by the Labour Research Department, an independent trade union oriented organisation. It shows that among the judges promoted under Labour to the Court of Appeal and House of Lords, the proportion who attended public school and Oxbridge was even higher than for those benches as a whole. While 78 per cent of Appeal Court Judges are products of public schools, the figure for those promoted under Labour was 86 per cent. On appointments to the bench, rather than promotions, Labour did better. While 87 per cent of high court family division judges went to public school and 57 per cent went to Oxbridge, of Labour's appointments 83 per cent went to public school and 20 per cent to Oxbridge.

(Adapted from the Guardian, December 6, 2002.)

Watchdog demands judicial shakeup

Commission scathing about "tap on shoulder" promotion system

Clare Dyer, legal correspondent

A "systemic bias" in the way the judiciary and the legal system operate leads women, ethnic minorities, and solicitors to lose out on appointments as judges and Q.C.s, the official watchdog on judicial appointments concludes in a report today.

The Commission for Judicial Appointments (CJA) welcomes the new independent Judicial Appointments Commission planned by the government to take over the selection of judges, but says it will not be enough on its own to cure the bias which has produced an overwhelmingly white, male judiciary. The whole system needs radical reform to produce a much more diverse judiciary, selected by a fairer, more transparent system, says the watchdog in its second annual report to the lord chancellor: "Action is needed by the government, the judiciary and the profession to address obstacles to diversity."

The CJA, set up two years ago, is limited to investigating the existing appointment procedures and dealing with complaints from aggrieved individuals. The new commission will play a much bigger role, largely taking over the current role of the lord chancellor in selecting judges. The eight members of the CJA, chaired by Sir Colin Campbell, the vice-chancellor of Nottingham University, are the first outsiders to be allowed inside the confidential system for selecting judges and queen's counsel, the elite top 10 per cent of barristers (and a few solicitors) allowed to put Q.C. after their names.

The selection processes for Q.C.s and judges rely heavily on "soundings" with judges and other senior legal figures, who give written comments on a candidate's suitability. Comments included: "I would reject X and Y as too primly spinsterish"; and "she does not dress appropriately." Sir Colin said: "If a woman dressed in a provocative way, that would attract comment." In the case of a candidate turned down for a part-time judicial appointment, comments "appeared highly subjective and were couched in inappropriate language".

The report endorses a new approach to selection of judges, piloted with deputy district judges. Candidates go through a range of exercises at an assessment centre to see whether they have the practical skills and legal knowledge for the job. The commissioners recommend an end to the "tap on the shoulder" mode of appointing high court judges, and recommend that all candidates should have to apply for the job and have an interview.

(Adapted from The Guardian, October 2, 2003.)

A Department for Constitutional Affairs Consultation paper: constitutional reform: a new way of appointing judges (July 2003)

Foreword

by The Lord Falconer of Thoroton, Secretary of State for Constitutional Affairs and Lord Chancellor

This consultation paper constitutes part of the Government's continuing drive to modernise the constitution and the legal system for the purpose of making it more relevant and effective for today's world. The paper seeks views on the form and responsibilities of a new, independent Judicial Appointments Commission which will take responsibility for the selection of judges in England and Wales . . .

In a modern democratic society it is no longer acceptable for judicial appointments to be entirely in the hands of a Government Minister. For example the judiciary is often involved in adjudicating on the lawfulness of actions of the Executive. And so the appointments system must be, and must be seen to be, independent of Government. It must be transparent. It must be accountable. And it must inspire public confidence. . .

There is a second point. As the existing Commission for Judicial Appointments pointed out in its first annual report, the current judiciary is overwhelmingly white, male, and from a narrow social and educational background. To an extent, this reflects the pool of qualified candidates from which judicial appointments are made: intake to the legal professions has, until recently, been dominated by precisely these social groups.

Of course, the fundamental principle in appointing judges is and must remain selection on merit. However the Government is committed to opening up the system of appointments, to attract suitably qualified candidates both from a wider range of social backgrounds and from a wider range of legal practice. To do so, and, to create a system which commands the confidence of professionals and the public, and is seen as affording equal opportunities to all suitably qualified applicants, will require fresh approaches and a major re-engineering of the processes for appointment . . .

. . . one of the Commission's central tasks will also be to look at the appointment procedures to see if new and better ways can help in attracting a wider range of people to the judiciary: more women, more minority members, and lawyers from a wider range of practice. Developing a judiciary more broadly reflective of society at large will not be easy and the introduction of an independent Commission will not be enough in itself to bring about change. It will need a close partnership with the current judiciary and the legal profession, as well as the Government to examine fresh ideas about the nature of judicial careers. The Government does not believe that a career judiciary on the continental model would be appropriate for the common law system of England and Wales but they do believe that new career paths should be looked at to promote other opportunities and diversity in appointments . . .

The need for a Judicial Appointments Commission

Despite this programme of improvements to the current system of appointments, many of the most fundamental features of the system, including the role of the Lord Chancellor, remain rooted in the past. Incremental changes to the system can only achieve limited results, because the fundamental problem with the current system is that a Government minister, the Lord Chancellor, has sole responsibility for the appointments process and for making or recommending those appointments. However well this has worked in practice, this system no longer commands public confidence, and is increasingly hard to reconcile with the demands of the Human Rights Act . . .

Different models of Commission

There are three main models on which the Government seeks views:

- an **Appointing Commission** which would itself make those appointments which the Lord Chancellor currently makes personally and directly advise The Queen on appointments above that level without any ministerial involvement;

- a **Recommending Commission** which would make recommendations to a minister as to whom he or she should appoint (or recommend that The Queen appoints); or

- a **Hybrid Commission** in which the Commission would act as an appointing commission in relation to the more junior appointments (for example, part-time judicial and tribunal appointments) and as a recommending commission in relation to more senior appointments.

(Adapted from the Department for Constitutional Affairs website.)

Summarise the main problems with the current system for appointing judges	
What changes are being proposed by the Government?	

Activity ❶

You have been asked to give a short **presentation** to a group of law undergraduates about the appointment and training of judges. Using relevant information (*e.g.* from the Judicial Studies Board website), prepare and deliver this presentation. In preparing this activity, you should also read **Chapter 11** of *A Level and AS Level Law: a Study Guide*. You must also produce a **one-page handout** for the audience, giving the main points of your presentation and where they can find further information. Your handout, in addition to the text, must include at least **one image**.

(**Evidence: Communications: 3.1b, C3.2, C3.3**)

Activity ❷

Working in **pairs** or **small groups**, and using the information in the articles above, together with any other information you may find (*e.g.* in books, journals, newspapers or on the internet), prepare the case for or against reforming the way judges are appointed. You should then **debate** this issue as a whole class.

(**Evidence: Communications: C3.1a, C3.2**)

Activity ❸

Using the information you have gathered for Activity 2 and any further information you have gained as a result of the debate, prepare an **appropriate document** (*i.e.* an article of approximately 1000 words for a broadsheet newspaper) that outlines the main arguments for and against reforming the way judges are appointed. This document must include at least one **image**.

(**Evidence: Communications: C3.2, C3.3**)

The Lord Chancellor

A Department for Constitutional Affairs Consultation Paper: Constitutional Reform—reforming the office of the Lord Chancellor (September 2003)

Foreword

by Lord Falconer of Thoroton, Secretary of State for Constitutional Affairs and Lord Chancellor

This consultation paper relates to the abolition of the office of Lord Chancellor. It forms a further part of the Government's continuing drive to modernise the constitution in order to make it more relevant and effective for the needs of today. . . The abolition of the office of

Lord Chancellor will put the relationship between the executive, the judiciary and the legislature on a modern footing, and clarify the independence of the judiciary. The office of Lord Chancellor has been the subject of criticism for some time. In particular by combining the three primary roles of Minister, Judge and Speaker of the House of Lords, these distinct functions have become obscured, even confused. Our existing arrangements have become increasingly hard to sustain, even as we seek to persuade developing countries to adopt clearer constitutional mechanisms and provide for the insulation of the judiciary from political pressures. But we have hitherto not followed our own advice. The Government believes that it is time to separate out the different roles of the Lord Chancellor to bring greater transparency and increased public confidence.

It can no longer be appropriate for a senior judge to sit in Cabinet or for a Government Minister to be our country's senior judge. I have myself made it clear that I shall not sit judicially, but it is now time to bring such anachronistic and questionable arrangements to an end . . . The Lord Chancellor has served as Speaker, as Head of the Judiciary and as Cabinet Minister. Each of these roles deserves to be given an important priority, which in practice is not possible . . . Each is demanding in its own right, and it is time this was recognised.

(Adapted from the Department for Constitutional Affairs website.)

What criticisms have been made of the current position of the Lord Chancellor?	
Does this mean we need to abolish the office of Lord Chancellor?	

13 Magistrates and Juries

? Issues to Explore

? What sorts of lay persons are involved in the administration of justice?

? How are they chosen?

? What sorts of duties do magistrates perform?

? What is the role of a jury in a criminal trial?

? What are the justifications for using ordinary people in such important roles?

? What criticisms can be made of using lay persons in this way?

Definition:

LAY PERSON:	People with no formal legal qualifications or training who are involved in the administration of justice.

- The English legal system is unusual in the extent to which it relies on the contribution of **lay persons** in the administration of justice. Some of these people are brought into the system because they have a **particular expertise**, such as **tribunal members** and **arbitrators**. Others are valued because they are **not trained lawyers**. The most prominent examples of these are **magistrates** and **jurors**.

Magistrates

A tradition of justice

Laws in this country are made and enforced on behalf of the people. It is a tradition that ordinary people, untrained in the law, should take part in the legal process—either as members of juries or as magistrates.

The part played by lay magistrates, also known as Justices of the Peace, in the judicial system of England and Wales can be traced to the year 1195. In that year, Richard I commissioned certain knights to preserve the peace in unruly areas. They were responsible to the King for ensuring that the law was upheld. They preserved the "King's Peace", and were known as Keepers of the Peace.

The title Justice of the Peace (JP) first appeared in 1361, in the reign of Edward III. By this time, JPs had been given the power to arrest offenders and suspects. They could investigate crime and, in 1382, were finally given the power to punish.

The duties and responsibilities of a magistrate

Magistrates work . . . covers a wide range of criminal and civil matters. Magistrates' courts dispose of over 95 per cent of all criminal cases.

In criminal cases heard in the Adult and Youth Courts, magistrates:

- decide on requests for remand in custody;

- decide on applications for bail;

- decide whether a case should be adjourned;

- determine whether a defendant is guilty or not;

- pass sentence on a defendant who has been found guilty;

- commit a defendant to the Crown Court for sentence;

- enforce financial penalties; and

- may determine the venue at which a case will be heard.

In civil cases heard in the Family Proceedings Court magistrates make decisions on a range of issues affecting children and families.

Magistrates are also asked to decide whether to grant certain . . . licences . . . for example, liquor licences.

In a magistrates' court the justices usually sit as a Bench of three; when sitting as a Youth or Family Proceedings Panel there must be at least one man and one woman justice on the Bench.

When hearing cases magistrates have to ascertain the facts and then apply the law to them with the help and advice of a qualified court clerk.

Magistrates may sit with a judge in the Crown Court to hear appeals from Magistrates' Courts against conviction or sentence.

Magisterial qualities

Magistrates must be of good character and have personal integrity; they should have sound common sense and the ability to weigh evidence and reach reasoned decisions. Magistrates must live or work in the area and need to have a good knowledge and understanding of the local community. They need to be firm yet compassionate and be able to work as a member of a team.

There is no requirement for any formal qualifications.

With a few exceptions anyone is eligible to serve as a magistrate. However, the Lord Chancellor will not appoint:

- anyone over 65 years of age or under 27 unless there are exceptional circumstances;
- anyone who is not of good character and personal standing;
- an undischarged bankrupt;
- anyone who, because of a disability, cannot carry out all of the duties of a magistrate;
- a serving member of Her Majesty's Forces; a member of a police force or a traffic warden or any other occupation which might be seen to conflict with the role of a magistrate; or
- a close relative of a person who is already a magistrate on the same Bench.

(Adapted from the Department for Constitutional Affairs website.)

Who are magistrates?

Magistrates are members of the local community appointed by the Lord Chancellor.

- No formal qualifications are required but magistrates need intelligence, common sense, integrity and the capacity to act fairly. Membership should be widely spread throughout the area covered and drawn from all walks of life.
- All magistrates are carefully trained before sitting and continue to receive training throughout their service.
- Magistrates are unpaid volunteers but they may receive allowances to cover travelling expenses and subsistence.

Dealing with criminal offences

Magistrates deal with two categories of crime.

- Serious (referred to as either-way offences), *e.g.* theft, fraud where magistrates may deal with the case or refer it to the Crown Court.
- Less serious (referred to as summary offences), *e.g.* traffic matters which are only dealt with by magistrates.

The maximum penalty available to magistrates is six months' imprisonment but magistrates can impose community penalties, compensation and fines.

A balanced bench

The Lord Chancellor requires that each bench should broadly reflect the community it serves in terms of gender, ethnic origin, geographical spread, occupation and political affiliation. Achieving a balance is, however, a secondary consideration to the essential and pre-eminent requirement that a candidate must be personally suitable for appointment, possessing the qualities required in a magistrate.

Age

The retirement age for magistrates is 70. The Lord Chancellor will not generally appoint a candidate under the age of 27 or over the age of 65.

Gender

Each bench should have a roughly equal number of men and women. There should be sufficient magistrates of each sex who are eligible to sit in the family proceedings and youth courts, which must be made up of three magistrates and include a man and a woman, unless this is impractical.

Ethnic origin

Advisory committees are making strenuous efforts to recruit suitable candidates from the ethnic minorities. Advisory committees should be aware of the ethnic composition of the area for which they are responsible and seek to recruit sufficient numbers from the ethnic minorities to reflect that composition.

Geographical spread

Advisory committees should aim to recommend candidates proportionally from the areas for which they are responsible but ensure that there are not too many magistrates on any one bench from the same village, neighbourhood or street.

Occupation

Advisory Committees should seek to recommend for appointment, candidates from a broad spectrum of occupations. No more than 15 per cent of the magistrates on a bench should be from the same occupational group.

Political affiliation

The political views of a candidate are neither a qualification nor a disqualification for appointment. However, the Lord Chancellor requires, in the interests of balance, that the voting pattern for the area as evidenced by the last two general elections, should be broadly reflected in the composition of the bench.

Membership of clubs/organisations including freemasonry

It is important that there are not too many magistrates on the bench from the same clubs or organisations. Candidates for the magistracy are specifically asked on the new application form if they are freemasons.

Who can become a magistrate?

Magistrates:

- Must be of good character.

- Have personal integrity.
- Have sound common sense.
- Have the ability to weigh evidence and reach reasoned decisions.
- Live or work in the area.
- Have good local knowledge and understanding of the local community.
- Be able to work as a member of a team.
- Be firm yet compassionate.

Who cannot become a magistrate?

Almost anyone can apply but the following will not be appointed:

- Anyone who is not of good character and personal standing.
- An undischarged bankrupt.
- A serving member of Her Majesty's Forces.
- A member of a police force.
- A traffic warden or any other occupation which might be seen to conflict with the role of a magistrate.
- A close relative of a person who is already a magistrate on the same bench.
- Anyone who, because of a disability, cannot carry out all the duties of a magistrate.

The application and appointment process

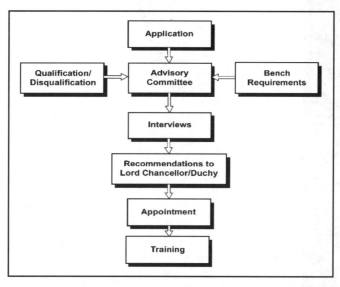

(Adapted from The Magistrates' Association website.)

What is a magistrate?	Lay magistrates: District Judges (Magistrates' Court):
What do magistrates do?	Civil matters: Criminal matters:
Who can be a magistrate?	
Who cannot be a magistrate?	
How are magistrate appointed?	
What are "Bench requirements"?	Examples:

Activity ❶

You have been asked to give a short **presentation** to a local community group about becoming a magistrate. Using the material in the extracts above, and any other relevant information you can find, prepare and deliver this presentation. In preparing this activity, you should also read **Chapter 12** of **A Level and AS Level Law: a Study Guide**. You must also produce a **one-page handout** for the audience, giving the main points of your presentation and where they can find further information. Your handout, in addition to the text, must include at least **one image**.

(Evidence: Communications: 3.1b, C3.2, C3.3)

Bench test

White, middle class, time-rich . . . that's an accurate stereotype of many magistrates. But it may be about to change as efforts are stepped up to recruit a wider range of "beaks". Christopher Middleton reports.

It's a warm Wednesday night in the Midlands and, at an extraordinary court sitting at Hinckley, Leicestershire, local magistrate Anne Knight finds herself in an embarrassing position. She is in the dock for shoplifting, charged with stuffing an £18.99 cardigan into her bag at Marks & Spencer, then walking out without paying for it. As the case proceeds, however, it emerges that she is only pretending to be a thief as Hinckley magistrates court hosts a special "outreach" evening for members of the local Ladies Tangent Circle—a senior female version of the Round Table.

"The reason we put on these events is twofold", says Sandra Blackbourn, chair of the Hinckley and Market Bosworth magistrates' bench. "First, we want to explain our work to the public. Second, we hope that some of these people will themselves want to become magistrates". To which end, the members of the Ladies Tangent Circle are given brochures and application forms as they leave. It's anyone's guess whether any of them will ever end up dispensing justice here, though there is no mistaking the relish with which they played their roles in the trial, some as lawyers, others as ushers and newspaper reporters.

There are just 47 Hinckley magistrates, yet 23 turn out regularly for events like this one—at sports clubs, schools and community associations. It is all part of a wider, national scheme called Magistrates in the Community, designed not just to recruit more magistrates, but also to ensure that they come from a broader range of social backgrounds. There are 30,000 magistrates currently serving in England and Wales, evenly spread as regards gender (51 per cent men, 49 per cent women) but not very representative as regards class (mainly middle) and race (only 4.5 per cent from ethnic minority communities). To help rectify this imbalance, magistrates on the 400–strong bench at Birmingham have joined with campaign Operation Black Vote to give members of the city's different ethnic minority communities a chance to "shadow" a magistrate as they preside, ponder, pass sentence and even visit prisoners at Winson Green jail.

"As in a lot of communities, there's this impression that magistrates are aloof and austere and that we could not possibly apply for a position", says Revinder Johal, a 31-year-old Sikh woman who is an equal opportunities officer with the city council and has been chosen to shadow magistrate and former food scientist Adrian Dence. "Basically, I want to find out whether or not that's true."

Johal admits she did not know what to expect, having never set foot inside a magistrates' court in her life. On her first two visits to court, however, the integrity scores seem to have been high. "In the cases I've seen, everyone seemed to be treated very fairly," she says. "Eventually, I'd like to set up a meeting at my temple, to explain to people the work that magistrates do. I might even like to become one myself. So far, I've seen nothing to put me off."

She is certainly old enough, 27 being the minimum age. And given that she lives locally and is of good character, as well as being possessed of intelligence, common sense and the capacity to act fairly—all are criteria—there is no obvious reason why she should not be accepted.

The other bonus is that she works for Birmingham council, and local authorities are traditionally better disposed than commercial employers towards giving staff time off to be magistrates. The minimum number of (half-day) sittings a magistrate must attend in one year is 25, with 35 the preferred figure. And while large banks and building societies profess 100 per cent readiness to let staff be magistrates in company time, the same is not true of smaller companies.

"I was secretary to my husband's building firm, and he always said that if I had just been another employee, he'd never have allowed me time off", says Anne Knight. This means that, unless local benches are careful, the only sufficiently time-rich people they will be able to recruit will be retired colonels and non-working women.

(Adapted from the Guardian, October 3, 2001.)

- On July 7, 2003 The Times reported that renewed attempts were being made to ensure that Magistrates "better reflect the country's social mix." A survey by the Lord Chancellor's Department highlighted that of the 24,419 people polled, 34.4 per cent voted Conservative, 25.5 per cent voted labour and 13.1 per cent Liberal Democrat. The remaining 20 per cent involved in the survey declared that they were uncommitted.

- The survey proved disproportionate representation for the Conservatives in the courts which decide the outcome of 99 per cent of criminal prosecutions.

- Following this survey reform plans were shelved "when no alternative way to ensure diversity of background and class among magistrates was forthcoming."

£4m drive to recruit younger magistrates

by Joshua Rozenberg, Legal Editor

A campaign to encourage young people, ethnic minorities and those with disabilities to become magistrates was launched yesterday by the Lord Chancellor. Lord Falconer said it was necessary to challenge the "generally held, but erroneous view that to become a magistrate you have to be white, middle-class, middle-aged and professional".

Advertisements would appear on buses as part of a three-year, £4 million recruitment campaign to increase the size and diversity of the justices' bench while bringing down the average age, he said. The aim was to make the bench a microcosm of the community it served. About 80 per cent of magistrates are currently over 50.

"We have a continuing problem reaching younger applicants, blue-collar workers, the self-employed and those from minority ethnic communities," he said, promising "targeted recruitment of ethnic minorities" in cities where they were under-represented. There was also a need to persuade employers that releasing an individual to sit in judgment for a day or two each month was good for their business, enhancing the employee's decision-making skills while investing in the local community.

(Adapted from the Daily Telegraph, October 8, 2003.)

What are the advantages of the lay magistracy?	
What are the disadvantages of the lay magistracy?	
Does the lay magistracy need reform?	

Juries

- Juries are regarded as one of the cornerstones of our system of justice. But, in fact, juries are only used to decide about 3 per cent of criminal cases. We also know very little about how effective English juries are in reaching their verdicts, because the **Contempt of Court Act 1981** prohibits the questioning of jurors (although a considerable amount of research has be carried out in other Common Law countries, such as New Zealand). Nevertheless, there is always considerable uproar whenever any changes to the role of the jury are proposed. The materials that follow discuss some of the major issues surrounding the jury and the cases for and against change.

Anyone know what the judge is on about?

A new study reveals some unsettling facts about the secret world of the juror—they often feel intimidated, scared and confused. Clare Dyer reports.

What goes on behind the door to the jury room and how do 12 ordinary mortals reach the verdict which could put a fellow human being behind bars for years? Try asking them and you could face a large fine and a spell in prison yourself.

No one questions the maxim that justice must not only be done but be seen to be done. Yet an impenetrable veil of secrecy hangs over the room where the final act of the criminal justice process—the determination of guilt or innocence—is played out. Researchers are banned from questioning jurors to find out how the system works in practice and how it could be improved. The appeal court has even refused to look into what happened in the jury room when faced with a claim that some irregularity made a conviction unsafe.

The jury, like royalty, is an ancient institution whose survival depends largely on its mystique. In the high-flown words of the late Lord Devlin, it is "the lamp that shows that freedom lives". But the lamp must not be lit too brightly—it could show up the warts and dent public confidence.

The result is that everything we think we know about how real juries operate is the result of anecdote, conjecture and studies of mock juries.

But now at last a window has been opened into the jury room. For the first time researchers have been able to systematically investigate how real jurors go about their job. It hasn't happened in Britain and the findings have so far gone unnoticed here. But a large-scale research project has been carried out in a criminal justice system so similar to our own that its conclusions shine an unprecedented light into the workings of our own jury system.

In New Zealand there is a convention that jurors may not be questioned about their experiences but not a blanket ban. Judicial approval was granted for the research to be carried out by a team from the Victoria University of Wellington . . . in collaboration with the New Zealand law commission, the country's official law reform body.

The findings explode some long-held myths. They show that while jurors are "overwhelmingly conscientious" in following the judge's instructions, they do have difficulty with the concept of "intent" and whether or not a defendant acted dishonestly.

The research also shows that "some jurors have particular difficulty assessing the credibility of witnesses, challenging the traditional view that juries are particularly adept at assessing credibility".

And juries have problems in fully grasping the law. In four out of the 48 trials, legal errors led to hung juries or questionable verdicts, concluded the researchers.

It was "a great deal to ask" of ordinary lawmen to take on board difficult concepts—such as the burden and standard of proof, the elements necessary to prove an offence, and rules of evidence—when they had heard them only once from the judge and were given no written record.

In 19 trials, one or more jurors misunderstood significant aspects of the ingredients of the offence. "Fairly fundamental" misunderstandings of the law emerged during deliberations in 35 of the 48 cases. Jurors were unsure about the difference between purpose and intent, and sometimes thought intent implied premeditation.

A significant number of jurors had difficulty concentrating on oral evidence, particularly in trials lasting more than two days, and problems in recalling the evidence.

In 22 cases, pressure to reach a verdict came from other members of the jury. Those on their own or in a small minority felt the worst pressure, with the pressure increasing as the other minority jurors changed their minds. In six cases jurors said feeling that time was running out or that people wanted to get home was an important factor in reaching a verdict.

Judges give standard directions to the jury when summing up, but at least some jurors did not realise these were standard. When the judge told them they could draw certain "inferences", some jurors, not knowing this was a standard direction, thought the judge was giving them hints on what the verdict should be. Others had no idea what the judge was talking about.

Feeling intimidated, like the juror in the trial of Tony Martin, the Norfolk farmer found guilty of murdering a burglar, is not, it seems, unusual. A number of jurors felt intimidated by being stared at by counsel, the accused and his family, and in four cases jurors felt "intimidated and scared" after the trial finished.

So far, the study has produced only preliminary recommendations. These include more guidance for jury foremen, providing the jury with a written summary of the judge's summing up on the law, more help with flow charts and other aids in multi-defendant cases, and more encouragement to ask the judge questions—all of which would no doubt help our own juries to reach better verdicts.

(Adapted from the Guardian, July 17, 2000.)

Perverting the course of justice?

They admitted it. The judge said they had no defence. But last week, two people who attempted to trash a nuclear submarine were acquitted. Marcel Berlins and Clare Dyer on why more and more juries are returning "perverse" verdicts.

On the very day that the appeal court described the jury's verdict in the Bruce Grobbelaar libel trial in the most damning terms that judges can muster, virtually calling the jurors mad, another 12 men and women, in Manchester, were doing their bit to be added to the roll-call of juries for whom "perverse" is an honourable label. They brought in a verdict of not guilty on two anti-nuclear protesters charged with conspiracy to cause criminal damage to a Trident submarine in a Barrow-in-Furness shipyard. The two happily admitted their intention to trash the sub but said they were doing so because nuclear weapons were immoral and illegal. The judge told the jury that such ideals formed no defence against the charge. He was ignored. Not guilty, said the jury.

It was not the first time that juries have, apparently contrary to the evidence, acquitted defendants charged with sabotage of defence equipment. But that strand of acquittals is itself part of a greater English tradition, going back to the trial of William Mead and William Penn, nonconformists charged in 1670 with unlawful preaching and conducting a seditious assembly. The jury was threatened by the judge and locked up for two nights "without meat, drink, fire or tobacco" after it refused to convict them but still stubbornly stuck to its verdict. The jurors were then fined and imprisoned till they paid, but were ultimately released by the Chief Justice, upholding "the right of juries to give their verdict by their conscience".

A perverse verdict could just mean—as in the *Grobbelaar* case—a totally unreasonable conclusion from the evidence presented. But the more distinguished form of jury perversity arises when jurors in a criminal trial, following their consciences and their moral beliefs, acquit a defendant even where the evidence and the law clearly point to conviction. Lord Devlin, one of the great law lords, regarded the jury's right to bring in a perverse acquittal as one of the glories of our jury system. "It gives protection against laws which the ordinary man regards as harsh and oppressive . . . an insurance that the criminal law will conform to the ordinary man's ideas of what is fair and just. If it does not, the jury will not be a party to its enforcement."

In 1985, Clive Ponting, a senior Ministry of Defence official, was tried under the Official Secrets Act for revealing to an M.P. that Government Ministers had misled Parliament over the sinking of the Argentine warship General Belgrano during the Falklands War. There was no doubt that he had done so and that he had no legal defence to the charge, as the trial judge made clear to the jury. Nevertheless the jury acquitted him. Jurors may not be asked why they reached a particular verdict, but it emerged that some of them resented the patronising and over-emphatic way in which the trial judge, in effect, ordered them to convict. Another factor was the feeling that the "catch-all" section of the Official Secrets Act under which Ponting was charged and which allowed no public interest defence was unfair and oppressive.

Even more striking was the acquittal at the Old Bailey in 1990 of Pat Pottle and Michael Randle, on a charge of helping the Soviet spy George Blake escape from Wormwood Scrubs in 1963, enabling him to flee to Russia. This was not just a case of a jury disregarding the judge's clear—and legally correct—instruction that the two men had no defence. The jury knew for a fact that they were guilty—not least because they had published a book entitled *The Blake Escape—How We Freed George Blake and Why*.

As if that wasn't enough, Pottle and Randle, defending themselves, confirmed their responsibility for the crime and made impassioned speeches from the dock. They argued that bringing them to court 26 years after the crime was an abuse of the legal process and showed a political motive behind their prosecution. The jury was clearly impressed and acquitted, knowing that it was delivering a perverse verdict, showing two fingers to a system that would behave in this way. Nor is it just in highly publicised cases raising quasi-political or social issues that juries have shown their bolshie independence. Away from the headlines, juries often acquit guilty defendants simply because they feel strongly that no prosecution should have been brought. Forgetful elderly shoplifters are frequent beneficiaries of jury anger at their being in the dock at all.

In the nineteenth century, juries used to find defendants not guilty of crimes they had clearly committed because the penalties—a death sentence or long imprisonment—were so disproportionate to the crime (stealing a sheep, for instance). The modern equivalent is the jury that refuses to convict a mercy killer of murder, even when all the ingredients of the crime are present, because a murder conviction means an automatic life sentence. The result is that mercy killers often escape with a conviction for manslaughter, and a lighter sentence, on the often spurious grounds of diminished responsibility.

Peace protestors have a long record of successful appeals to the jury's conscience. In the 1970s a group led by the well-known campaigner Pat Arrowsmith were charged under the 1934 Disaffection Act for leafleting troops at Aldershot and acquitted after a 51–day trial, despite overwhelming evidence against them. The trial took place before the Contempt of Court Act 1981 put a firm lid on jury revelations, and some jurors revealed afterwards that they had made up their minds to clear the defendants after just five days.

In another series of prosecutions, people with Multiple Sclerosis or other painful illnesses charged with using, growing or supplying cannabis have pleaded that the drug was the only means of relieving their pain. Juries have acquitted almost all those accused. Last September, Lord Melchett, executive director of Greenpeace, and 27 other environmental activists who trashed a field of genetically modified maize in Norfolk in July 1999 successfully pleaded that their action was justified to prevent the contamination of nearby organic crops. Under the Criminal Damage Act 1971, an accused has a defence if he acted to protect other property that he believed was in imminent danger, using means that he believed reasonable in the circumstances. Maybe the jury really believed the Greenpeace 28 were justified in their aim of uprooting the whole crop to prevent flowering and pollination, possibly contaminating nearby crops. Or maybe, like many of their fellow citizens, they just didn't like the idea of GM foods. Scimac, the industry body representing the company that developed the GM maize, said after the trial that the verdict raised "fundamental questions about the ability of our legal system to cope with the gradual erosion of respect for public rights and authority".

Perverse verdicts show that juries don't like stigmatising people they don't really regard as criminals. It offends them to have to convict an MS sufferer who takes a few illegal puffs to alleviate pain. They're also reluctant to make criminals out of defendants who think like them and have the same world view. And jurors don't want to risk sending to prison those who act out of genuine public interest or moral concern, even if they break the letter of the law. Most juries heed the judge's warnings and convict on the evidence, not on their feelings. But more and more jurors, it seems, are following their consciences. Perverse verdicts are on the rise.

(Adapted from the Guardian, January 19, 2001.)

Perverse verdicts

99. There are many, in particular the Bar, who fervently support what they regard as the right of the jury to ignore their duty to return a verdict according to the evidence and to acquit where they disapprove of the law or of the prosecution in seeking to enforce it. Lord Devlin . . . saw it as a protection against laws that the ordinary man might regard as "harsh and oppressive" and an insurance "that the criminal law will conform to the ordinary man's idea of what is fair and just". E.P. Thompson, expressed a similar view in a memorable passage in 1980:

"The English common law rests upon a bargain between the Law and the People. The jury box is where people come into the court; the judge watches them and the jury watches back. A jury is the place where the bargain is struck. The jury attends in judgment, not only upon the accused, but also upon the justice and humanity of the law. . .."

100. The *Clive Ponting*, and *Randle* and *Pottle* cases and, more recently, a number of acquittals in cases of alleged criminal damage by anti-war and environmental campaigners cases may be modern examples of juries exercising such "dispensing" ability. But not all perverse verdicts have the attractive notion of a "blow for freedom" that many attach to them. There are other prejudices in the jury room that may lead to perverse acquittals, for example, in sexual offences where the issue is consent or in cases of serious violence where a lesser verdict than that clearly merited on the evidence may be returned.

101. However, although juries may have the ability to dispense with or nullify the law, they have no right to do so. Indeed, it is contrary to their oath or affirmation "faithfully [to] try the defendant and give a true verdict according to the evidence". But, at present there is no procedural means of stopping them exercising their ability to return what in law may be a perverse verdict of not guilty. . .

102. Dr Glanville Williams has pointed out that, though juries had long had this ability, there was no evidence of their wide use of it:

> "Most of the great pronouncements on constitutional liberty, from the eighteenth century onwards, have been the work of judges, either sitting in appellate courts or giving directions to juries. The assumption that political liberty at the present day depends upon the institution of the jury . . . is in truth merely folklore.
>
> The notion that an English jury will, as anything like a regular matter, take the law into its own hands and acquit in defiance of the judge's direction upon the law rests on a misapprehension of its function. The English jury is a trier of fact only. . . .
>
> A lawyer, if he is true to his calling, must have some reservations about any instance whereby jurymen gain applause by disregarding their oath to give a true verdict according to the evidence. If we really wish juries to give untrue verdicts, why do we require them to be sworn?"

104. Despite the illogicality of this "dispensing" ability of juries, I can understand why there is such an emotional attachment to it. It has been an accepted feature of our jury system for a long time and is seen as a useful long-stop against oppression by the State and as an agent, on occasion, of law reform. And illogicality is not necessarily an obstacle to the retention of deeply entrenched institutions, especially where, as here, there may be infrequent recourse to them. There is the further point that under our present procedures the courts cannot prevent juries from acquitting perversely; as yet their verdicts are unreasoned and there is no appeal against an acquittal.

105. However, I regard the ability of jurors to acquit, and it also follows, convict, in defiance of the law and in disregard of their oaths, as more than illogicality. It is a blatant affront to the legal process and the main purpose of the criminal justice system—the control of crime—of which they are so important a part. With respect to Lord Devlin, I think it unreal to regard the random selection, not election, of 12 jurors from one small area as an exercise in democracy, "a little parliament", to set against the national will. Their role is to find the facts and, applying the law to those facts, to determine guilt or no. They are not there to substitute their view of the propriety of the law for that of Parliament or its enforcement for that of its appointed Executive, still less on what may be irrational, secret and unchallengeable grounds. Moreover, I do not see why this form of lay justice, responsible for only about 1 per cent of criminal cases, should be distinguished in this way from the lay justice administered by magistrates who, like their professional colleagues, are accountable for any perversity revealed on appeal by way of case stated.

107, . . . I consider that the law should be declared, by statute if need be, that juries have no right to acquit in defiance of the law or in disregard of the evidence.

Adapted from "The Review of the Criminal Courts of England and Wales" by The Right Honourable Lord Justice Auld (September, 2001).

Advantages of juries	
Disadvantages of juries	

Activity ❷

Working in **pairs** or **small groups**, and using the information in the articles above, together with any other information you may find (e.g. in books, journals, newspapers or on the internet), prepare the case for or against the use of juries in criminal trials. You should then **debate** this issue as a whole class.

(Evidence: Communications: C3.1a, C3.2)

Activity ❸

Using the information you have gathered for Activity 2 and any further information you have gained as a result of the debate, prepare an **appropriate document** (e.g. an article of approximately 1000 words for a broadsheet newspaper) that outlines the main arguments for and against the use of juries in serious criminal trials. This document must include at least one **image**.

(Evidence: Communications: C3.2, C3.3)

14 Access to Legal Services

? Issues to Explore

? Why is access to legal services an important issue?

? What provision exists for those who cannot pay the market rate for private legal services?

? What role does public funding play in seeking to ensure access to justice?

? What is the future for access to justice?

Definition:

ACCESS TO JUSTICE:	The various providers of legal services and sources of funding that exist to ensure that those who need legal services are able to access those services.

- The principle of the rule of law is at the heart of the English legal system holding that all citizens are equal before the law. For this notional equality to have any practical meaning, individuals must have access to the systems and institutions that uphold it. Equal access to legal services is a fundamental issue if all citizens are to benefit from the law and its protections. However, this equality of access does not exist. Rather, there is an **unmet need** for legal services. Research in the 1970s by Abel-Smith, Zander and others identified three forms of unmet need:

- where someone does not recognise their problem as a legal one;

- where the problem is recognised as legal, but the person is unable to access the services available; and

- where the problem is recognised as legal, but no developed service exists to provide the appropriate help.

Why is access to legal services an important issue?

Legal and Advice Services: A pathway out of social exclusion (November 2001)

How can we help tackle social exclusion?

The paper defines social exclusion in terms of the availability of legal help and advice and explains what is meant by these terms. It points out that legal rights are useless if people do not know what those rights are or do not know how to enforce them, and they are unable to receive expert independent help.

It describes the wide range of providers of legal and advice services, and points out that whilst solicitors' firms make up the largest number of legal service providers, there are a growing number of other sources of help, such as Law Centres, Citizens Advice Bureaux, independent advice centres and local authority services.

What problems do people need help with?

Professor Hazel Genn's report *Paths to Justice* was a major breakthrough in this area, as it identified the type of civil legal problems faced by people and how they dealt with them. For the first time we had real evidence about the levels and types of need for legal help and advice. The research showed that those people who fall within the commonly understood definitions of socially excluded are the ones least likely to take any action and seek help to resolve their problems. As a follow-up the Department for Constitutional Afairs (DCA) has commissioned a long-term project to measure and characterise levels of unmet legal need in England and Wales every three years. The surveys will provide a comprehensive national picture of the extent of unmet legal need in the social welfare field.

Lack of access to advice

Lack of access to reliable legal advice can be a contributing factor in creating and maintaining social exclusion. Poor access to advice has meant that many people have suffered because they have been unable to enforce their legal rights effectively, or have even been unaware of their rights and responsibilities in the first place. They are unable to get justice. Many socially excluded individuals and groups will at some point come into contact with the legal process, whether it is because of the condition of their housing, an inability to access essential services, or problems paying their bills and so on. These are just a few examples of the problems faced. They will therefore need the means by which they can find out about their legal rights and responsibilities and whether their problems can be resolved. Some will also require the means and expertise to enforce their rights. Legal and advice services therefore have a key role to play in addressing the situation that many people find themselves in.

Good advice and assistance at an early stage can prevent a problem getting any worse, and hopefully lead to its early resolution and justice being done. Early intervention can avoid the need to go to the expense and trouble of involving the courts. Indeed, the courts themselves may advise a person to seek legal advice when a case is brought before them if they have not sought expert help and advice in advance. Good legal advice can therefore result in cases being resolved without the involvement of the courts.

It is no good a person having rights in theory, if they:

- do not know what those rights are;
- do not know how to exercise them; or
- have no idea where to turn for advice if they need expert help enforcing their rights.

Without those things, legal rights and justice are illusory.

Government departments and public agencies are taking greater steps to increase awareness of new rights and responsibilities. However, many people remain unaware of their rights, and even if they are aware, they often need expert and independent help and advice. That is the role of legal and advice services.

What do we mean by legal and advice services?

Legal services are provided by a wide range of private, public and voluntary sector agencies, and are not just restricted to solicitors and barristers in private practice. The range of services include Law Centres, Citizens Advice Bureaux, independent advice centres, Age Concern, Shelter offices, local authority services, such as housing advice centres, welfare rights units or trading standards, Race Equality Councils, and a range of smaller community and voluntary groups. Indeed, many of the smaller groups may not recognise what they provide as legal services, as it might be just one aspect of the work they do with their local community or target client group.

Solicitors' firms make up the majority of legal service providers, but there are a large and growing number of public, community and voluntary sector agencies involved as well, such as Law Centres and Citizens Advice Bureaux.

(Adapted from the Department for Constitutional Affairs website.)

Why is access to legal services an important issue?	
Summarise the range of providers of legal services	

The main providers of legal services

- The legal profession—solicitors and barristers—remains the main providers of legal services, and the profession does make a contribution to ensuring access through, for example, *pro bono* initiatives. An increasingly important contribution is also made by a range of alternative providers, such as Citizens Advice Bureaux and Law Centres.

Bar *Pro Bono* Unit

Pro bono publico describes work done for the public good. For the legal profession, *pro bono* refers to the *provision of free legal services*. The Unit was established by Lord Goldsmith Q.C., the Unit's President, in May 1996 to provide *pro bono*—free—legal advice and representation in deserving cases where public funding (Legal Aid) is not available or where the applicant is unable to afford legal assistance. Since opening, over 4000 applications for assistance have been received, with help given in more than 1500 cases. The Unit helps by putting solicitors, advice agencies and members of the public in touch with barristers who can: give **advice**—either in **writing** or in **conference**; **represent** applicants in **any court/tribunal** in **England** or **Wales**; assist with **mediation**, free of charge. The Unit is able to call on the services of over 1500 barristers from all over England and Wales.

(Adapted from the Bar Pro Bono Unit website.)

The Solicitors *Pro Bono* Group

The Solicitors *Pro Bono* Group (SPBG) is a small, national charity whose aim is to enable and encourage lawyers to provide free legal help to individuals and community groups in need. The SPBG delivers free legal advice through a number of projects under the Law Works banner:

- **Law Works Clinics** promotes partnership between Law firms and Community Advice agencies. It produces written materials for individuals and law firms, arranges training sessions and provides support for lawyers and clinic workers.

- **Law Works for Community Groups** provides free business law advice to not for profit community groups through a network of volunteer lawyers. Tthe work must be non-urgent and non-contentious.

- **Law Works Mediation** has been set up to offer mediation free of charge in various situations.

- **Law Works Web** works with advice agencies to deliver advice and assistance using the Internet as the means of communications.

- **Law Works Students** encourages students to help with *pro bono* work, organises conferences, runs the Student Challenge and much more.

(Adapted from the Solicitors Pro Bono Group website.)

Citizens Advice Bureau

The Citizens Advice Bureau Service offers free, confidential, impartial and independent advice. From its origins in 1939 as an emergency service during World War II, it has evolved into a professional national agency.

Every Citizens Advice Bureau is a registered charity reliant on volunteers. Citizens Advice Bureaux help solve nearly six million new problems every year which are central to people's lives, including debt and consumer issues, benefits, housing, legal matters, employment, and immigration. Advisers can help fill out forms, write letters, negotiate with creditors and represent clients at court or tribunal.

Many bureaux provide specialist advice, often in partnership with other agencies such as solicitors and the probation service. There are over 2,800 locations where CAB advice is regularly availible in England, Wales and Northern Ireland.

(Adapted from the Citizens Advice Bureau website.)

The Law Centres Federation

What do Law Centres do?

Law Centres provide a free and independent professional legal service to people who live or work in their catchment areas.

Law Centres were to set up to overcome the obstacles faced by people who need access to the legal system. Free, publicly provided legal advice should be available to everyone, not just to those with financial resources or to those few that can get Legal Aid because of their income, there are many areas of law where Legal Aid is simply not available. This means that even in areas where fundamental rights are in dispute there is no access to the legal system. Legal Aid is not available, for example, for representation at Industrial Tribunals or Immigration Appeals Tribunals.

Law Centres are managed democratically by individuals and organisations from their local areas. They work closely with their communities and provide the kind of services that are most suitable for that area. This accountability means that they complement the services of other community groups and advice agencies in the area, ensuring that there is no duplication of work and providing the local groups with back-up legal advice when needed.

What areas of law do they deal with?

Law Centres are grant aided. To make the most of their limited resources, Law Centres have to prioritise areas of work that they feel are most in demand, and where the needs are greatest. They specialise in those areas of law including welfare rights, immigration and nationality, housing and homelessness, employment rights, and sex and race discrimination.

Other areas of work vary according to local need and may include mental health, disability rights, education rights, juvenile crime and children's rights. Law Centres were set up with a vision—that of providing a more complete and responsive service to people than the individual service provided by private lawyers. This means providing a more efficient and comprehensive service for their users. They employ solicitors, barristers, legal advisers and community workers. In addition to dealing with individual cases (including test cases, judicial reviews and representation), they use their grants to:

- work with whole groups of people, rather than just helping one person at a time;

- provide training and information about the law and people's rights;

- go out into their communities and identify legal problems at an early stage;

- take on cases that clarify and extend rights for the public;

- comment on and propose improvements in the law as it affects their clients; and

- provide legal advice and services for community organisation provide initial quick advice and/or referral.

(Adapted from the Law Centres Federation website.)

How does the legal profession try to ensure access to justice for all who need it?	
Outline the role of Citizens Advice Bureaux	
Outline the role of Law Centres	

Public funding for legal services

The **Legal Aid** system (state subsidies for private legal services) was first introduced in 1949. For the following 50 years (together with the **Green Form Scheme**, established in 1972, and **ABWOR**—assistance by way of representation—established in 1979) this was the main strategy to ensure access to justice. This covered assistance with the cost of litigation and representation (legal aid) and cost of preliminary and non-contentious work (legal advice and assistance). However, the demand-led nature of the scheme saw costs escalate while the proportion of the population eligible for help declined dramatically (creating the "middle-income trap").

The Government's plans for reforming legal services and the courts (the "Modernising Justice" White Paper)—Presented to Parliament by the Lord High Chancellor by Command of Her Majesty (December 1998)

Weaknesses of the current legal aid system

The Government does not believe that the existing Legal Aid system, now 50 years old, is capable of meeting its objectives and priorities.

- Legal Aid is too heavily biased towards expensive, court-based solutions to people's problems. Because the scheme is open-ended, it is impossible to target resources on priority areas, or the most efficient and effective way of dealing with a particular problem. Legal Aid is spent almost entirely on lawyers' services. In practice, it is lawyers who determine where and how the money is spent.

- Legal Aid is sometimes criticised for backing cases of insufficient merit; and for allowing people to pursue cases unreasonably, forcing their opponents to agree to unfair settlements.

- The scheme provides few effective means or incentives for improving value for money. Because any lawyer can take a Legal Aid case, there is little control over quality, and no scope for competition to keep prices down. Lawyers' fees are calculated after the event, based on the amount of work done, so there is little incentive to work more efficiently. In recent years, higher spending has supported fewer cases. The number of full civil legal aid cases started each year has fallen by 31 per cent, from 419,861 in 1992–93 to 319,432 in 1997–98.

- It is not possible to control expenditure effectively. The few means of control available, for example cutting financial eligibility, are crude and inflexible. Spending on all forms of civil and family legal aid has risen rapidly, from £586 million in 1992–93, to £793 million in 1997–98. This level of growth in expenditure—35 per cent compared to general inflation of 13 per cent—cannot be sustained in future.

- The cost of criminal legal aid is rising at an alarming rate. In 1992–93, the taxpayer spent a total of £507 million on all forms of criminal legal aid; by 1997–98, the figure was £733 million. This is an increase of 44 per cent, compared to general inflation of 13 per cent. Over the same period, the number of criminal legal aid orders (for representation at court) rose by only 10 per cent, from 563,788 in 1992–93 to 618,621 in 1997–98. The position is worst in relation to the higher criminal courts (Crown Court and above), which is the single most expensive element of the criminal Legal Aid system. Here, spending has risen from £221 million in 1992–93 to £349 million in 1997–98 (an increase of 58 per cent), while the number of cases remained constant at 124,000.

- The system for assessing defendants' means, to decide whether they can contribute towards the cost of their case, is also flawed. About 94 per cent of defendants in the Crown Court obtain Legal Aid without making a contribution. So in most of these cases, the means assessment is a waste of time and money. On the other hand, free legal aid is sometimes granted to a defendant with an apparently wealthy lifestyle. This is usually because the defendant's assets have been frozen for the duration of the case, which is the only period when contributions are payable. This has undermined public confidence in legal aid.

(Adapted from the Department for Constitutional Affairs website.)

What were the main failings of civil Legal Aid?	
What were the main failings of criminal Legal Aid?	

The Legal Services Commission

On April 1, 2000 the Legal Aid Board was replaced by the Legal Services Commission. Under the Access to Justice Act 1999, the Legal Services Commission has responsibility for two schemes—the Community Legal Service which provides advice and legal representation for people involved in civil cases, and the Criminal Defence Service, which provides advice and representation for people facing criminal charges.

The Legal Services Commission will only pay solicitors and other organisations to provide help if they can meet certain standards. Organisations which have met the Commission's standards will display the Community Legal Service Quality Mark or CDS logo.

The **Community Legal Service**, which from April 1, 2000 replaced the old civil scheme of Legal Aid, bringing together networks of funders (*e.g.* Local Authorities) and suppliers into partnerships to provide the widest possible access to information and advice. Since April 2, 2001 only organisations with a contract with the LSC have been able to provide advice or representation funded by the LSC. For family cases and specialist areas like immigration and clinical negligence only specialist firms are funded to do the work. claims for personal injury other than clinical negligence are not usually funded by the LSC. Such cases can instead be pursued under "conditional fee agreements" between solicitors and clients.

The **Criminal Defence Service** which from April 2, 2001 replaced the old system of criminal Legal Aid and provides criminal services to people accused of crimes. The purpose of the CDS is to ensure that people suspected or accused of a crime have access to advice, assistance and representation, as the interests of justice require. Since April 2, 2001, private practice solicitors' offices must hold a General Criminal Contract to carry out criminal defence work funded by the Commission. Firms are audited against the Contract to ensure they continue to meet quality assurance standards. Since May 2001 the Commission has also directly employed a number of criminal defence lawyers, known as public defenders. The Public Defender Service is able to provide services in exactly the same way as lawyers in private practice.

(Adapted from the Legal Services Commission website.)

Community Legal Service Partnerships

The CLS provides the framework for local networks of legal and advice services, which are based on local needs and priorities, and supported by local CLS Partnerships. The local partnerships bring together the Legal Services Commission, local authorities, local solicitors' firms, Citizens Advice Bureaux, Law Centres, and other independent advice centres, and a range of other organisations and agencies. The CLS Partnerships have four main tasks:

- to assess the extent of need in their area for legal and advice services;

- to identify how well the current service provision meets the need in priority categories;

- to plan together how best to organise their funding to meet priority needs more effectively; and

- to support the local networks and develop active referral systems between the individual providers.

(Adapted from the Department for Constitutional Affairs website.)

Outline the role of the LSC	
Outline the role of the CLS	
Outline the role of the CLS Partnerships	
Outline the role of the CDS	

Activity ❶

You have been asked to give a short **presentation** to a local community group about the Criminal Defence Service. Using the material in the extracts above, and any other relevant information you can find, prepare and deliver this presentation. In preparing this activity, you should also read **Chapter 13** of *A Level and AS Level Law: a Study Guide*. Make sure your presentation covers:

- advice at the police station; and

- advice and representation in court.

You must also produce a **one-page handout** for the audience, giving the main points of your presentation and where they can find further information. Your handout, in addition to the text, must include at least **one image**.

(Evidence: Communications: 3.1b, C3.2, C3.3)

Activity ❷

Working in **pairs** or **small groups**, and using the information in the articles above, together with any other information you may find (e.g. in books, journals, newspapers or on the internet), prepare the case for or against the view that people of limited financial means have adequate access to legal advice and representation. You should then **debate** this issue as a whole class.

(Evidence: Communications: C3.1a, C3.2)

Activity ❸

Using the information you have gathered for Activity 2 and any further information you have gained as a result of the debate, prepare an **appropriate document** (e.g. an article of approximately 1000 words for a broadsheet newspaper) that outlines the main arguments for and against the view that people of limited financial means have adequate access to legal advice and representation. This document must include at least one **image**.

(Evidence: Communications: C3.2, C3.3)

INDEX